OECD Economic Surveys: Slovenia 2015

OECD
BETTER POLICIES FOR BETTER LIVES

Please cite this publication as:
OECD (2015), *OECD Economic Surveys: Slovenia 2015*, OECD Publishing, Paris.
http://dx.doi.org/10.1787/eco_surveys-svn-2015-en

ISBN 978-92-64-23222-8 (print)
ISBN 978-92-64-23223-5 (PDF)
ISBN 978-92-64-23224-2 (ePub)

Series: OECD Economic Surveys
ISSN 0376-6438 (print)
ISSN 1609-7513 (online)

OECD Economic Surveys: Slovenia
ISSN 1995-3585 (print)
ISSN 1999-0642 (online)

Photo credits: Cover © iStockphoto.com/Erik Zunek.

Corrigenda to OECD publications may be found on line at: *www.oecd.org/about/publishing/corrigenda.htm*.

Table of contents

Thematic chapters

Boxes

Tables

Figures

BASIC STATISTICS OF SLOVENIA, 2013

(Numbers in parentheses refer to the OECD average)*

LAND, PEOPLE AND ELECTORAL CYCLE

Population (million)	2.1		Population density per km^2	102.9	(34.7)
Under 15 (%)	14.4	(18.2)	Life expectancy (years, 2012)	80.2	(80.2)
Over 65 (%)	16.9	(15.6)	Men	77.1	(77.5)
Foreign-born (%, 2011)	11.2		Women	83.3	(82.9)
Latest 5-year average growth (%)	0.6	(0.6)	Latest general election	July 2014	

ECONOMY

Gross domestic product (GDP)			Value added shares (%)		
In current prices (billion USD)	48.0		Primary sector	2.1	(2.5)
In current prices (billion EUR)	36.1		Industry including construction	32.0	(26.8)
Latest 5-year average real growth (%)	-2.0	(0.8)	Services	65.8	(70.5)
Per capita (000 USD PPP)	38.8	(39.2)			

GENERAL GOVERNMENT

Per cent of GDP

Expenditure	59.7	(43.1)	Gross financial debt	78.9	(113.2)
Revenue	45.2	(38.3)	Net financial debt	18.9	(72.7)

EXTERNAL ACCOUNTS

Exchange rate (EUR per USD)	0.753		Main exports (% of total merchandise exports)		
PPP exchange rate (USA = 1)	0.605		Machinery and transport equipment	35.6	
In per cent of GDP			Manufactured goods	21.0	
Exports of goods and services	74.7	(53.4)	Chemicals and related products, n.e.s.	18.5	
Imports of goods and services	68.7	(49.4)	Main imports (% of total merchandise imports)		
Current account balance	5.8	(-0.1)	Machinery and transport equipment	29.2	
Net international investment position	-39.1		Manufactured goods	18.0	
			Mineral fuels, lubricants and related materials	15.1	

LABOUR MARKET, SKILLS AND INNOVATION

Employment rate for 15-64 year-olds (%)	63.3	(65.2)	Unemployment rate, Labour Force Survey (age 15 and over) (%)	10.1	(7.9)
Men	67.1	(73.1)	Youth (age 15-24, %)	21.7	(16.1)
Women	59.2	(57.4)	Long-term unemployed (1 year and over, %)	5.1	(2.7)
Participation rate for 15-64 year-olds (%)	70.5	(71.1)	Tertiary educational attainment 25-64 year-olds (%, 2012)	26.4	(32.2)
Average hours worked per year	1,547	(1 771)	Gross domestic expenditure on R&D (% of GDP, 2012)	2.6	(2.4)

ENVIRONMENT

Total primary energy supply per capita (toe)	3.1	(4.2)	CO_2 emissions from fuel combustion per capita (tonnes, 2012)	7.1	(9.7)
Renewables (%)	17.2	(8.8)	Water abstractions per capita (1 000 m^3, 2012)	0.4	
Fine particulate matter concentration (urban, PM_{10}, µg/m^3, 2011)	31.4	(28.0)	Municipal waste per capita (tonnes, 2012)	0.4	(0.5)

SOCIETY

Income inequality (Gini coefficient, 2011[a])	0.245	(0.308)	Education outcomes (PISA score, 2012)		
Relative poverty rate (%, 2011[a])	8.9	(11.1)	Reading	481	(497)
Median equivalised household income (000 USD PPP, 2010)	19.2	(20.4)	Mathematics	501	(494)
Public and private spending (% of GDP)			Science	514	(501)
Health care (2012)	9.4	(9.2)	Share of women in parliament (%, October 2014)	26.9	(26.7)
Pensions (2011)	11.6	(8.7)	Net official development assistance (% of GNI)	0.13	(0.37)
Education (primary, secondary, post sec. non tertiary, 2011)	3.8	(3.9)			

Better life index: www.oecdbetterlifeindex.org

a) 2010 for the OECD aggregate.

* Where the OECD aggregate is not provided in the source database, a simple OECD average of latest available data is calculated where data exist for at least 29 member countries.

Source: Calculations based on data extracted from the databases of the following organisations: OECD, International Energy Agency, World Bank, International Monetary Fund and Inter-Parliamentary Union.

This Survey *is published on the responsibility of the Economic and Development Review Committee of the OECD, which is charged with the examination of the economic situation of member countries.*

The economic situation and policies of Slovenia were reviewed by the Committee on the 1st April 2015. The draft report was then revised in the light of the discussions and given final approval as the agreed report of the whole Committee on the 15th April 2015.

The Secretariat's draft report was prepared for the Committee by Urban Sila, Natasa Jemec and Peter Walkenhorst, under the supervision of Piritta Sorsa. Statistical research assistance was provided by Hermes Morgavi with general administrative assistance provided by Anthony Bolton and Mikel Inarritu. The authors would like to thank Alvaro Pereira, Robert Ford and Jeanne Dall'Orso for their contributions at different stages.

The previous Survey of Slovenia *was issued in April 2013.*

Acronyms

AETR	Average effective tax rate
AJPES	Agency of the republic of Slovenia for public legal records and related services
ALMP	Active labour market programme/policy
AMC	Asset management company
AQR	Asset quality review
BAMC	Bank asset management company
BERD	Business enterprise expenditure on R&D
CC	Competence centres
CEEC	Central Eastern European countries
CoE	Centres of excellence
CPA	Competition protection agency
CPC	Corruption prevention commission
EBITDA	Earnings before interest, taxes, depreciation and amortisation
ECB	European central bank
EPL	Employment protection legislation
FDI	Foreign direct investment
GDP	Gross domestic product
GVA	Gross value added
GVC	Global value chain
HERD	Higher education spending on R&D
HLY	Healthy life years
KAD	State-owned pension fund (Kapitalska družba)
LTC	Long-term care
NHEP	National higher education programme
NPL	Non-performing loan
PMR	Product market regulation
PPP	Purchasing power parity
R&D	Research and development
RISS	Research and Innovation strategy of Slovenia
SEF	Slovene enterprise fund
SMA	Securities market agency
SME	Small- and medium-sized enterprise
SOD	State-owned restitution fund
SOE	State-owned enterprise
SSH	Slovenian sovereign holding
STRI	Services trade restrictiveness index
TFP	Total factor productivity
ULC	Unit labour cost
VAT	Value-added tax
VET	Vocational education and training
ZZZS	Health insurance institute of Slovenia

Executive summary

- Main findings
- Key recommendations

Main findings

After independence in 1991, Slovenia experienced impressive growth and today compares well internationally on well-being indicators. Nevertheless, the 2008 crisis revealed important weaknesses in the growth model. Prior to the crisis, easy access to credit and mispricing of risk led to an unsustainable investment boom. Rigid product and labour markets in conjunction with widespread state involvement in the economy hindered adjustment. Yet, Slovenia maintained the lowest degree of income inequality, despite deep and protracted drop in GDP. In response to the crisis important reforms have been implemented, including fiscal consolidation, pension reform, labour market reform, restructuring and recapitalisation of banks, and initiation of privatisation procedures. The reform drive has raised the credibility of Slovenia in the financial markets and boosted confidence. Together with rising competitiveness it supported a return to economic growth in 2014.

Strengthening the banking and corporate sectors. Excessive credit growth, poor risk assessment and lax lending standards in the run up to the 2008 crisis led to unsustainable debt build-up in (largely state-owned) banks and in the corporate sector. A weak framework for the governance of state-owned banks and weak supervision contributed to poor credit standards, excessive risk taking and misallocation of credit. The authorities and banks were slow in recognising and tackling the problem. So far, major state-owned banks have been recapitalised, and part of their non-performing loans (NPLs) have been transferred to the Bank Asset Management Company. However, banks are still importantly exposed to credit risk as well as profitability risk, due to relatively high NPL ratios. The corporate sector remains highly indebted, but indebtedness is heavily concentrated in certain companies. Viable firms have access to financing abroad and increasingly rely on retained profits. Lengthy insolvency procedures still impede needed restructuring, although important reform was implemented in 2013.

Stabilising debt and tackling pressures from population ageing. Public debt has risen rapidly from 22% of GDP in 2008 to over 80% of GDP in 2014. Despite a growth surprise on the upside, the fiscal deficit in 2014 was bigger than planned, partly due to one-offs. The government goal is nevertheless to reduce the deficit below 3% in 2015. Consolidation has relied too much on one-off measures instead of structural efforts, making longer-term expenditure control challenging. Moreover, the fiscal framework has no credible mechanism to reach medium-term objectives. The rapid rise in age-related public expenditure from pensions, health care and long-term care is further complicating future consolidation. Slovenia is aging faster than many other OECD countries. Recent pension reform has improved sustainability, but further steps are needed. Although somewhat improving, the health care system is in urgent need of reform, and the government is undertaking a thorough review of health expenditures. Long-term care lacks a stable source of funding and relies too much on high-cost institutional care.

Boosting jobs and growth. Prevalence of long-term unemployment is high and unemployment among the young has increased steeply. The relatively high minimum wage compared to average wage and a high tax burden on labour reduces employment opportunities. Slovenia spends relatively little on active labour market programmes, which are not well-targeted to the long-term unemployed and the low-skilled. Public ownership and control of enterprises is widespread in Slovenia, and the profitability of state-owned enterprises is low. Corporate governance and management practices in the state-owned sector have been weak, and have deterred foreign direct investment.

Key recommendations

Continuing with structural reform

- Focus fiscal consolidation on structural measures to increase cost efficiency in education, public administration and local government.
- Enhance the leading role of the Bank Asset Management Company to ensure swift restructuring of companies and effective liquidation of assets.
- Continue privatising state-owned enterprises and do not hold controlling interests in firms operating in competitive markets.

Strengthening the banking and corporate sectors

- For the most important firms to be restructured, ensure that all assets in a company group are transferred to the Bank Asset Management Company.
- Bank Asset Management Company should maintain its independence and ability to attract highly professional staff, while adhering to the highest standards of corporate governance and transparency.
- Monitor the implementation of the new insolvency regulation and improve institutional capacity by training judges and insolvency administrators. Make out-of-court restructuring faster and more attractive.

Stabilising debt and tackling pressures from population ageing

- Adopt a fiscal rule with a credible and transparent expenditure rule, and ensure that an independent and effective fiscal council is charged with assessing adherence.
- Increase the statutory and minimum pension ages and link them explicitly to life expectancy. Calculate pension rights over lifetime contributions.
- Thoroughly reform the health sector to improve efficiency, including of organizational and governance structures and public procurement.

Boosting jobs and growth

- Increase resources for active labour market policies and better target assistance to the long-term unemployed and the low-skilled, based on evaluation of individual programmes.
- Introduce the "silence is consent' rule for issuing licences required to open up a business and make obtaining construction permits and registering property faster.
- Implement the government's unified innovation policy and monitor its progress. Improve collaborative links between major stakeholders of innovation policy.

Assessment and recommendations

- Macroeconomic outlook
- Restoring the financial sector and corporate deleveraging
- Ensuring sustainable public finances
- The economic consequences of population ageing
- Raising living standards and long-term growth by improving the business environment

The statistical data for Israel are supplied by and under the responsibility of the relevant Israeli authorities. The use of such data by the OECD is without prejudice to the status of the Golan Heights, East Jerusalem and Israeli settlements in the West Bank under the terms of international law.

After independence upon the break-up of Yugoslavia in 1991, Slovenia experienced robust growth (Figure 1) and incomes rose steadily towards the EU average (Figure 2). The catch-up was facilitated by a relatively skilled labour force and modern industrial base, for instance in

Figure 1. **Growth was strong after independence**

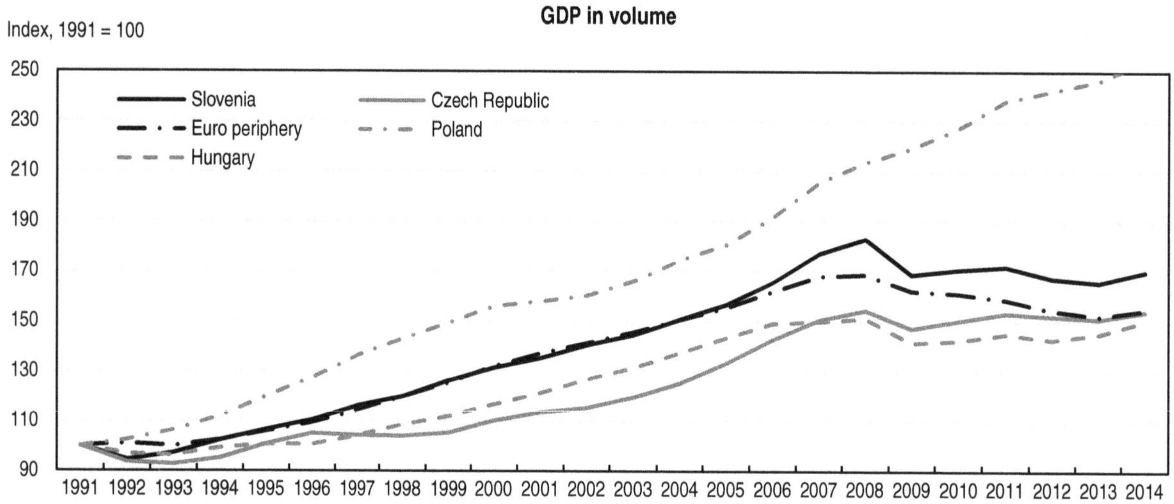

Source: *OECD Economic Outlook 96 Database.*

StatLink http://dx.doi.org/10.1787/888933204771

Figure 2. **Rapid catch-up stalled after the crisis**

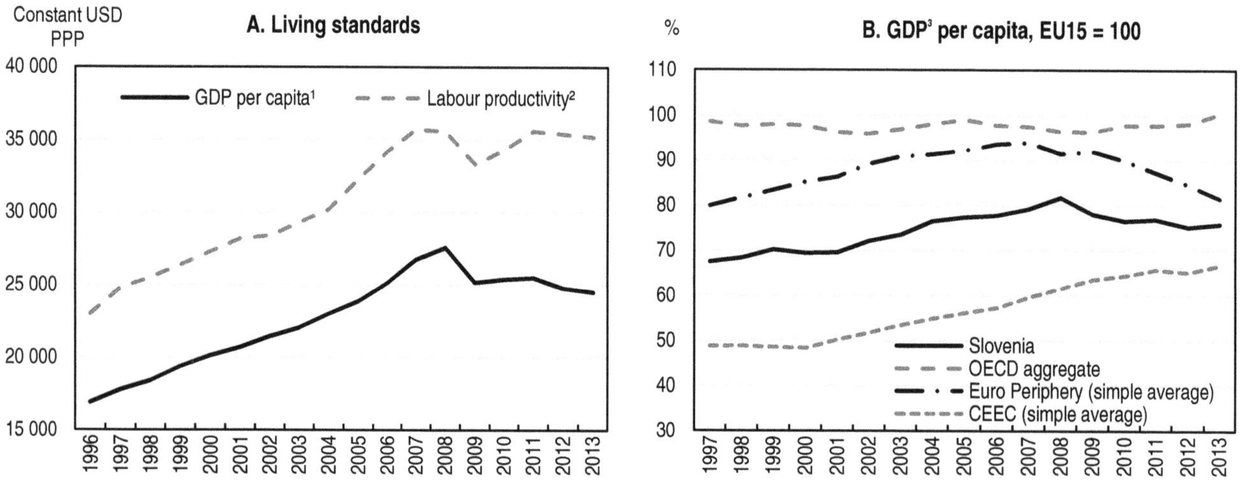

Note: CEECs include Poland, Hungary, Slovak Republic and Czech Republic; Euro Periphery includes Spain, Portugal, Greece and Ireland.
1. GDP in USD constant prices, constant PPP (base year 2005).
2. Labour Productivity measured as GDP per thousand hours.
3. GDP in million USD, current prices, current PPP per thousand persons/thousand hours worked.

Source: *OECD Level of GDP per Capita and Productivity Database.*

StatLink http://dx.doi.org/10.1787/888933204789

pharmaceuticals and household appliances. Production was reoriented to new markets in Europe, while Slovenia remained a competitive provider of goods and capital to the countries in the Balkans. Significant structural reforms, including trade reform and financial liberalisation, paved the way to European Union (EU) accession in 2004 and euro adoption in 2007. Growth was relatively widely shared (Figure 3), which has helped to boost well-being (Figure 4). Slovenia currently exceeds the OECD average in education, social connections, civic engagement and security.

Figure 3. **Income inequality is low**

Income inequality[1] – 2011 or latest data available

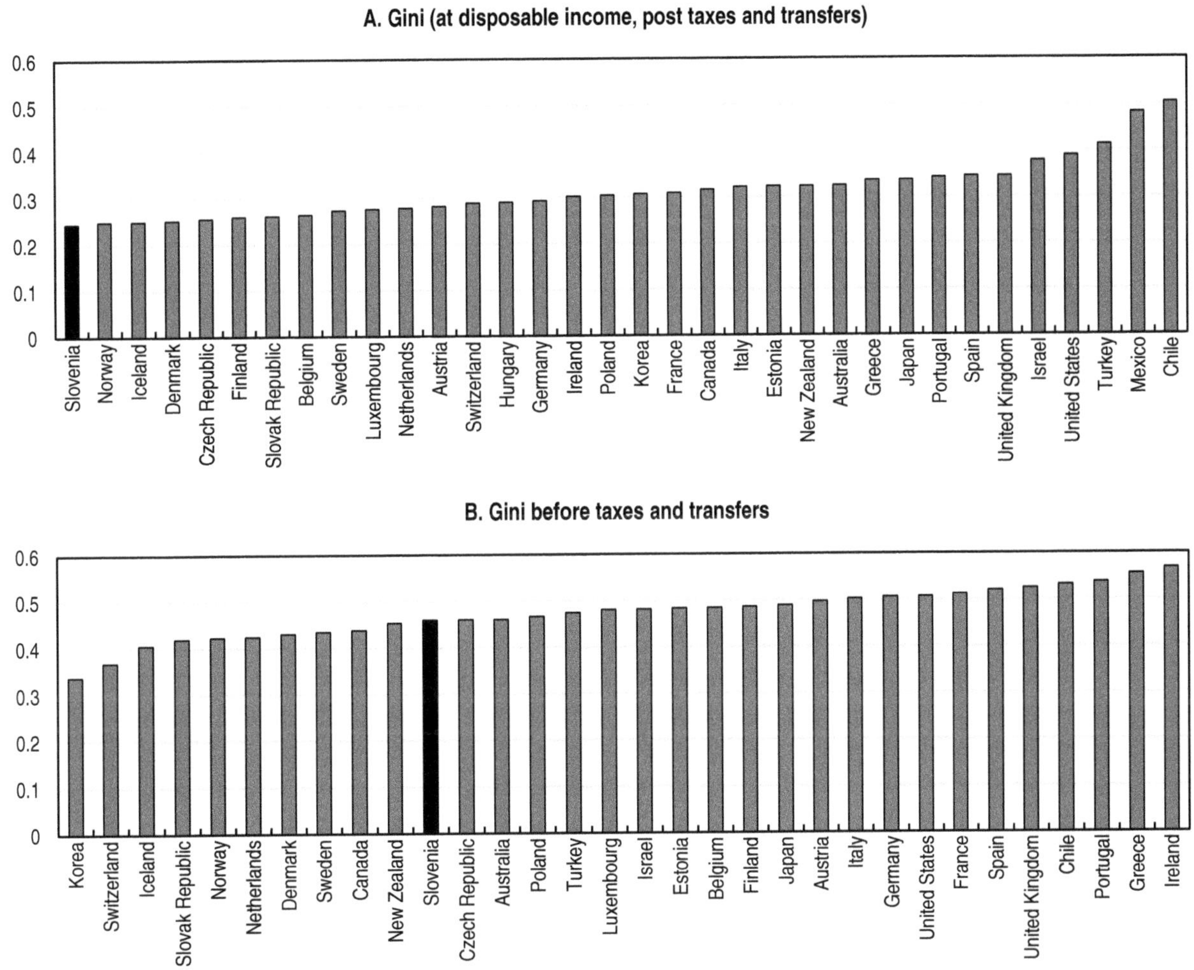

1. The Gini coefficient has a range from zero (everybody has identical incomes) to 1 (all income goes to only one person). Increasing values of the Gini coefficient thus indicate higher inequality in the distribution of income. Market income includes incomes from wages and salaries, self-employment income and cash property income together with occupational and private pensions. Disposable income is obtained by subtracting income tax and employees' social security contributions from gross income and adding transfers. Both income measures are adjusted to reflect differences in household needs depending on the number of persons in the household.

Source: OECD Income Distribution and Poverty Database.

StatLink http://dx.doi.org/10.1787/888933204792

In spite of this impressive economic performance, the 2008 crisis exposed important weaknesses and imbalances. In the run up to the crisis, easy and cheap wholesale credit raised by banks abroad, overly optimistic growth expectations and mispriced risk taking led to an unsustainable investment boom in construction and much of the corporate sector. In

Figure 4. **Well-being outcomes: Better Life Index**

From 0 (worse) to 10 (best), 2014[1]

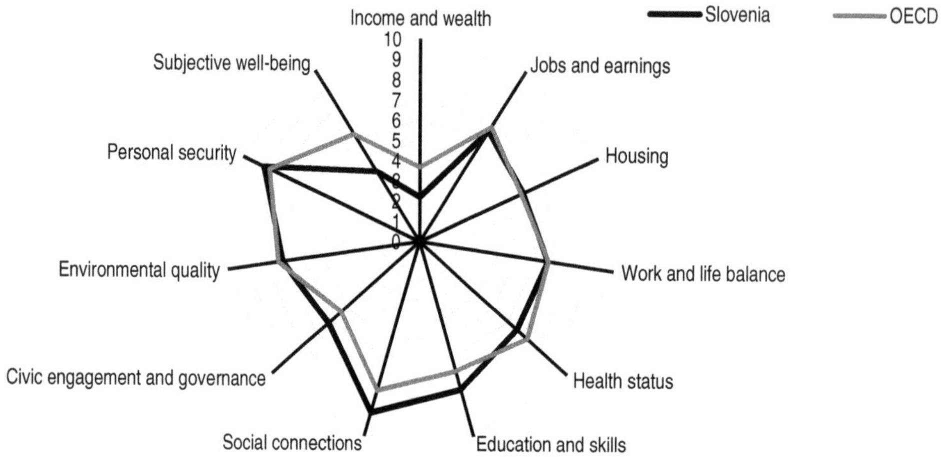

1. Each well-being dimension is measured by one to four indicators from the OECD Better Life Index set. Normalised indicators are averaged with equal weights. Indicators are normalised to range between 10 (best) and 0 (worst) according to the following formula: *(indicator value – minimum value)/(maximum value – minimum value)* x 10.

Source: OECD Better Life Index, www.oecdbetterlifeindex.org.

StatLink http://dx.doi.org/10.1787/888933204809

addition, the optimism facilitated highly leveraged management buyouts. The resulting high indebtedness made corporates and banks vulnerable to changes in market conditions. Adjustment was also complicated by rigidities in labour and product markets and weak corporate governance, including in the extensive state-owned sector. The subsequent drop in output was one of the largest in the OECD. Recovery has been slow and difficult as the authorities initially reacted hesitantly and with delay in dealing with the causes of the crisis. The persistent weakness of the banking sector, overleveraged corporate sector, and a rapid rise in the public debt call for more action to restore sustainable growth.

Some important structural reforms have been implemented in recent years (Table 1). A pension reform increased statutory and minimum retirement ages, and increased incentives for continued work of older people, making the pension system more sustainable. A labour market reform enhanced flexibility and reduced duality between permanent and fixed term contracts, and subjected student work to pension and healthcare contributions. The business environment benefitted from simpler rules on opening a business and reduced administrative burdens. Parliament approved a list of 15 companies to be privatised and the government committed to privatise state-owned banks. Changes to the fiscal framework are expected to limit public expenditure growth in the future, lowering public debt and freeing resources for more growth-enhancing spending. The weakened banking system was recapitalised and part of non-performing assets were transferred to the newly established Bank Asset Management Company (BAMC). Bank supervision is being strengthened. Meanwhile, insolvency procedures were reformed to speed up restructuring of companies.

These reforms will – if fully implemented – have a positive impact on growth. The labour market reforms, changes to the product market regulation and effects of pension reform on employment should boost GDP by 1% in five years and 2% in ten years compared to the baseline projection (Table 2). This translates to about 0.2 percentage point faster GDP growth per year. The effect on GDP comes through improved productivity and higher employment and assumes full and swift implementation. However such estimates should

Table 1. **Reforms approved and being implemented**

Area	Reform (fully implemented or on-going*)	Approved	Brief description
Reforms quantified			
Pensions	Pensions	Jan. 2013	Pension reform increased the statutory and minimum retirement ages and increased the number of years on which pensions are based. It increased penalties for early retirement and increased rewards for continued work.
Labour	Labour market reform	Apr. 2013	Increase of labour market flexibility and reduction in segmentation (shorter notice periods, reduction in severance payments for permanent employees, severance payments for temporary contracts, simplification of administrative procedures related to hiring and firing).
Business environment	Regulatory procedures and administrative burden	Since 2008	Processes to open a business were simplified, single contact points for getting information on all notifications and licenses were introduced, administrative burdens on start-ups and sole proprietors were simplified.
	Privatisations*	2013	Parliament approved a list of 15 companies to be privatised. By early 2015 four companies were privatised and seven are in the process. The government committed to privatise state-owned banks.
	Reforms via EU commitment*	Since 2014	EU commitment on Single Telecom Market. EU commitment in the energy sector. EU commitment in transport.
Reforms not quantified			
Fiscal	Fighting tax evasion*	Jul. 2013, Jan. 2015	Increased oversight and the mandatory use of cash register software; recently measures to increase transparency in cash transactions.
	Fiscal framework*	May 2013	Adoption of the fiscal rule in the Constitution that requires a balanced budget over the medium term. Implementing law is still pending.
Labour	Student work	Feb. 2015	Healthcare and pension contributions for student work have been introduced and a minimum hourly gross wage rate was set. Students will accumulate years of pensionable service from their work.
Business environment	Governance of SOEs*	Apr. 2014	Slovenian Sovereign Holding (SSH) was established and made operational. The role of the SSH is to manage and dispose of the state-owned assets (SOEs).
	Insolvency procedures	Jun. 2013, Dec. 2013	To facilitate early restructuring of viable companies and speed up liquidations of unviable ones.
Banking	Measures for stabilisation of banks	Dec. 2012	In December 2012, the parliament adopted amendments to the Banking Act entrusting Bank of Slovenia with additional resolution powers, and the Act Defining the Measures of the Republic of Slovenia to Strengthen Bank Stability that, among others, established conditions for setting up a Bank Asset Management Company (BAMC). BAMC has the power to seek a quick resolution of impaired assets. Many bad assets from state-owned banks were transferred to BAMC.
	Enhancing bank supervision*	2014	The National Assembly passed a law establishing a bank resolution fund, to be financed by banks and managed by the central bank, to become operational in 2015. Macroprudential institutional framework for macroprudential oversight of the financial system was established by the Bank of Slovenia.

be thought of as a broad guide to the expected impact of reforms rather than precise estimates. Delays, or less than full implementation, would reduce the gains.

This survey will point out that to enhance growth a reform drive needs to persist:

- Decisive action is needed to strengthen the banking and corporate sectors.
- Further fiscal consolidation is needed to put the rising debt on a downward path, particularly in view of looming pressures on expenditures from population ageing.
- Structural reforms in product and labour markets, including privatisation of state owned assets, will help create more and better jobs, boost FDI and increase innovation.

Macroeconomic outlook

Economic recovery remains fragile

After two years of recession, economic growth returned to Slovenia in 2014, driven by net exports and domestic demand (Figure 5, Panels A and B). Investment was boosted by local infrastructure projects co-financed with EU funds that have to be used before the expiry of the financial perspective by end-2015. Private consumption benefitted from improvements in consumer confidence and job creation in industrial and construction

Table 2. **The impact of recent structural reforms on GDP over 5 and 10 years**

	GDP	Via employment growth	Via productivity growth
*Impact on GDP growth over the horizon of **5 years** (in %)*			
Product market reform	0.7		0.7
Labour market reform			
Employment protection legislation	0.2		0.2
Pension reform	0.1	0.1	
Total	**1.0**	**0.1**	**0.9**
*Impact on GDP growth over the horizon of **10 years** (in %)*			
Product market reform	1.3		1.3
Labour market reform			
Employment protection legislation	0.3		0.3
Pension reform	0.4	0.4	
Total	**2.0**	**0.4**	**1.6**

1. OECD estimates for the impact of product market reform include changes to the product market regulation (PMR) as captured by the change in the OECD PMR indicator between 2008-13, announced privatisations and reforms via EU commitments. The 2008-13 change in the PMR is assumed to start having an effect on growth two years before other reforms.
2. Impact on the labour market reform is assessed via the effect of the change in the employment protection legislation (EPL) on growth. Effect of the pension reform is based on a judgement and assesses the effect on employment via increased incentives for older people to stay in the labour market.

Source: OECD calculations.

activity. However, the recovery is fragile. Corporate investment remains low as companies are deleveraging, and banks' capacity to lend is constrained by still elevated non-performing loans.

Unemployment has slightly declined from its peak of 11% reached in late 2013 (Figure 5, Panel C), but it remains high and more than half of the unemployed have been out of work for one year or more. Youth unemployment increased steeply and stood at about 20% in 2014. Due to the large slack in the economy, inflation has been low, and recent declines in the price of oil and other commodities have pushed inflation even lower. Slovenia's cost competitiveness and export market performance deteriorated and still lag behind some peers. Recently, however, competitiveness started to improve markedly and Slovenia has gained market shares (Figure 5, panels E and F). The tradable part of the economy, and manufacturing in particular, has made considerable unit labour cost (ULC) adjustments since 2010. And while in previous years cost competitiveness improved mainly owing to the adjustments in employment and earnings, in 2014, improvements have been mostly due to rises in value added (IMAD, 2014a).

Growth is likely to remain weak going forward (Table 3). Rising export growth is projected to be the main driver of growth, as global trade recovers and competitiveness improves further. Restructuring in the banking and corporate sectors, corporate deleveraging and weak credit will hold back private investment. Continued fiscal consolidation and a slow improvement in the labour market are projected to limit consumption growth. Private domestic demand will gain momentum, but only in 2016. Unemployment will decline slowly and inflation will remain low due to continued slack in the economy.

The risks are more balanced than in the past, but there are still certain important risks on the downside. Lack of progress in corporate restructuring, consolidation in the banking sector, and privatisation can hold back investment and reduce access to finance. Fiscal slippage can also worsen markets' perception of Slovenia. Corporate financial and operational restructuring could raise unemployment in the short run, weighing on growth.

Figure 5. **Key macroeconomic developments**

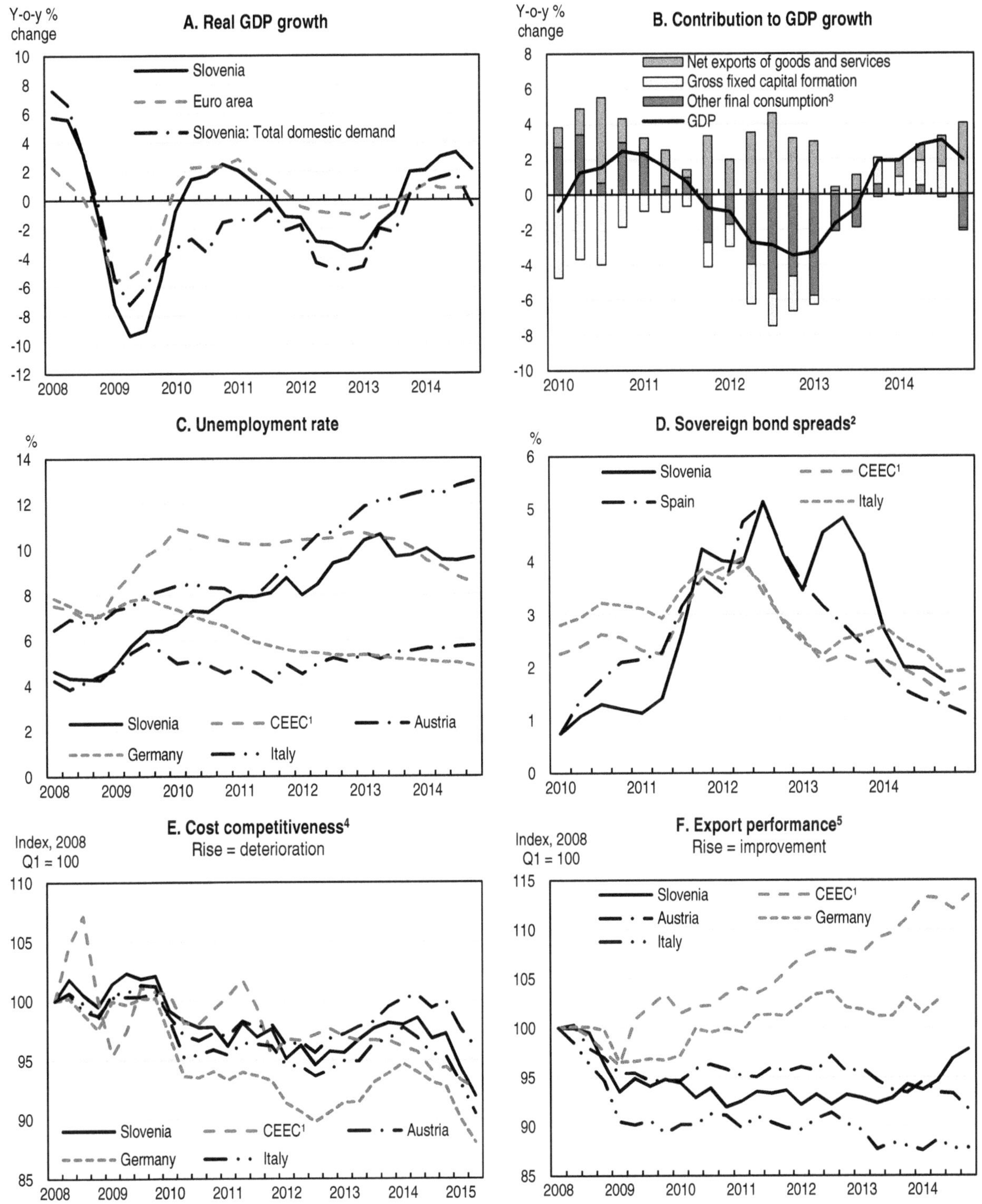

1. Unweighted average of Central and Eastern European Countries (Czech Republic, Hungary, Poland and Slovak Republic).
2. Ten-year government bond yields relative to the German rate.
3. Other final consumption include household, government and no-profit expenditure in final consumption, changes in inventories and acquisitions less disposals of valuables.
4. Real effective exchange rate based on unit labour costs for the total economy.
5. Ratio between export volumes and export markets for total goods and services.

Source: *OECD Economic Outlook 96 Database.*

StatLink http://dx.doi.org/10.1787/888933204818

Table 3. **Macroeconomic indicators and projections**

	2010	2011	2012	2013	2014	2015	2016
GDP	**1.2**	**0.6**	**-2.6**	**-1.0**	**2.6**	**1.8**	**1.9**
Private consumption	1.0	-0.1	-3.0	-3.9	0.3	0.3	1.3
Government consumption	0.1	-1.3	-1.5	-1.1	-0.5	-0.3	-0.2
Gross fixed capital formation	-13.7	-4.6	-8.9	1.9	4.8	2.3	-0.4
Housing	-20.4	-12.4	-7.3	-8.8	-4.4	-1.6	1.9
Final domestic demand	-2.8	-1.4	-3.9	-2.1	1.1	0.6	0.6
Stockbuilding[1]	1.9	0.6	-1.8	0.1	-0.2	-0.1	0.0
Total domestic demand	-0.9	-0.8	-5.7	-2.1	0.8	0.5	0.6
Exports of goods and services	10.1	7.0	0.3	2.6	6.3	5.2	5.5
Imports of goods and services	6.6	5.0	-3.9	1.4	4.1	3.1	4.4
Net exports[1]	2.1	1.4	2.9	1.0	1.9	1.9	1.4
Other indicators (growth rates, unless specified)							
Potential GDP	0.6	0.2	0.2	0.3	1.0	1.3	1.6
Output gap[2]	-1.5	-1.1	-4.0	-5.2	-3.7	-3.2	-2.9
Employment	-1.5	-3.1	-1.3	-1.9	1.2	0.5	0.4
Unemployment rate	7.2	8.2	8.8	10.1	9.7	9.4	9.1
GDP deflator	-1.1	1.2	0.3	1.4	0.4	0.8	-0.5
Consumer price index	2.1	2.1	2.8	1.9	0.4	-0.4	0.7
Core consumer prices	-0.4	-0.4	0.7	0.9	0.7	0.6	1.0
Household saving ratio, net[3]	6.2	5.8	3.5	6.8	5.3	6.4	5.7
Trade balance[4]	1.6	2.0	4.4	6.0	8.1	10.5	11.1
Current account balance[4]	-0.1	0.2	2.7	5.6	5.9	7.9	7.8
General government financial balance[4]	-5.6	-6.6	-4.0	-14.9	-4.9	-2.9	-2.4
Underlying government primary balance[2]	-4.4	-4.0	-1.6	-0.6	-1.0	0.2	1.4
Gross government debt (Maastricht)[4]	38.2	46.5	53.7	70.3	80.9	83.2	85.2
General government net debt[4]	-0.4	2.1	7.9	18.9	23.2	25.5	27.5
Three-month money market rate, average	0.8	1.4	0.6	0.2	0.2	0.0	0.0
Ten-year government bond yield, average	3.8	5.0	5.8	5.8	3.3	1.2	1.1

1. Contribution to changes in real GDP.
2. As a percentage of potential GDP.
3. As a percentage of household disposable income.
4. As a percentage of GDP.

Source: OECD Economic Outlook: Statistics and Projections Database, April.

The pace of export growth will depend largely on the growth of Slovenia's trading partners, and a possibility of a euro area slowdown therefore poses a downside risk. Having said that, euro depreciation and quantitative easing by the ECB could have more positive impact on European trading partners than expected, boosting exports further. Euro depreciation also opens opportunities to expand trade to new markets. Lower commodity prices will have a positive effect on terms of trade and profits of exporting firms and will boost import demand from Slovenia's trading partners. Further declines in oil prices, however, could also bring more persistent deflation, increasing the real value of financial debt and deterring investment and hiring.

Restoring the financial sector and corporate deleveraging

The banking sector was hit hard by the boom-bust credit cycle. The loan-to-deposit ratio (Figure 6, Panel A), and the credit-to-GDP ratio more than doubled from 2003 to 2011. Loans were mainly directed to the corporate sector, whereas household indebtedness remained low. The big drop in economic activity led to a high proportion of non-performing loans (NPLs), (Figure 6, Panel B), mostly in the large state-controlled banks. The deterioration in asset quality

Figure 6. **The banking sector was hit hard by the boom-bust credit cycle, but restructuring efforts have resulted in improvements**

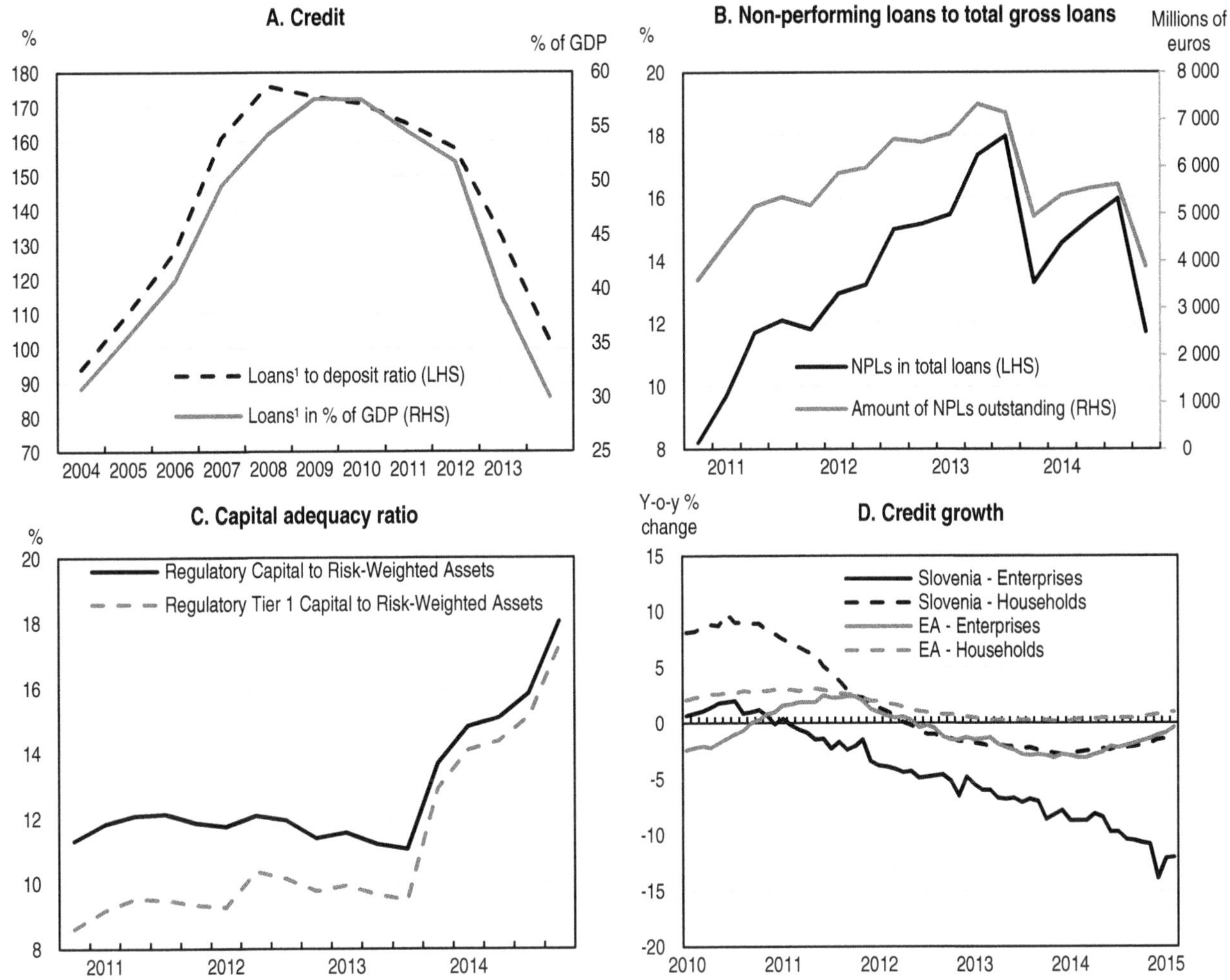

1. Outstanding amount at the end of the period.

Source: *ECB Statistical Data Warehouse*, for Panels A and D; and *IMF Financial Soundness Indicator Database*, for Panels B and C.

StatLink http://dx.doi.org/10.1787/888933204820

left Slovenian banks poorly capitalised and ill-equipped to extend further credit to the private sector (Figure 6, Panels C and D), holding back investment and consumption.

The banking sector had to be restructured and recapitalised. Comprehensive stress tests and the Asset Quality Review (AQR) of 8 banks in December 2013 showed a large shortfall in capital under the adverse scenario (Bank of Slovenia, 2013). Two small private loss making banks [4.5% of total assets, (IMF, 2014)] that had been under a supervised wind-down were recapitalised, and other small banks were asked to raise private capital, and if they were unsuccessful the state promised to provide funds. The three largest state-owned banks (NLB, NKBM and Abanka) have been recapitalised, while the shareholders and holders of subordinated debt have been wiped out. Since December 2013, the state has provided close to EUR 4 billion of capital to banks in total (11% of GDP).

To reinforce the banking sector further, the authorities committed that in the medium term they were going to fully privatise two banks (NKBM and Abanka), and reduce the state's share in the largest (NLB) to 25% plus one share. The NKBM bank was expected to be sold in the first quarter of 2015 but there are delays. The process should be finalised as soon as possible.

The transfer of bad assets of the banks to the state-owned Bank Asset Management Company (BAMC) was also facing delays (BAMC, 2014). BAMC was established in 2013 to have a key role in managing, liquidating and restructuring of bad assets, with the principal goal to recover the highest possible value for the transferred assets. The physical transfer of the loan files to the BAMC from NLB and NKBM was completed in 2014, while the Abanka transfer was finalised in the first half of 2015. In total, the three large state-owned banks and another small bank have transferred EUR 4.86 billion in assets to the BAMC, at the transfer value of EUR 1.56 billion, or with a 68% average haircut. Only about half of corporate NPLs have been transferred to the BAMC (IMF, 2015a), so there is room for further transfers. Foreign NPLs – consisting of lending to companies and subsidiaries of domestic banks in the Balkans – have not been transferred to the BAMC and constitute close to one quarter of total remaining NPLs (European Commission, 2015a).

Restructuring has stabilised the banking sector, but there are still weaknesses. The level of non-performing loans remains elevated (Figure 7, Panel A) and capital ratios are not high compared to banks in other euro area countries (Figure 7, Panel B). The level of provisioning however is higher than before and NPLs pose a lower risk to the solvency of banks (European Commission, 2015a). The results of the ECB's Comprehensive Assessment of European banks' balance sheets, announced in October 2014 showed a small capital shortfall (less than 0.2% of GDP) under the adverse scenario for NLB and NKBM. The two banks, however, will not require additional public recapitalisation, as they will be able to cover the capital shortfalls from retained earnings (ECB, 2014). Yet, profitability of banks remains low and credit activity to the corporate sector is still declining (Figure 7, Panels C and D).

Enhancing the role of BAMC in dealing with bad assets

The BAMC has the legal instruments and power to seek a quick resolution of impaired assets, either by restructuring the company (when it holds more than 50% of claims) or by liquidating it. Bankruptcy procedures with BAMC involvement are to be concluded within six months. The BAMC can acquire additional assets from other banks to facilitate corporate restructuring, but has to purchase them at market prices. The BAMC can issue of up to EUR 4 billion of government-guaranteed bonds in total (about 11% of GDP) to acquire assets. The life-span of the BAMC is set to five years (until the end of 2017) after which the remaining assets are to be transferred to the Slovenia Sovereign Holding (SSH) (BAMC, 2014; IMF, 2014).

Many countries have used asset management companies (AMCs) to deal with bad assets, as for example Finland, Mexico, Spain, Sweden and the USA, but results have been mixed (Klingebiel, 2000; Laeven and Valencia, 2008). The advantages include economies of scale in consolidating scarce skills and resources within one agency, and the fact that AMCs can have enhanced bargaining power versus debtors by concentrating assets and collateral in one place. However, the transfer from originating banks means some loss of institutional knowledge about borrowers (Klingebiel, 2000; Woo, 2000). In practice, AMCs have been more successful in selling off assets of unviable bankrupt institutions than in corporate restructurings. It has also been easier to sell real estate than other assets. When AMCs only had a small fraction of the banking system on their balance sheets, it was easier to maintain independence from political pressures (Klingebiel, 2000).

About two thirds of the BAMC's current exposures are in default, where BAMC is to acquire the collateral – real estate but also equity and company assets – and sell it to the private sector. The other exposure is corporates that have a viable core activity but need to be financially and operationally restructured (European Commission, 2014a). Past

Figure 7. **The banking sector remains weak and credit activity is subdued**

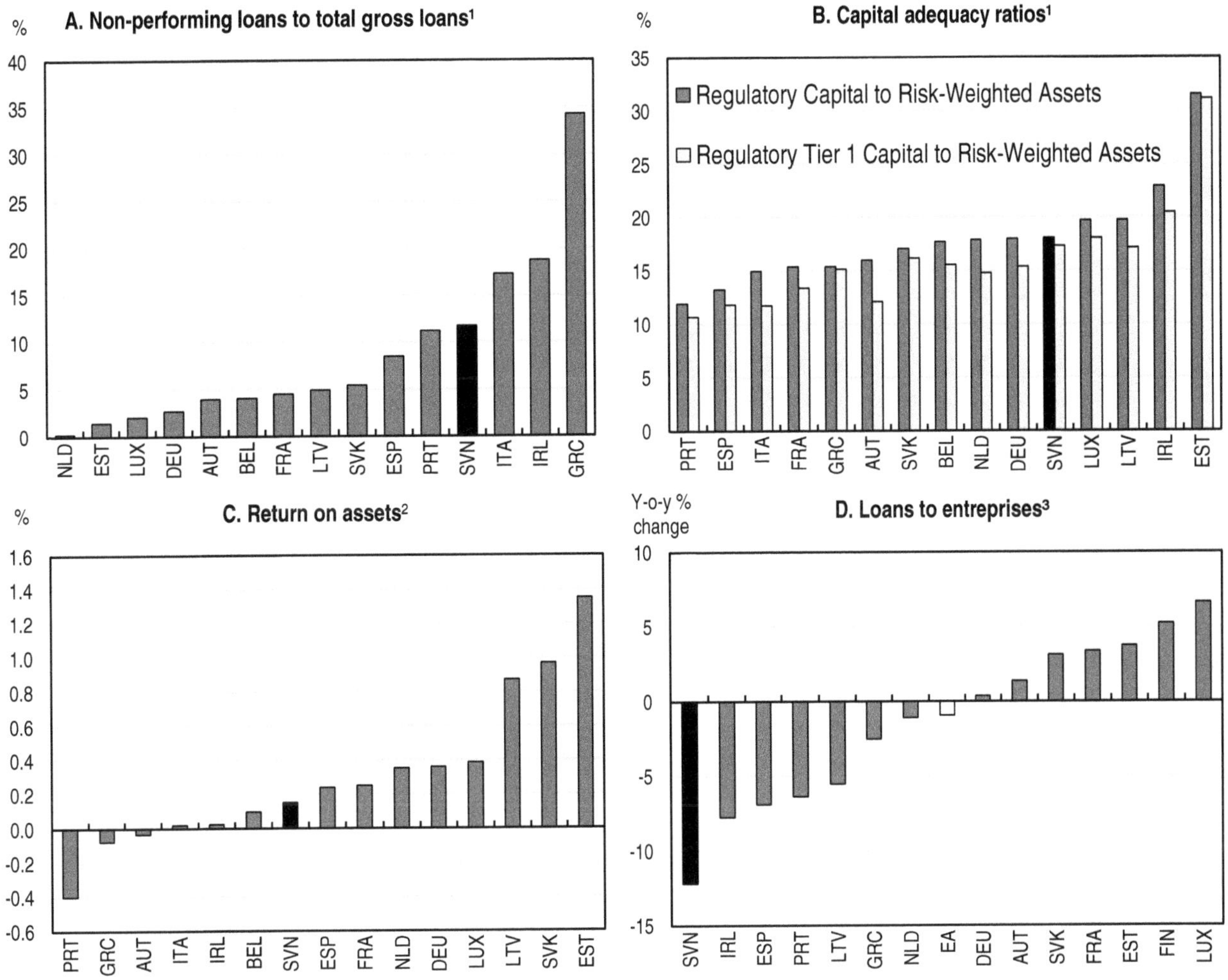

1. 2014 Q4 or latest data available.
2. Average return on assets in the four quarters of 2014, except for France and Germany whose data refers to 2013.
3. Average of annual growth rates between November 2014 and February 2015. Loans adjusted for sales and securitisation of all types of maturity.

Source: IMF Financial Soundness Indicator Database, for Panels A, B and C; and *ECB Statistical Data Warehouse*, for Panel D.

StatLink http://dx.doi.org/10.1787/888933204831

experience shows that corporate restructuring can be challenging, and the situation in Slovenia is exacerbated by the presence of numerous complex, inter-connected group loans with several bilateral contracts and conflicting interests (Bank of Slovenia, 2014a). Transferring all assets in a company group to BAMC will give it a majority position *vis-à-vis* other creditors. BAMC in co-ordination with the authorities should decide strategically which are the most urgent and important cases in the economy to be restructured, and ensure that additional exposures are transferred to the BAMC. This will also alleviate the problem of NPLs on banks' balance sheets. But action needs to be taken swiftly. Past experience shows that ambiguity on what additional assets may eventually be transferred to the AMCs limit banks' incentives to engage in corporate restructuring of assets remaining on their balance sheets (Klingebiel, 2000).

Independence and professionalism are also important for BAMC's success (Klingebiel, 2000). Restructuring companies requires specialised expertise which is highly valued on the market. BAMC therefore needs to have freedom to set its own remuneration policy to attract adequate talent. In addition, extending the life-span of the BAMC would reduce pressure for fire sales and enhance independence of the BAMC. The authorities are planning to change legislation in order to extend the life of BAMC to 2022 from current 2017, which is a step in the right direction. Successful AMCs in the past have relied on a detailed set of directives and guidelines to staff and contractors that cover a wide range of operations, including asset management and disposition, contract policies, bidding procedures and marketing. This minimised the possibility of fraud, made policy and cost evaluation more transparent, and hence expedited the resolution process (Klingebiel, 2000). The Slovenian Corruption Prevention Commission (CPC) and the Court of Audit in their reports voiced concerns about conflict of interest, significant corruption risks and irregularities in BAMC with respect to hiring of external consultancies, remuneration policies, internal processes and corporate governance. BAMC has taken measures to strengthen its own governance in 2014 by adopting strategic guidelines and a business strategy for asset management.

Effective restructuring and disposal of assets also requires sound financial institutions and other available markets, where the AMCs can find potential buyers for the assets. Deep and liquid capital markets also help in this regard. Slovenia lacks fresh equity, and BAMC is unable to lend money to companies, while banks are weak and unwilling to extend credit. In fact, the authorities are planning to change the law to enable BAMC to lend to companies, which will facilitate restructuring. In addition, more openness to privatisation and foreign investors could bring more fresh capital. Swift restructuring of the banking sector and resumption of credit activity is equally important. BAMC can use tools at its disposal to encourage banks to lend afresh to viable restructured companies, for example, by putting up their collateral for fresh loans or assigning super-seniority status.

Improving bank supervision and business practices of banks

The weak framework for the governance of state-owned banks contributed to poor credit standards, excessive risk taking and misallocation of credit before the crisis (OECD, 2013a). The Slovenian Corruption Prevention Commission reports (CPC, 2013) that corrupt practices in allocation of credit had been wide spread in the state-dominated banking system. The planned bank privatisations are welcome in this regard as they are expected to improve corporate governance. However, the plan to retain a blocking minority shareholding should be dropped as it opens the door to political interference.

The Asset Quality Review (AQR) from December 2013 identified several weaknesses in the banks' risk management systems (European Commission, 2014b). The data integrity validation highlighted deficiencies in IT systems and paper records, with significant gaps in several loan files. Most banks did not assign rating classes in line with the regulations issued by Bank of Slovenia and in many instances the collateral valuations were out of date. BAMC (2014) likewise notes that credit files received from the banks were in many cases incomplete and of poor quality. The risk management in banks should be of higher standard and bank supervisors should more closely follow that regulations and guidance are properly followed by the banks.

The ECB Single Supervisory Mechanism, in place from November 2014, will bring unified supervisory methodologies and standards at the Eurosystem level. New legislation was adopted in March 2015 in line with EU directives, to introduce capital shock absorbers, enhanced risk management and bank governance requirements, and improved transparency of bank operations through additional disclosure and assessment of systemic risks. Furthermore, a bank resolution fund has been established, to be financed by banks and managed by the central bank. To foster higher standards of the risk management and non-performing exposures management in banks, the Bank of Slovenia has introduced number of measures, such as additional reporting of banks and requirements for individual plans for non-performing exposure management. As the absence of credit information sharing between banks is likely to have contributed to poor risk outcomes (OECD, 2013a), the upgrading of the Central Credit Registry (Bank of Slovenia, 2014a) is welcome.

An improved insolvency framework will speed up corporate restructuring

Indebtedness of corporates remains high (Figure 8, Panel A), despite debt reduction since 2009 (Figure 9, Panel A). The debt is fairly concentrated (Bank of Slovenia, 2014c; European Commission, 2014b; IMAD 2014b; Damijan, 2014). Only one-third of all companies have a debt overhang – financial debt exceeding EBITDA by a factor of five – but they account for around 80% of total financial debt (Figure 8, Panel B). State-owned and state-controlled enterprises are also highly leveraged and continue to be at risk of default (European Commission, 2015a). Despite the concentration of debt overhang, evidence shows that deleveraging is having significant negative effects on overall economic activity and investment (IMAD, 2014c). Moreover, compared to other vulnerable countries the economic distress is not only concentrated in real estate and construction, but widely spread across sectors, with many service sectors also affected (European Commission, 2014b). Profitability is low, due to high interest burden, and the bank funding costs of Slovenian corporates remain elevated (Figure 9, Panel B), but many viable companies have been able to tap alternative sources of funding at lower cost.

Figure 8. **The debt overhang is concentrated in a few companies**

A. Debt to equity ratio
2013 or latest data available

B. Corporate health of companies by debt leverage ratio (2013)[1]

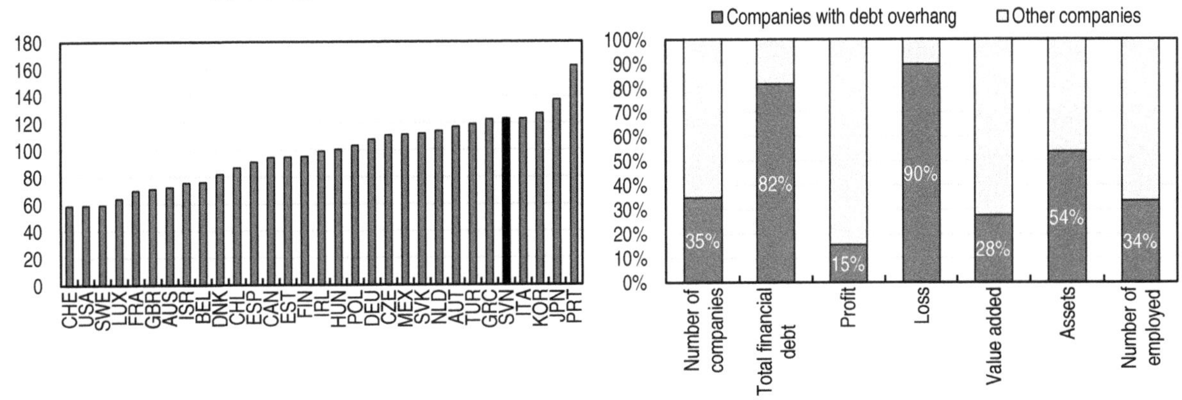

1. Companies with debt overhang are those with negative EBIDTA (earnings before interest, tax, depreciation and amortisation) and those with debt leverage ratio (financial debt over EBITDA) larger than 5.

Source: *OECD Financial Indicators Database*, for Panel A; and Calculations by IMAD, based on raw micro level data (firm-by-firm) from AJPES, for Panel B.

StatLink http://dx.doi.org/10.1787/888933204848

The European Commission (2014b) found that between 2007 and 2012 Slovenia's expenditures on state aid to the real economy more than tripled, to 1.3% of GDP. Yet, many of the companies that received aid still ended up in financial difficulties. Given the fiscal pressures, it is important to shift from state aid to an effective framework for swift

Figure 9. **Deleveraging has been under way, while corporates still face elevated funding costs**

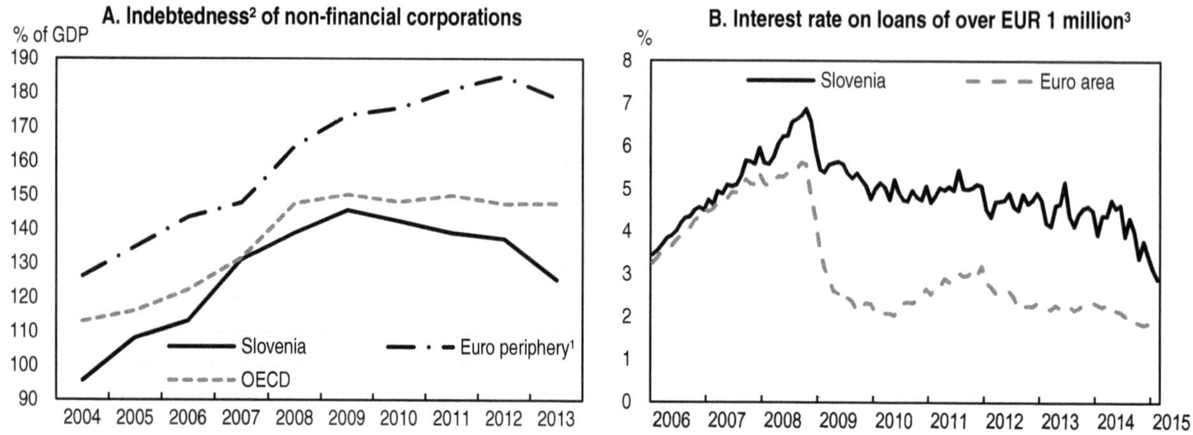

1. The euro periphery is composed of Greece, Portugal, Spain and Ireland.
2. Debt is defined as all liabilities that require payment or payments of interest or principal by the debtor to the creditor at a date or dates in the future. It comprises of all debt instruments except for shares, equity and financial derivatives.
3. Interest rate on loans to non-financial corporations of amount over EUR 1 million.

Source: *OECD Financial Indicators Database*, for Panel A; and *ECB Statistical Data Warehouse*, for Panel B.

StatLink http://dx.doi.org/10.1787/888933204852

liquidation of unviable companies and effective restructuring of viable ones. The authorities are already replacing subsidies by low cost loans to companies. Furthermore, in an important step, in January 2015, the government appointed a task force for corporate restructuring and deleveraging, comprising government and central bank officials, tasked with monitoring and co-ordinating restructuring and deleveraging of companies, and proposing measures to make the processes more effective. Better co-ordination and communication among the major stakeholders will facilitate the process, so this is a welcome step.

Resolving insolvency in Slovenia is very time consuming and recovery rates are low. According to the *2015 World Bank Doing Business Survey*, it takes an average of 2 years to complete a standard bankruptcy procedure (involving a main secured creditor and several unsecured ones). In Slovenia, investors recover only about 50% of assets, while other countries (Finland, Japan and Norway) achieve recovery rates above 90%. Such high rates are achieved by rapid bankruptcy procedures that last 5 to 11 months. In addition, in Slovenia insolvency procedures are often initiated too late, usually when it is already impossible to save the enterprise.

In 2013, the parliament passed important reforms to facilitate early restructuring of viable companies. The framework provides for preventive restructuring of large and medium-sized companies that are viable, but that could become insolvent within a year. The framework also gives more powers to creditors and smaller creditors now enjoy better protection. The absolute priority rule now ensures that if equity is zero, equity will be eliminated, preventing existing owners from blocking the restructuring process. The amendments also improved corporate restructuring features such as debt-for-equity swaps and corporate spin-offs to facilitate viable firms continuing as a going concern (IMF, 2014). The overall procedure of court-mandated debt restructuring has been streamlined by broadening the scope of companies eligible for a "simplified procedure".

Reforms have significantly improved the corporate insolvency regime, which, if properly implemented, can facilitate the rehabilitation of viable firms (IMF, 2014). During 2013-14, about 30 compulsory settlements were completed per year, simplified compulsory settlements increased from 10 in 2013 to 90 in 2014. Furthermore, in 2014, 8 pre-insolvency restructuring proceedings were concluded for the first time. Nevertheless, corporate bankruptcy procedures remain widespread, amounting to close to 1 000 per year in 2013-14, twice as many as in 2012 (IMF, 2015a). The effectiveness of the reform should be closely monitored and evaluated based on appropriate indicators, such as recovery rates in all types of insolvency procedures (European Commission, 2014c). Indeed, Slovenia has already started evaluating the reform (European Commission, 2015a). Institutional capacity could also be improved further to promote successful implementation. The number of judges specialised in commercial law is low. The number of insolvency administrators is insufficient and many lack relevant knowledge in the areas of accounting and finance. Furthermore, there is lack of meaningful co-operation between judges and insolvency administrators (IMF, 2015a and 2015b).

Slovenia could achieve speedy and cost effective debt settlement through better use of voluntary out-of-court restructuring, as recently introduced in Portugal and Spain. *2013 Economic Survey of Slovenia* reports that although allowed under the Slovenian insolvency law, out-of-court restructuring is not explicitly regulated and average time of such restructuring is high in international comparison. Additional incentives could be introduced to promote the use of out-of-court restructuring. Sufficient debt hair-cuts should be permitted for such procedures and tax and social security should be equalised with other liabilities.

Recommendations on restructuring and deleveraging the banking sector and the corporate sector

Key recommendations

- Enhance the leading role of the Bank Asset Management Company to ensure swift restructuring of companies and effective liquidation of assets.
- For the most important firms to be restructured, ensure that all assets in a company group are transferred to the Bank Asset Management Company.
- Bank Asset Management Company should maintain its independence and ability to attract highly professional staff, while adhering to the highest standards of corporate governance and transparency.
- Monitor the implementation of the new insolvency regulation and improve institutional capacity by training judges and insolvency administrators. Make out-of-court restructuring faster and more attractive.

Other recommendations

- Privatise state-owned banks as planned, without retaining blocking minority shareholdings.
- In the context of the single supervisory mechanism framework, the bank supervisor should more closely monitor banks' adherence to regulations and guidance, and encourage banks to improve their risk management.

Ensuring sustainable public finances

The costs of the banking crisis, persistent deficits and the drop in output have strained public finances and led to a rapid rise in public debt from 22% of GDP in 2008 to over 80% of GDP in 2014 (Figure 10). Together with a period of high uncertainty about capital needs of

Figure 10. **The government pursues fiscal consolidation but public debt keeps rising**

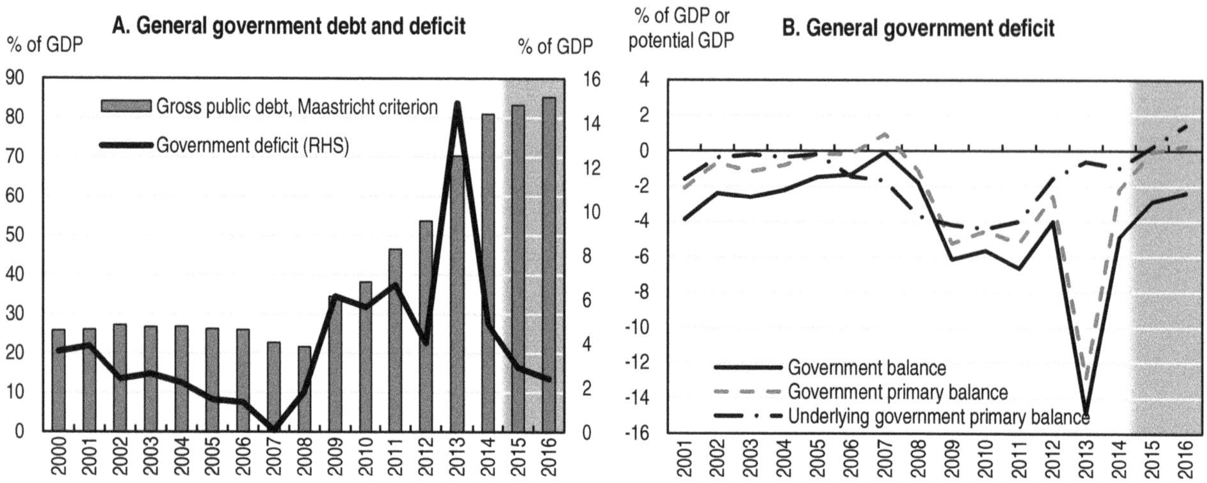

Note: Data for years 2014-16 represent OECD projections. The large shift in 2013 includes the cost of bank recapitalisation.
Source: OECD Economic Outlook 96 Database.

StatLink http://dx.doi.org/10.1787/888933204864

the banking sector and political difficulties, this pushed sovereign yields close to 7% during 2013. Subsequent bank rescue and fiscal measures, coupled with lower risk perception in the euro area, brought the sovereign yield to below 2% (Figure 5, Panel D), and the government has substantially prefinanced its 2015 and 2016 fiscal needs.

To contain the debt build-up the government has pursued fiscal consolidation since 2010. The measures have included cuts in public investment, consumption and subsidies, reduction in the public-sector wage bill, and a temporary freeze of pension indexation. The government also increased VAT and excise duties on alcohol, tobacco and fuel. The personal income tax was adjusted with elimination of the automatic indexation of tax brackets and tax allowances. The fight against the grey economy and tax evasion was stepped-up. Between end-2010 and end-2014 the fiscal effort in terms of the underlying government primary balance amounted on average to over 1 percentage points of GDP per year. In line with its commitments under the EU Excessive Deficit Procedure, the government aims to bring the deficit to below 3% of GDP by end-2015. The plan is to reach a roughly balanced budget by the end of 2019.

The path has not been easy. The deficit at the end of 2014 at 4.9% of GDP was larger than planned despite better than forecast economic growth. The expenditures were higher due to higher spending on subsidies to some public expenditures and increased absorption of EU funds (IMF, 2015a). At the same time, the newly adopted real estate tax was repealed by the Constitutional Court, lowering revenue. The government aims to lower the headline deficit to 2.9% of GDP in 2015 by further cutting the public wage bill, more efficient public procurement and changes to the system of financing of municipalities. On the other hand, it plans a 30% year-on-year increase in investment spending to support growth. On the revenue side the government plans to raise taxes on financial services and insurance, to reverse the abolition of the bank balance sheet tax, increase CO_2 and energy efficiency levies, and gain savings from a further simplification of tax collection procedures.

Simulations by the OECD show that to stabilise public debt at 60% by 2030 Slovenia needs to consolidate on average 0.9 percentage points of GDP per year beyond 2015 (the

Figure 11. **Structural primary surpluses will be needed to stabilise debt while age-related expenditures will exert additional pressure**

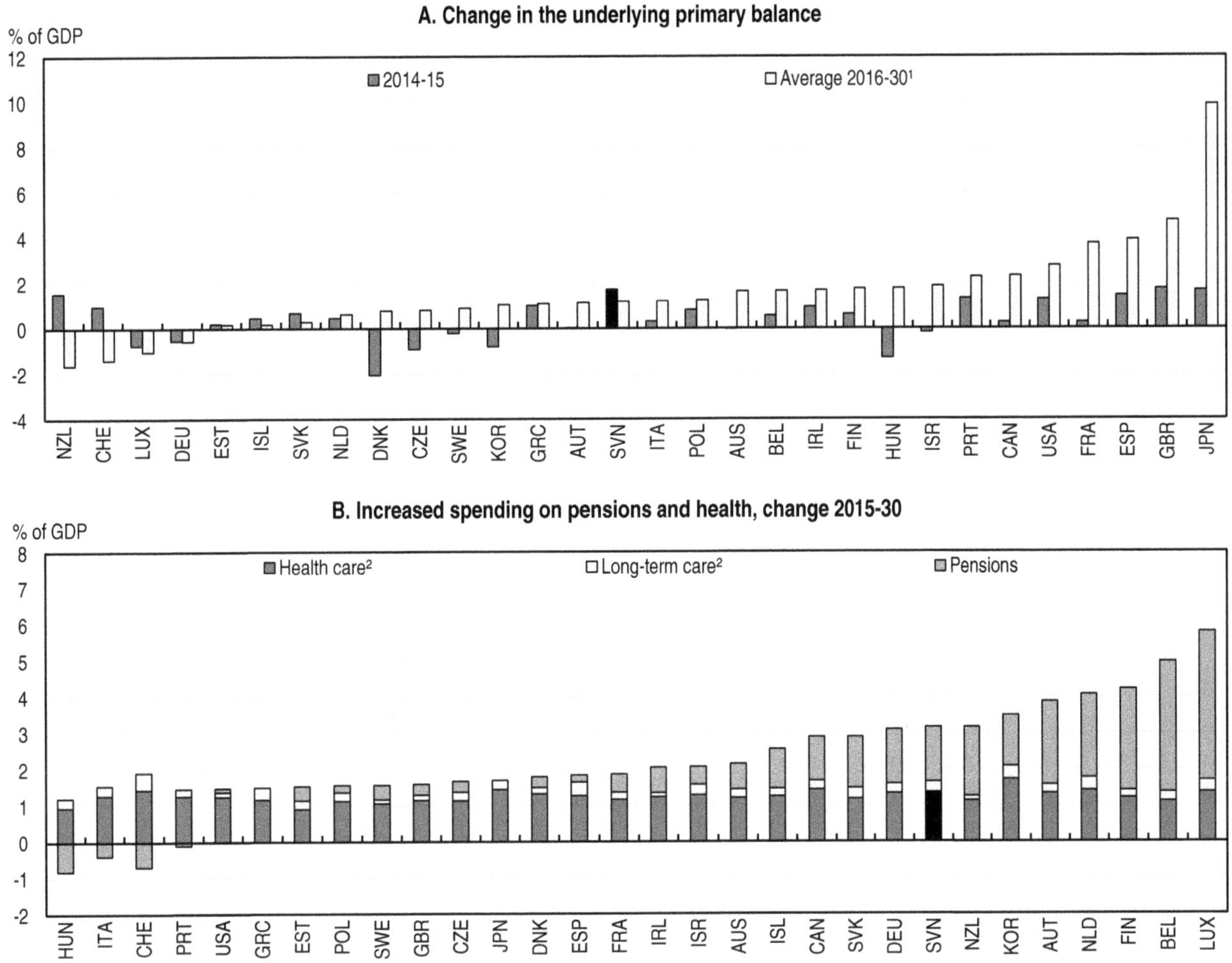

1. The average measure of consolidation is the difference between the underlying primary balance in 2015 and the average underlying primary balance between 2016 and 2030, except for those countries for which the debt target is only achieved after 2030, in which case the average is calculated up until the year that debt target is achieved.
2. Based on "Cost-containment scenario", (Oliveira Martins and de la Maisonneuve, 2014). Where projections are not available over the period 2015-30, linear interpolation has been applied.

Source: OECD calculations based on *OECD Economic Outlook 96* projections.

StatLink http://dx.doi.org/10.1787/888933204875

difference between the projected underlying primary balance in 2015 and the average underlying primary balance to 2030) (Figure 11, Panel A). This, however is made challenging by a projected rise in age-related public expenditure by about 3.1 percentage points of GDP over the years 2015-30 (OECD, 2014a) (Figure 11, Panel B). Despite the recent pension reform, the public expenditure on pensions is expected to increase by 6 percentage points of GDP between 2015 and 2050 (OECD, 2014b). This comes on top of already high levels of public expenditure in terms of GDP and the steeply rising trend in recent years (Figure 12).

With public debt high and prospect of it rising further, it is appropriate that the government aims at fiscal consolidation. Given the still weak economic recovery and the impact of automatic stabilisers, the chosen pace – not too abrupt – correctly balances consolidation and growth concerns. However, the government should set out more clearly a credible medium-term consolidation plan, and the quality of the measures should be

Figure 12. **Public expenditure is high and rising**

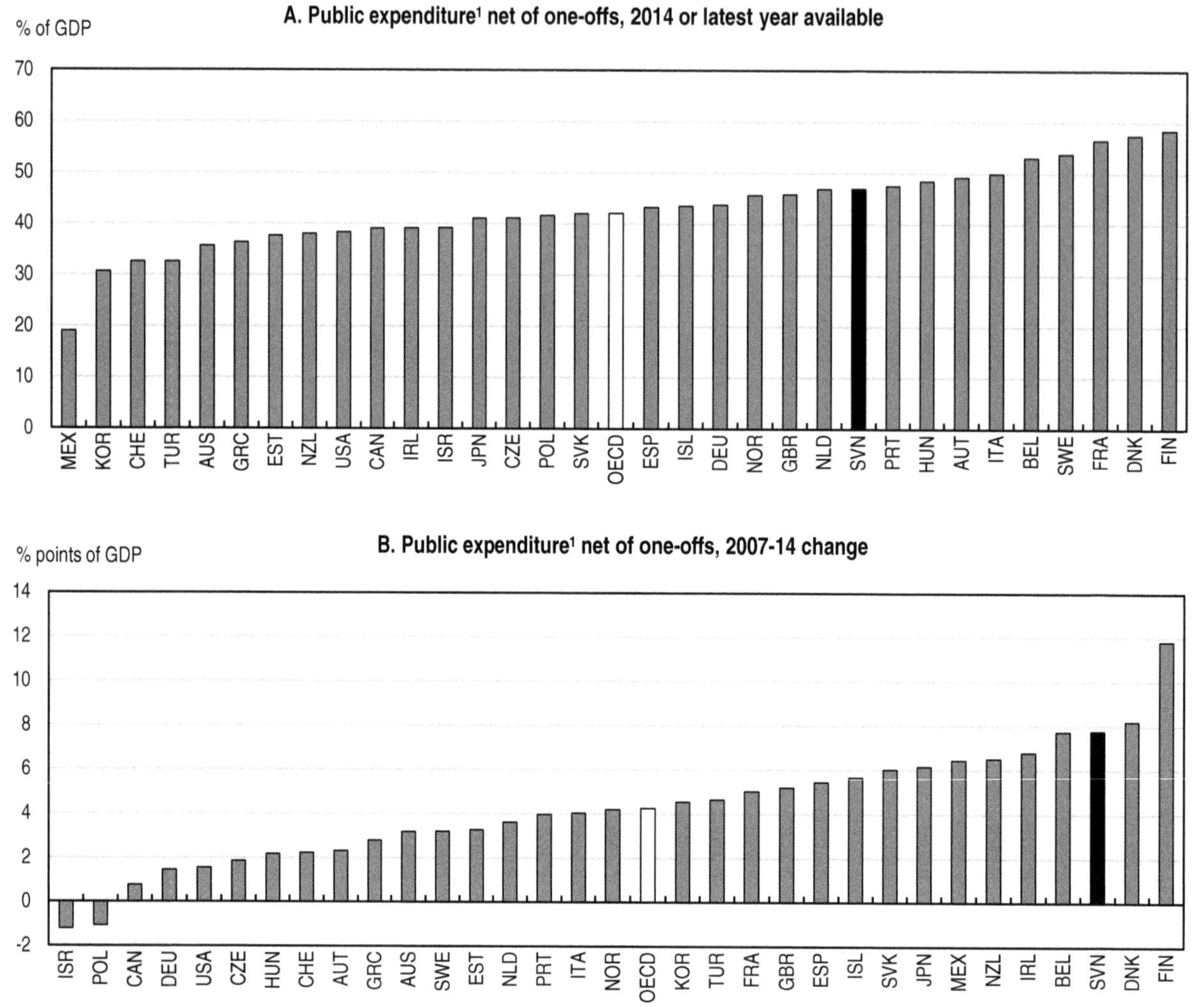

1. Total general government expenditure corrected for exceptional net capital transfers and payments and other exceptional transfers.
Source: OECD Economic Outlook 96 Database.

StatLink http://dx.doi.org/10.1787/888933204888

improved. Policy decisions have relied too heavily on temporary measures instead of structural efforts to rein in public expenditure growth.

Structural reform of public expenditure is key to reducing public debt

Restructuring welfare spending and better targeting social transfers – family, unemployment and disability – could go a long way in tackling the budget deficit and improving fiscal sustainability. Inactivity and unemployment traps are high in Slovenia. The combined effects of unemployment benefits, social assistance and other transfers, together with taxes, act as disincentives for the unemployed or the inactive to return to work (OECD, 2013a; Table 4). Reform could boost work incentives if, at low income levels, benefits could be withdrawn at a lower rate than the after-tax increase in earnings, to allow a more generous net increase in income. Furthermore, the progressivity of cash transfers is relatively low (Joumard et al., 2012; OECD, 2014c). With the 2012 reform, the eligibility of high-income earners for cash transfers was reduced, by taking into account all income and also property of individuals and families. Better means testing could further reduce the share of high-income earners eligible for support and boost fiscal savings.

Table 4. **Inactivity traps and unemployment traps are high in international comparison**

Average effective tax rate when moving from unemployment/inactivity into work, per cent, 2012

	Wage level (% of average worker)	Inactivity trap[1]			Unemployment trap[2]		
		Slovenia	Other CEEC	OECD average	**Slovenia**	Other CEEC	OECD average
One-earner married couple	67	**65**	55	63	**88**	62	70
	100	**63**	46	54	**76**	57	65
	150	**56**	43	48	**65**	51	59
Lone parent with two children	67	**71**	43	56	**84**	66	69
	100	**63**	48	55	**78**	68	68
	150	**64**	44	51	**69**	58	62
One-earner married couple with two children	67	**81**	57	66	**88**	59	69
	100	**64**	50	60	**75**	55	67
	150	**65**	46	54	**66**	50	61
Two-earner married couple with two children	67	**45**	35	35	**93**	68	70
	100	**49**	34	36	**80**	63	66
	150	**48**	33	37	**68**	55	60

Note: Participation tax rates measure the extent to which taxes and benefits reduce the financial gain of moving into work.

1. Average effective tax rate when moving from inactivity into work for selected family types and earnings levels. The estimates here relate to the situation of a person who is not entitled to unemployment benefits (e.g. because the entitlements have expired). Instead, social assistance and other means-tested benefits are assumed to be available subject to relevant income conditions.
2. Average effective tax rate for a transition into full-time work for persons receiving unemployment benefits at the initial level, for selected family types and earnings levels (same in new job as in previous).

Source: OECD Tax-Benefit Models.

Increasing efficiency of expenditures in education, public administration and local government can also increase sustainability of public finances (Hribernik and Kierzenkowski, 2013). In education, increasing pupil-teacher ratios and class sizes in primary and lower secondary education would lower cost and ensure a more effective use of staff. Employing better qualified teachers, with good working conditions, is more important for student performance than the number of teachers (Sutherland and Price, 2007; Hattie, 2009; OECD, 2009). The allocation of tertiary education services could also be better targeted, as it is currently very regressive, largely benefiting households at the top of the income distribution (OECD, 2013a). The number of municipalities in Slovenia has grown over the last 20 years, in contrast to pattern observed in most other OECD countries. Many municipalities are too small to provide public services efficiently and municipal mergers and financial incentives for inter-municipal co-operation should be a policy priority (OECD, 2011a). The revenue formula is more generous to smaller and less dense municipalities, and local revenues rely heavily on income tax. Hence, many small municipalities can survive as "bedroom communities" with revenue based on economic activities outside the local area. Changes to local finances could further reduce the incentives for fragmentation (OECD, 2011a).

There is also scope for improved efficiency in the public administration. Certain administrative units could be merged and the proliferation of agencies should be resisted. There is a lack of strategy in reducing public sector employment and the wage bill. Wage cuts were applied across the board, including in performance related pay. Yet, public sector salaries (Figure 13) and motivation of workers are already comparatively low. The authorities should reinstate performance-related pay as soon as possible, while strengthening performance assessment systems. Non-monetary incentives, such as training and options for a better work-life balance, could be used too. Furthermore, when cutting staff, reductions should be focused on inefficient programmes, and avoid aggravating shortages of certain skills and competences (OECD 2013b, 2012a and 2012b).

Figure 13. **Salaries in the public sector are low**

Average annual compensation of central government officials relative to compensation of tertiary-educated workers

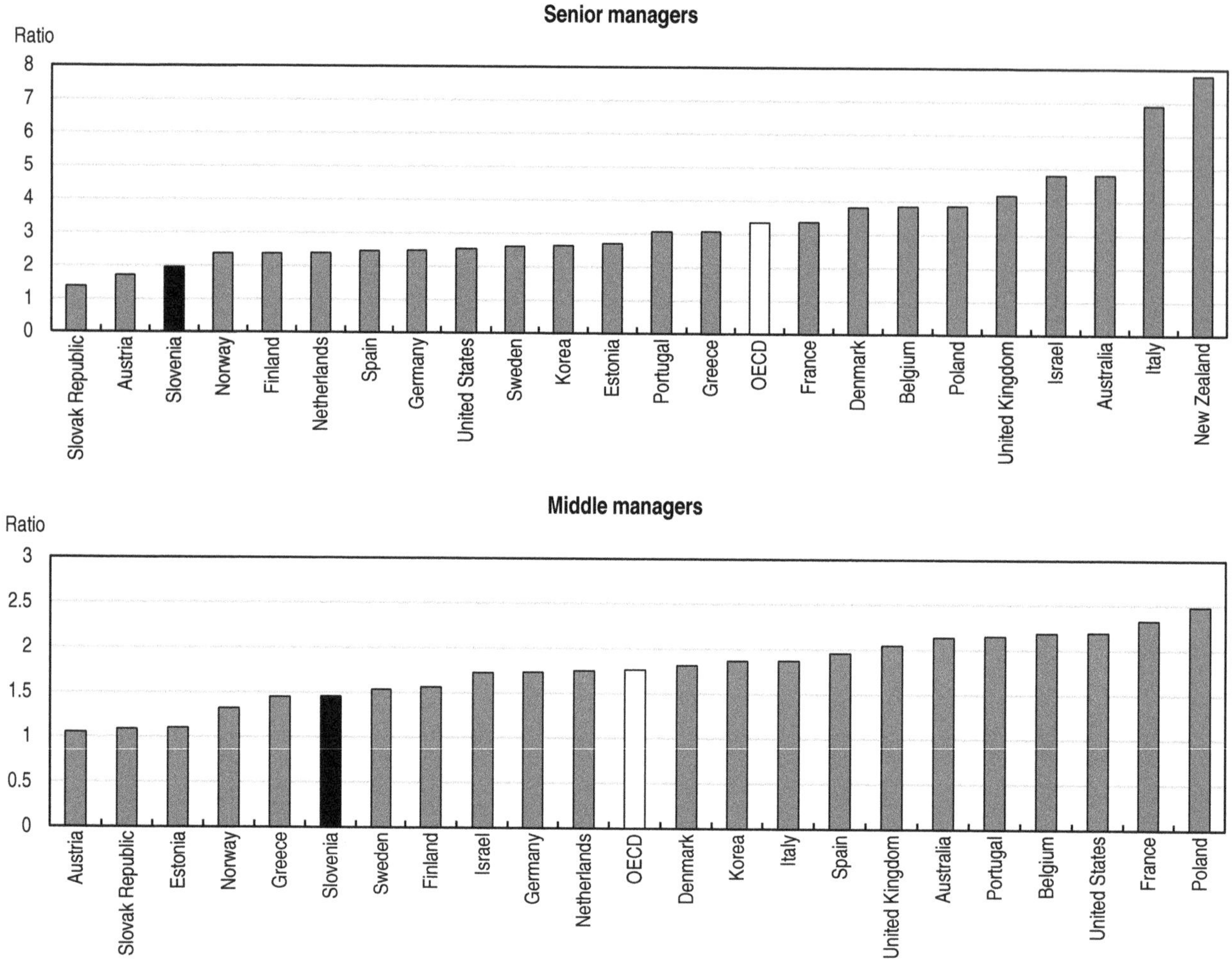

Source: *Government at a Glance*, 2013.

StatLink http://dx.doi.org/10.1787/888933204898

Weaknesses in the fiscal framework contributed to poor control over expenditure growth. The fiscal council set up in 2009 and the fiscal rule of 2010 have not effectively controlled spending. After some delays, the government in December 2014 adopted legislation to implement a Constitutional fiscal rule that requires a balanced budget over the medium term, but it still needs to be passed in parliament with a two-thirds majority. As spending growth has been hard to contain, Slovenia should adopt a credible and transparent expenditure rule (for example, a multi-year nominal expenditure ceiling) with well-defined escape clauses. Expenditure rules target the part of budget that the government controls most directly and tend to be less uncertain compared to cyclically-adjusted deficit rules, raising transparency and accountability. Successful examples – Denmark, Finland, the Netherlands and Sweden – show that expenditure rules can be effectively combined with a cyclically adjusted budget balance rules (Ayuso-i-Casals, 2012). Together with medium-term budgetary objectives based on a structural budget within the Stability and Growth Pact, the expenditure rule could provide a good basis for medium-term fiscal framework. Finally, the fiscal council should be charged with assessing both adherence to the rules and the rationale for the use of escape provisions (OECD, 2013a).

Tax mix to better support growth

Taxes on labour are relatively high in Slovenia as a result of high social security contributions and progressive personal income tax, especially at the high end of the wage distribution (Figure 14). After introducing the additional 50% tax bracket for those earning more than 5 times the average wage, the marginal tax wedge for top earners stands at 66% (OECD, 2014d). This can have large costs in terms of work incentives, deter hiring and investment in skills, while bringing very little in terms of additional government revenue (OECD, 2011b; Guner et al., 2014). Better labour market outcomes could be achieved by reducing the top marginal personal income tax rate.

Figure 14. **Marginal tax wedge is high – % of total earnings, 2013**

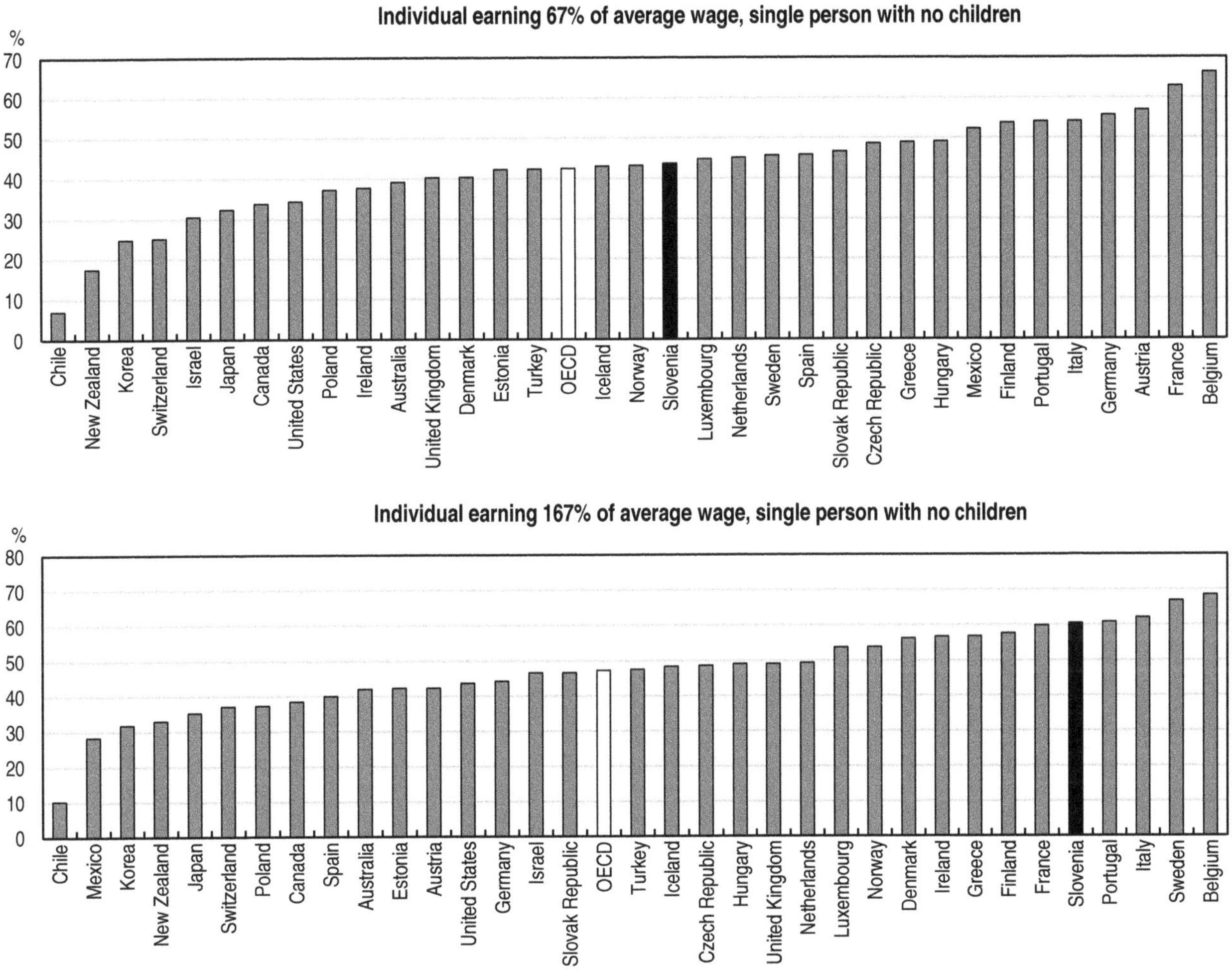

Source: Public Sector, *Taxation and Market Regulation Database.*

StatLink http://dx.doi.org/10.1787/888933204901

Revenues from taxes on property were only 0.7% of GDP in 2013, one third of the OECD average (Figure 15). Recurrent taxation of real estate is a key element of a tax system that supports inclusive and sustainable growth. This form of taxation has been found to have relatively limited negative effects on economic growth (Arnold et al., 2011). In fact, Slovenia enacted a Real Estate Tax Law in 2014, but this law was repealed by the Constitutional Court. Slovenian government plans to prepare an alternative property tax reform with the same policy objectives while satisfying legal requirements, which is a positive step.

Figure 15. **There is room to raise property taxes**

Property taxation revenues, 2013 or latest year available

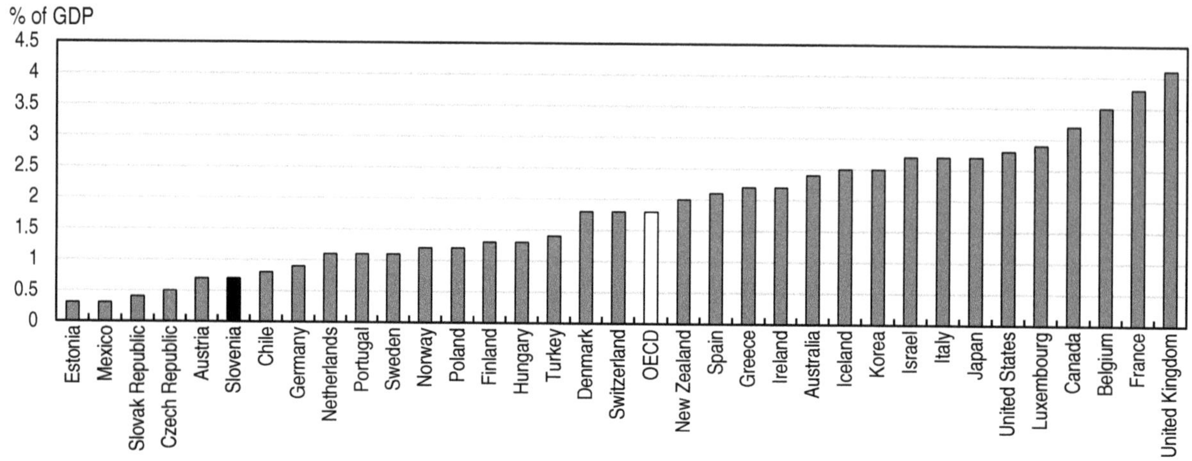

Source: Public Sector, *Taxation and Market Regulation Database.*

StatLink http://dx.doi.org/10.1787/888933204911

Recommendations on fiscal sustainability

Key recommendations

- Focus fiscal consolidation on structural measures to increase cost efficiency in education, public administration and local government.
- Adopt a fiscal rule with a credible and transparent expenditure rule and ensure that an independent and effective fiscal council is charged with assessing adherence.

Other recommendations

- Restructure the combined effects of unemployment benefits, social assistance and taxes so that, at low income levels, benefits would be withdrawn at a lower rate than the after-tax increase in earnings, in order to increase work incentives for the unemployed and inactive persons.
- Reduce top tax rates on labour income. Better target family benefits and strengthen means testing of education-related benefits.
- Avoid across the board cuts in reducing the public sector wage bill. Reinstate the performance pay provisions and use non-monetary incentives for public sector workers. When cutting employment, reductions should avoid aggravating shortages of certain skills and competences.
- Increase recurrent taxes on real estate.

The economic consequences of population ageing

Slovenia is aging faster than many other OECD countries. The share of the elderly (aged 65 and above) is projected to increase from 17% in 2013 to 29% in 2060 (European Commission, 2014d), doubling the old-age dependency ratio (Figure 16, Panel A). Policy makers will need to contain ageing-related outlays and pursue efficiency-enhancing reforms of social support systems and labour markets.

Figure 16. **Old-age dependency ratio and projected public pension expenditure**

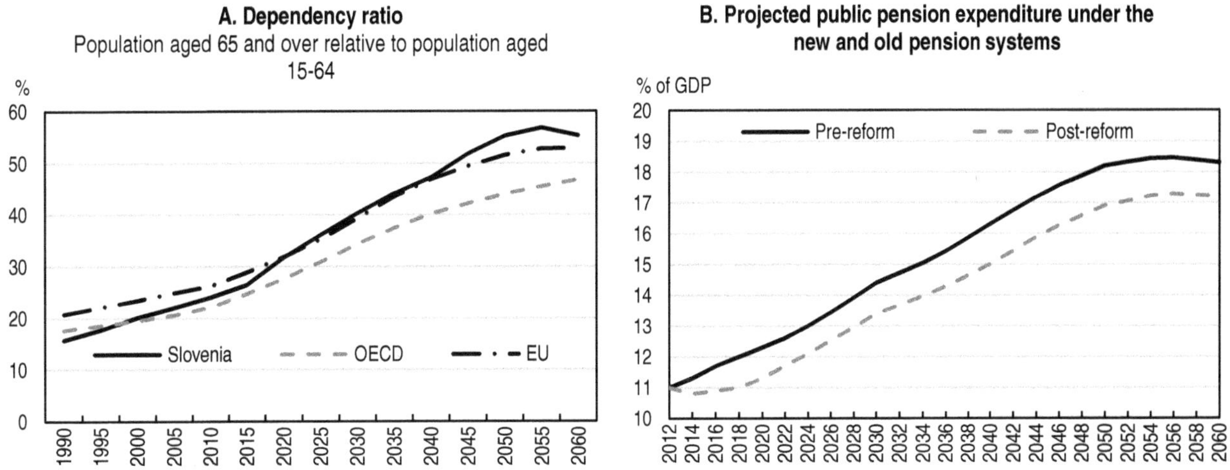

Source: UN, *World Population Prospects: The 2012 Revision* for Panel A; and Majcen et al., 2012 for Panel B.

StatLink http://dx.doi.org/10.1787/888933204921

The pension system is not sustainable despite recent reforms

The new pension legislation, implemented in January 2013, strengthens the link between contributions paid and pensions received and equalises the statutory retirement age for men and women; for both it will be gradually raised to 65 years by 2020. Pensions are no longer fully indexed to gross salaries, but 60% to the increase in the average gross wage and 40% to inflation. The new measures have helped to slow the inflow of new applicants into the pension system, increase the average retirement age, and raise the share of retirees that have completed the full duration of the statutory working life (MDDSZ, 2014). These achievements, however, have to be seen in the context of a strong inflow into the pension system and related expenditure increases just before 2013 in anticipation of the reforms. In any case, the undertaken policy changes will only temporarily ease the spending pressure (Majcen et al., 2012) (Figure 16, Panel B). In more recent analysis, the European Commission's Ageing Working Group projects a less pronounced increase of pension expenditure in the long term (European Commission, 2015b), but confirms the near-term need for additional measures to contain expenditure growth.

To ensure sustainability after 2020 and to take account of longer life expectancy, the effective retirement age will have to be further increased by adjusting upwards the minimum and statutory retirement ages. Also, there is a need to further tighten eligibility for early retirement and raise the minimum contribution period required to obtain a full pension. Indeed, about half of OECD countries have elements in their mandatory retirement-income provision that provide an automatic link between pensions and a change in life expectancy (OECD, 2011c).

The 2013 pension reform increased the number of years on which pensions are based from the best 18 to the best 24. However, the reform stopped short of adopting a system based on lifetime contributions, which would further increase sustainability of the system. Further, placing an even greater weight on prices in the indexation of pensions will make it possible to maintain the purchasing power of pensioners, while avoiding that labour productivity gains translate into higher pension expenditures. Countries such as France, Japan, Spain, the United Kingdom and the United States, take only price inflation into account when indexing pensions. One of the key challenges in this context is to balance fiscal sustainability and adequacy of pensions.

Expenditures on health and long-term care will grow strongly

Public outlays on health and long-term care in Slovenia are in line with the OECD average, but higher than in many countries with a similar level of GDP per capita. However, they are expected to grow strongly over the next 50 years as the population ages and life expectancy increases, as in many other countries. Under the European Commission's reference scenario, the total increase in health and long-term care expenditures would amount to 2.7 percentage points of GDP by 2060 (European Commission, 2015b, Figure 17).

Figure 17. **A big rise in health and long term care expenditures is projected in the future**

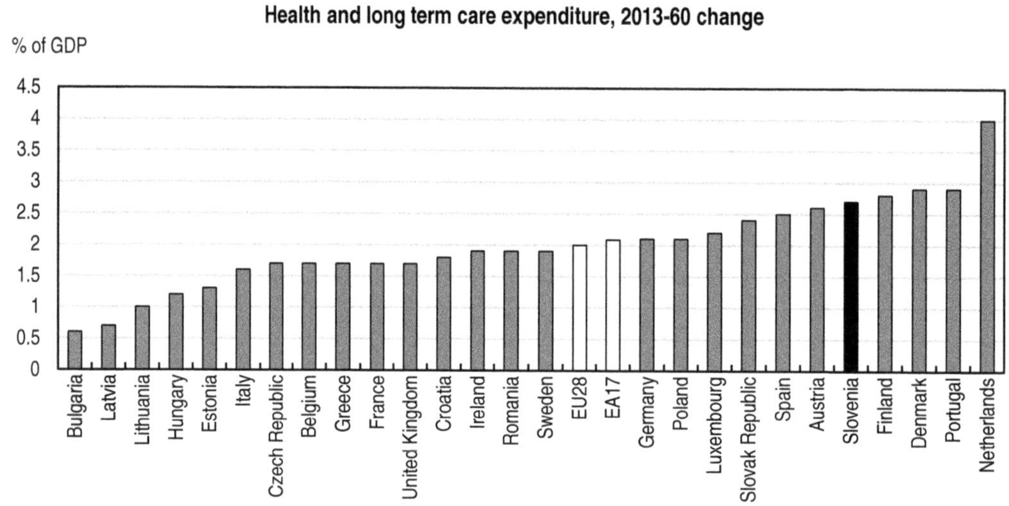

Source: European Commission, 2015 *Ageing Report.*

StatLink http://dx.doi.org/10.1787/888933204938

Although somewhat improving, the health care system is in urgent need of reform, and the government is undertaking a thorough review of health expenditures. Rising costs and the economic downturn following the global financial crisis have resulted in the emergence of severe financial constraints. Some of the cost drivers are endemic to the system. Despite recent growth in the number of general practitioners, their share among all doctors is still low and the allocation of resources is skewed to more costly specialist care. A third of overall healthcare spending is on inpatient care, and more could be done to further develop ambulatory care (OECD, 2013a). The Commission for the Prevention of Corruption reports that the public procurement in the public health system is inefficient and susceptible to conflicts of interest. Slovenian health providers pay significantly higher prices for equipment and materials in comparison to their EU counterparts (CPC, 2014). In this context, the Insurance Institute of Slovenia has undertaken several cost-cutting initiatives, and the Ministry of Health has started to centralise the procedures for purchasing of drugs and pharmaceutical products. Finally, the government is undertaking a comprehensive review of health expenditure, scheduled for the first half of 2015. The findings of the review will serve as inputs into a comprehensive health sector reform, expected to be launched towards the end of 2015.

The health insurance system in Slovenia has a number of redistribution elements. There is no upper contribution threshold for the compulsory health insurance, so that high income employees pay much more into the insurance pool than would be actuarially needed to cover their health risks. Pensioners face a lower contribution rate than employees and despite higher contributions from the self-employed since the beginning of 2014, they contribute less than comparable wage earners. Moreover, the voluntary complementary insurance consists of a flat fee, which represents a heavy burden on low income individuals. Hence, contribution rates of different groups within society might need to be reviewed in order to reduce or avoid distortions in the system.

Another element in need of reform is voluntary complementary health insurance. It currently covers the full remaining part of the costs of most treatments that are not fully reimbursed by the compulsory health insurance. Hence, neither medical practitioners nor patients have an incentive to ensure that the treatments and drugs prescribed are effective and necessary. In this context, the authorities should reform the system to limit insurance cover to a basket of proven and effective drugs and services and let patients pay for any additional treatments they desire out-of-pocket or through private insurance.

The health care reform will also provide an occasion to put the financing and delivery of long-term care services on a more solid basis. Up to now, long-term care has been provided by the general health system and paid for out of resources from compulsory health insurance, pension insurance, and general tax revenues. Similarly, the regulations governing the sector are spread across several social security laws, and the oversight of long-term care activities is split between the Ministry of Labour and the Ministry of Health. A unifying framework is therefore missing. A dedicated source of funding for long-term care would be welcome to better monitor and control the expanding costs due to ageing. Moreover, long-term care is currently oriented too much towards costly institutional care. A move towards home care would generate savings, and at the same time would improve the quality of life of those under care. The government has already taken measures to further develop home care, and these should be extended and accelerated, and complemented by efforts to promote prevention and healthy ageing.

Increasing the labour market participation of older workers

Another challenge for policy makers is to raise the low labour force participation rate of workers aged 55-64 (Figure 18). The 2013 pension reform increases the statutory and minimum retirement ages and provides benefits in the form of higher pension pay-outs for continued work beyond the normal retirement age and penalties for early retirement. Yet, employers are often reluctant to hire or retain older workers. Besides being more expensive due to seniority-related pay structures, they are frequently considered as having low technological skills, being slow in processing information, and lacking openness to new ideas (European Commission, 2012). Targeted training programmes and life-long learning could help older workers adapt to new tasks and technologies, and facilitate the migration of workers from arduous jobs to less exacting work after a certain age. Programs that encourage employers to make working conditions more accommodating for older workers open the door for longer working lives. Respective initiatives in other OECD countries include the sustainable employability programme in the Netherlands and the Centre for Senior Policy in Norway.

Figure 18. **The labour force participation rate of older workers is low**

Labour force participation rate, 2013 - population aged 55-64

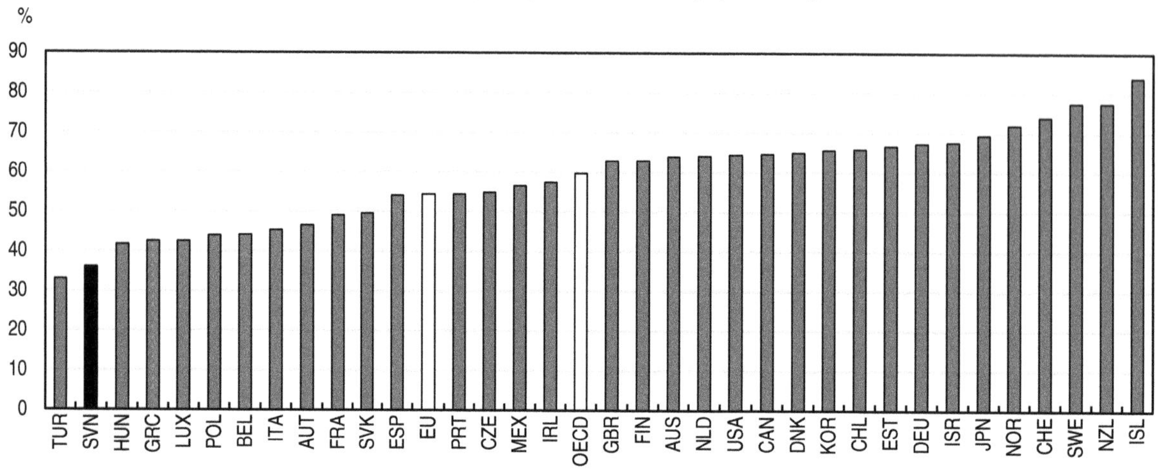

Source: OECD Short-Term Labour Market Statistics Database.

StatLink http://dx.doi.org/10.1787/888933204945

Recommendations to deal with the consequences of population ageing

Key recommendations

- Increase the statutory and minimum pension ages and link them explicitly to life expectancy. Calculate pension rights over lifetime contributions.
- Thoroughly reform the health sector to improve efficiency, including of organisational and governance structures and public procurement.

Other recommendations

- Increase the weight of inflation, as opposed to wages, in the pension indexation rule.
- Equalise the contribution rates of different population groups to the compulsory health insurance and move coverage for health-critical services from the voluntary complementary insurance to the compulsory insurance system.
- Ensure transparent and sufficient funding for long-term care, based on contributions from the working-age population and pensioners.
- Develop home care by creating a level playing field with institutional care in the accessibility to health services, and by giving patients more freedom to organise their own care.
- Help older workers adapt to new tasks and technologies through life-long learning and targeted training programmes, and facilitate shifts of workers from strenuous jobs to less extorting work after a certain age.

Raising living standards and long-term growth by improving the business environment

Labour market policies for more jobs

The labour market has been reformed in recent years. The 2013 labour market reform reduced employment protection and reduced labour market duality between permanent and fixed-term contracts (Figure 19). The reform increased flexibility by simplifying hiring

Figure 19. **Employment protection was reduced in 2013**

A. Strictness of employment protection – individual and collective dismissals (regular contracts)[1]

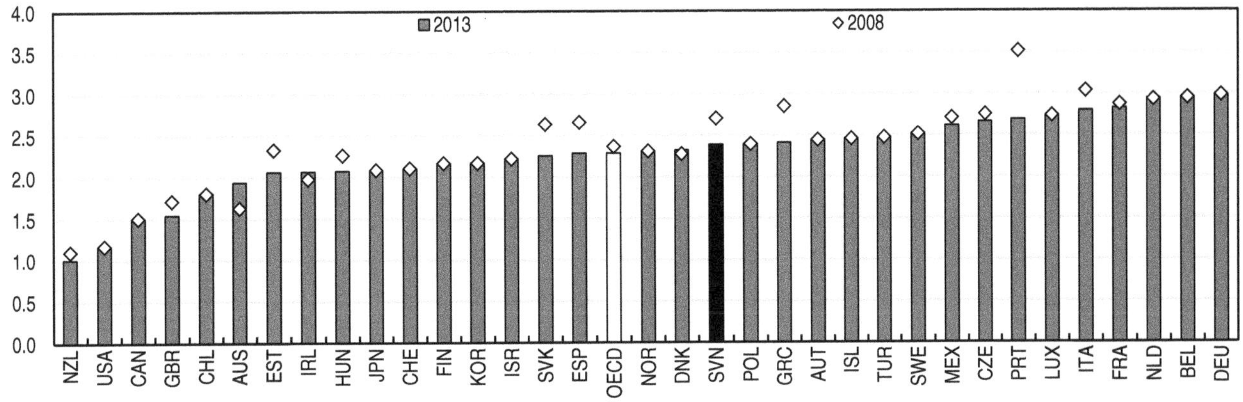

B. Strictness of employment protection – regulation on temporary contracts[2]

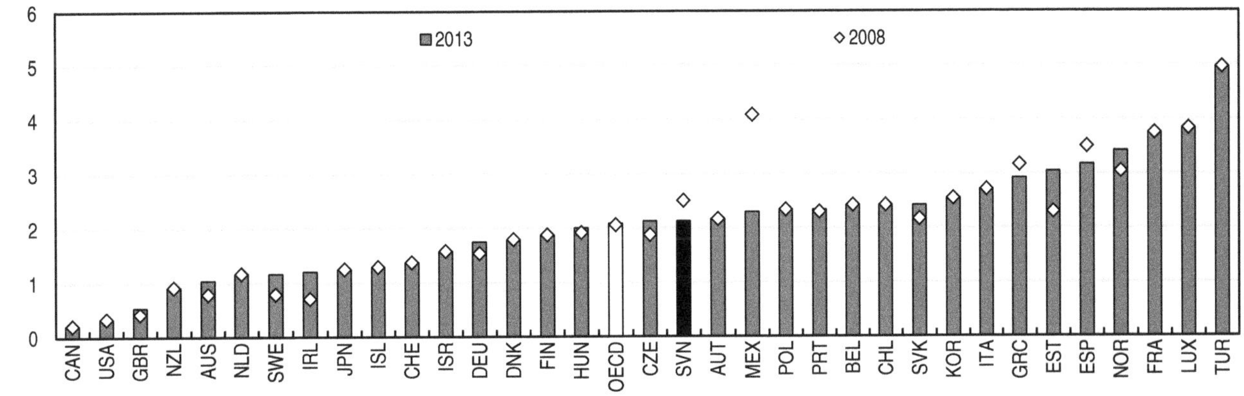

1. The OECD indicator of employment protection legislation (EPL) for regular employment measures the procedures and costs involved in dismissing individual regular employees. The indicator runs from 0 to 6, representing the least to most restrictive EPL.
2. The OECD indicator of regulation on temporary contract (EPT) measures the restrictions on the use of temporary employment by firms, with respect to the type of work for which these contracts are allowed and their duration.

Source: *OECD Employment Protection Database*, 2013 update.

StatLink http://dx.doi.org/10.1787/888933204954

and firing, and lowered costs of permanent contracts. For fixed-term contracts it introduced redundancy payments and limited duration to two years. Bank of Slovenia (2014b) survey shows that only 14% of companies reported a change in their human resources policy due to the new legislation. Duality, however, may have indeed decreased as the share of permanent contracts among all new contracts is increasing (IMAD, 2014d). Another reform, from February 2015, phased out the preferential treatment of student work. This was another major factor behind labour market duality in Slovenia. The reform introduced healthcare and pension contributions for student work and a minimum hourly gross wage rate, increasing the cost of student work, but keeping its flexibility. Both reforms were important steps in the right direction.

More than 50% of the unemployed in Slovenia have been out of work for a year or more and youth unemployment has increased steeply, to about 20% in 2014 (Figure 20). Only 0.3% of GDP was spent on active labour market programmes (ALMPs) in 2012, half the

Figure 20. **Long-term unemployment is high and youth unemployment has risen**

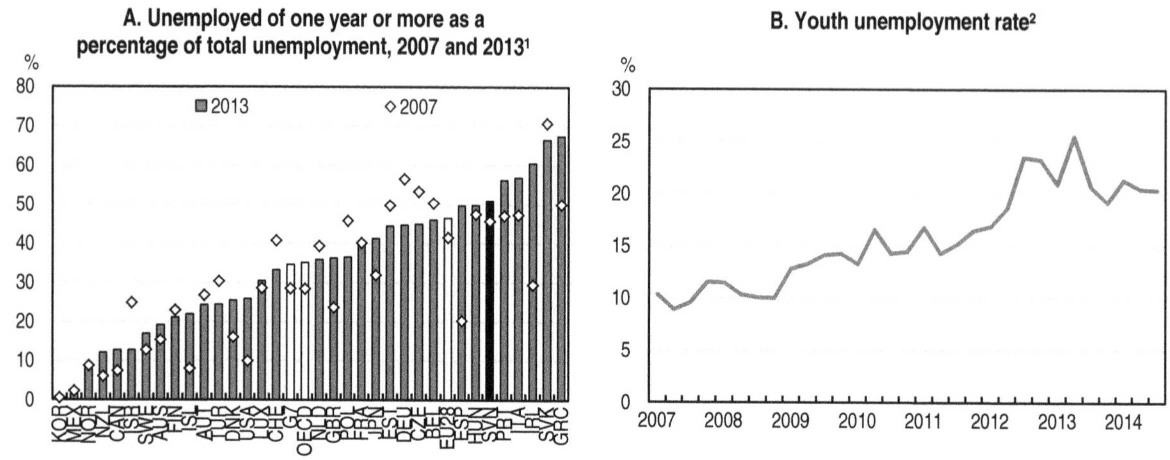

1. Countries are shown in ascending order of the incidence of long-term unemployment in 2013. Data are not seasonally adjusted but smoothed using three-quarter moving averages. OECD is the weighted average of 33 OECD countries, excluding Chile.
2. Data are seasonally adjusted and refer to the unemployment rate of individuals aged 15-24.

Source: OECD calculations based on quarterly national labour force surveys, for Panel A; and *OECD Short-Term Labour Market Statistics Database*, for Panel B.

StatLink http://dx.doi.org/10.1787/888933204966

Figure 21. **Slovenia spends less on active labour market programmes than most other countries**

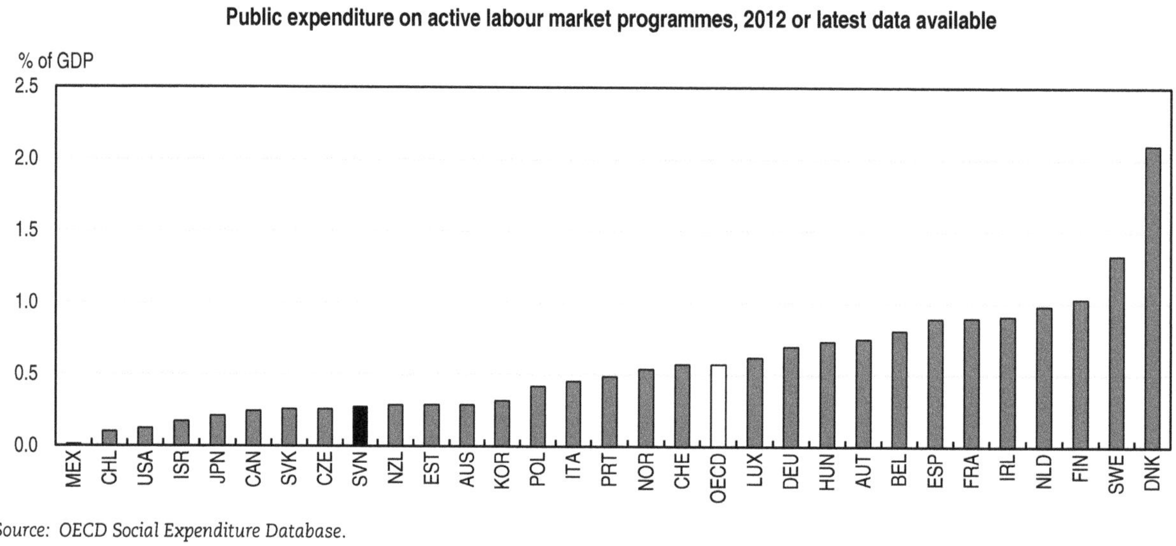

Source: OECD Social Expenditure Database.

StatLink http://dx.doi.org/10.1787/888933204973

amount spent on average across the OECD (Figure 21). The resources currently devoted to training and job search services should therefore be increased to enhance placement prospects for the unemployed upon comprehensive evaluation of existing programmes. To maximise the effect, given restricted fiscal space, active labour market programmes should also be better targeted on the long-term unemployed and the low-skilled. Currently, less than half of the unemployed participate in ALMPs. All unemployed should therefore be encouraged to participate in job counselling and activation programmes, by increasing awareness and specifically targeting those groups that do not participate.

Figure 22. **Slovenia is one of the countries with the highest minimum wage relative to the median**

Ratio of minimum wage (gross) to median wage of full-time employees, 2013

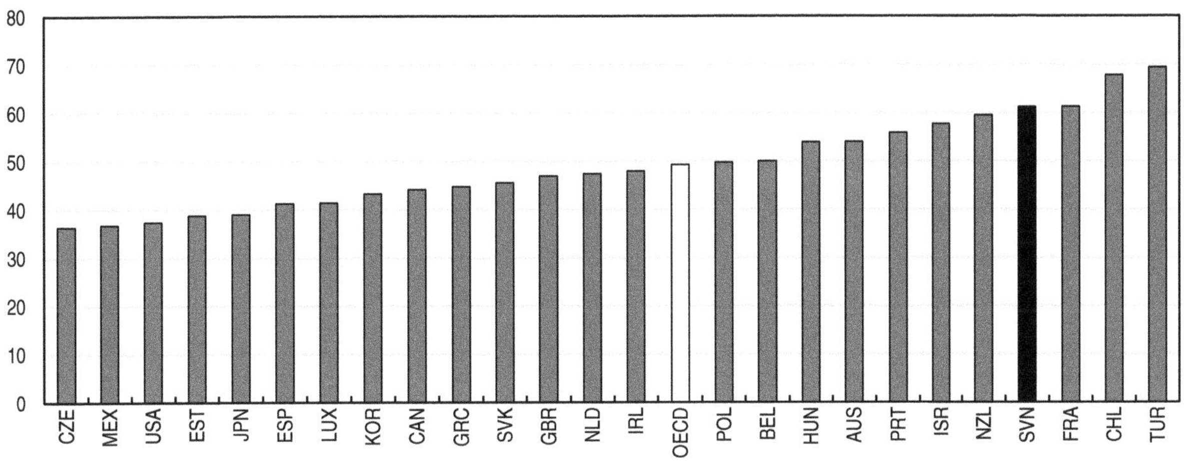

Source: *OECD Minimum Wage Database.*

StatLink http://dx.doi.org/10.1787/888933204981

The high minimum wage relative to the median wage (Figure 22) potentially reduces employment prospects of low-skilled workers. The Law on Minimum Wage stipulates that minimum wage should be increased by at least the inflation rate each year, but cites other benchmarks for adjustment, such as wage trends, economic growth and employment trends. Evidence shows that earned income tax credits, rather than minimum wage increases, have been successful in supporting the incomes and employment of lower-income families in the USA (Eissa and Hoynes, 2006; Clemens and Wither, 2014). Going forward, minimum wage growth should be moderated, with a view to restoring the link to productivity and boosting employment opportunities. Incomes of low-skilled workers can be better protected through social transfers and tax measures that incentivise employment.

Recommendations on the labour market

Key recommendations

- Increase resources for active labour market policies and better target assistance to the long-term unemployed and the low-skilled, based on evaluation of individual programmes.

Other recommendations

- Moderate growth in the minimum wage, with a view to restoring the link to productivity and gradually increasing the gap between the minimum and median wage.

Making product market regulation less restrictive

Slovenia's overall regulatory framework is among the most restrictive in the OECD, as indicated by the OECD product market regulation (PMR) indicator (Figure 23, Panel A). Slovenia's PMR score has improved since 2008, but remains worse than in most Central and Eastern European countries (CEEC) and euro area countries. This underperformance stems largely from the pervasive state involvement in the economy, but there is also room to reduce the complexity of regulatory procedures and administrative burdens on start-ups (Figure 23, Panel B).

There has been improvement in some areas. The number of regulated professions has decreased from 323 to 242 (European Commission, 2015a) and the number of days required to open up a business was shortened. According to the PMR survey, Slovenia has set up single contact points for information on opening up a business, but these do not issue or accept all notifications and licenses, and are not sufficiently established at the local level. Furthermore, Slovenia could introduce the "silence is consent" rule for issuing licences required to open up a business, as they have been successfully implemented in Portugal and the Slovak Republic. Dealing with construction permits and registering property still takes a lot of time. According to the *Doing Business Survey* (World Bank, 2015) it takes 109.5 days in Slovenia to register a property compared to one day in Portugal and New Zealand. Obtaining construction permits in Slovenia takes 212.5 days, more than three times the time in Finland or Denmark.

Slovenia should also further ease regulation of such professional services such as accounting, legal, engineering and architecture services (Figure 23, panel C). Regulation of professional services is strict in many European countries, although successful examples like Sweden, Denmark, Finland, Norway and Switzerland show that reduced regulation can increase competition and the quality of professional services. Education requirements to enter a profession are excessively high in Slovenia. According to the PMR survey, in the four professions, a university degree, in many cases another specialised degree, and a compulsory practice lasting up to 5 years are required to become a full member of the profession. Each profession also requires compulsory membership in a chamber of the profession.

Rationalising public ownership

Public ownership and control of enterprises is widespread (Figure 23, panel B) and enterprises owned (or indirectly controlled) by the state are most dominant in network industries, but are also common in banking, insurance and even manufacturing. Rojec (2014) estimates that enterprises directly or indirectly owned by the state (higher than 50% equity share) account for 18% of the corporate sector's total assets and 23% of total equity. The profitability and productivity of state-owned enterprises (SOEs) is lower than of privately and foreign-owned companies operating in same sectors (Rojec, 2014; European Commission, 2015a and 2014b). SOEs also pose risks to public finances via potential recapitalisation needs and as receivers of a major share of state guarantees (Georgieva and Riquelme, 2013). In 2013, the parliament approved a list of 15 SOEs to be privatised, including one state-owned bank and a major telecom provider. By early 2015, five companies had been privatised and six are in the process. The government should continue with privatisations.

For the SOEs that remain under state ownership, it is important to set up a solid asset management framework to enhance performance. In April 2014, the new Slovenian Sovereign Holding (SSH) became fully operational and its capacity to manage and dispose of state-owned assets was strengthened (OECD, 2014d). The role of the SSH is to consolidate and manage all state assets under one structure, and to execute privatisation of some of these assets. Among the important next steps will be the appointment of professional and independent SSH board members. The remaining SOEs must be held to high standards of disclosure and transparency (OECD, 2014d). When setting up its own

Figure 23. **Product market regulation is overly strict**

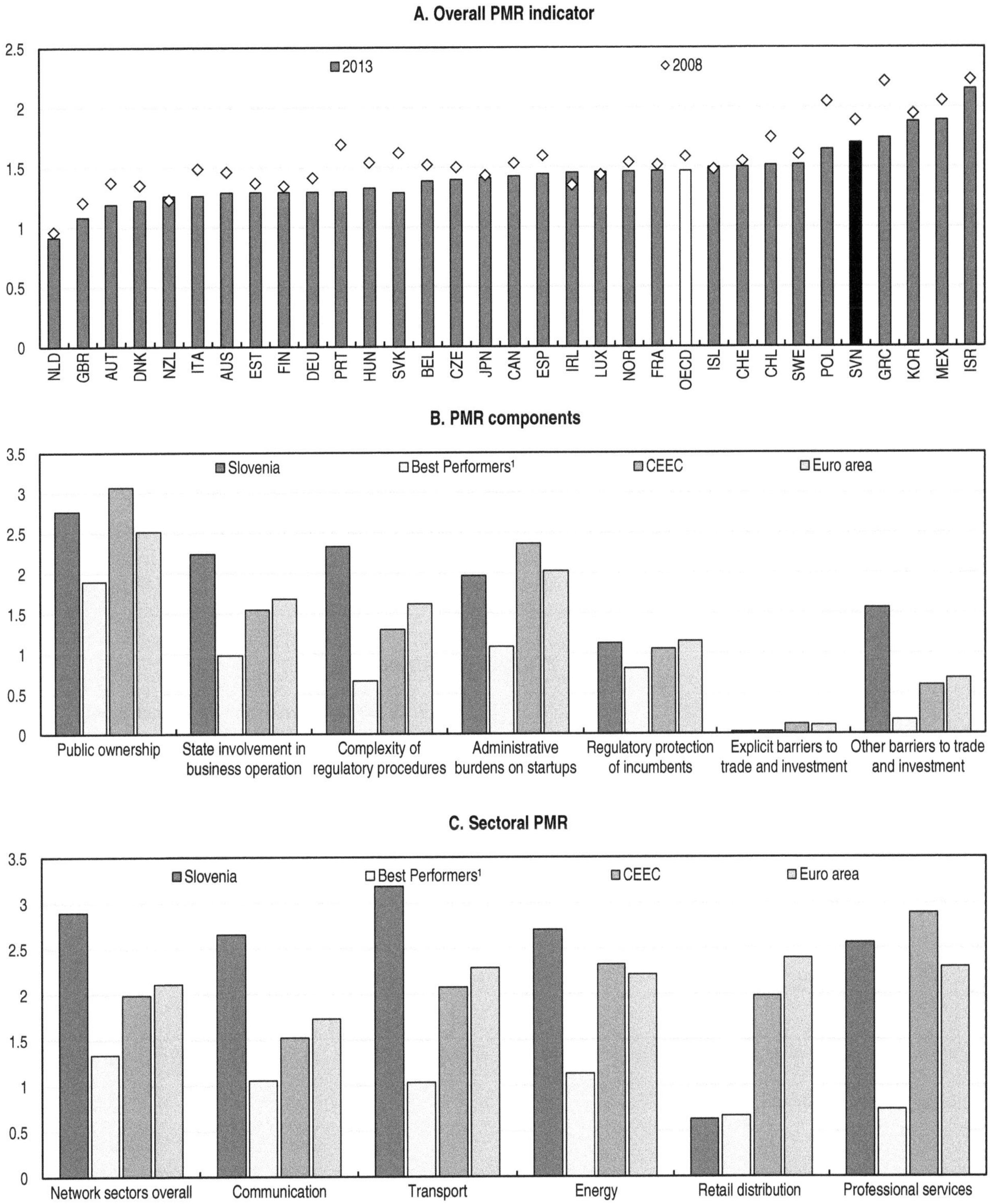

Note: The numerical PMR indicators represent the stringency of regulatory policy in specific areas on a scale of 0 to 6 with a higher number indicating a policy stance that is deemed less conducive to competition. In each case, it characterises the stance of regulation as it stood in early 2013 and does not reflect the reforms implemented since then.

1. The simple average of the five countries with the lowest values of each indicator is shown.

Source: OECD PMR Indicators Database.

StatLink http://dx.doi.org/10.1787/888933204990

corporate governance framework for SOEs the SSH should closely follow the OECD Guidelines on Corporate Governance of SOEs (OECD, 2005).

Another priority is to develop an asset management strategy. According to the SSH law, assets are to be classified into three types: strategic, important and portfolio assets. The minimum share in strategic assets is 50% plus one vote, in important assets 25% plus one vote, while the SSH is permitted to freely dispose of portfolio assets. The government has yet to agree on an asset management strategy, which will eventually have to be confirmed by the parliament. It is critical that the strategy provide a rigorous rationale for why assets should be owned by the state at all, rather than privatised. SOEs that are in direct competition with the private sector deserve especially strict scrutiny in this regard (OECD, 2011d).

Less public ownership and deeper capital markets would attract more FDI

A large body of empirical evidence shows that FDI is good for growth and productivity and that companies with FDI perform better when compared to domestically owned ones (Simoneti et al., 2002; Bijsterbosch and Kolasa, 2009; Damijan, Rojec, Majcen and Knell, 2013; Dall'Orso and Sila, 2015). In the last 15 years, the growth of inward FDI stock has been much slower in Slovenia than in other new EU members (Figure 24). Inward stock of FDI is just above 30% of GDP, less than half the share in Estonia, Hungary or the Czech Republic. The reason for such low FDI, despite the efforts of government to create a friendly regulatory and tax environment, lies in pervasive state ownership and political unwillingness to undertake privatisations. At a time when the deleveraging process in the corporate sector is dragging down investment and activity, Slovenia has the opportunity to open up more to FDI to bring in needed fresh capital.

Figure 24. **FDI has remained low**

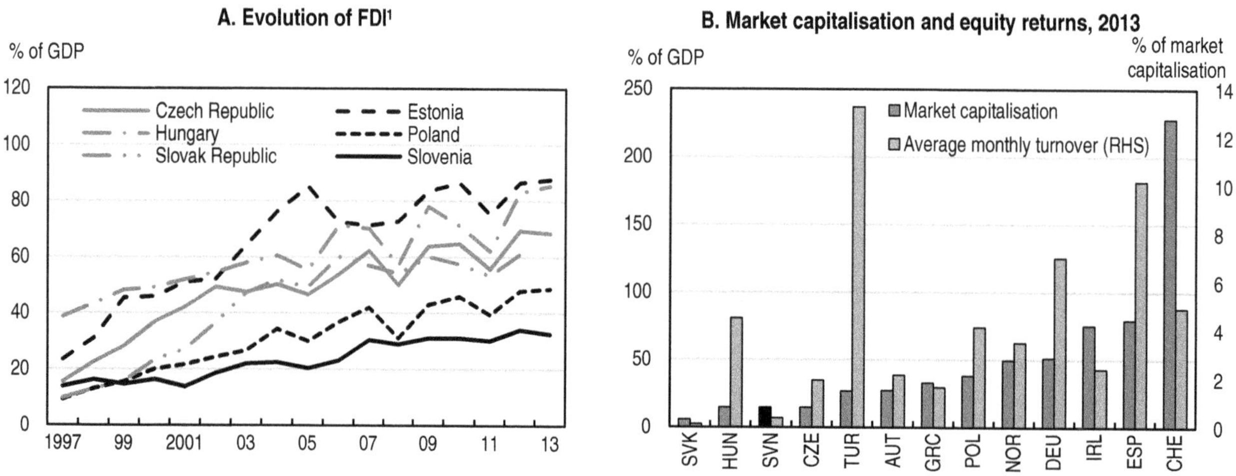

1. Inward position at year end.

Source: OECD FDI series of BOP and IIP aggregates database for Panel A; and Federation of European Securities Exchanges for Panel B.

StatLink http://dx.doi.org/10.1787/888933205005

Recommendations on product market regulation and business environment

Key recommendations

- Continue privatising state-owned enterprises and do not hold controlling interests in firms operating in competitive markets.
- Introduce the "silence is consent' rule for issuing licences required to open up a business and make obtaining construction permits and registering property faster.

Other recommendations

- Prepare an asset management strategy for assets in public ownership and strengthen the corporate governance of SOEs by appointing professional board members.
- Reduce entry barriers in professional services (accounting, legal, engineering and architecture).

Boosting innovation and R&D

In terms of expenditure and human resources in science and technology Slovenia performs above the OECD average, but there is a low number of innovative firms, patents and trademarks (Figure 25). As argued in the 2011 Economic Survey of Slovenia, the disappointing innovation outcomes can be linked to the lack of entrepreneurial dynamism, general barriers to doing business and the overly complex national innovation policy. The Research and Innovation Strategy of Slovenia 2011-20 (RISS) and the National Higher Education Programme 2011-20 (NHEP) propose measures towards a unifying innovation policy (OECD, 2014e). The lack of planning, implementation and co-ordination in national innovation policy nevertheless hold back innovation. The current public research system is marked by administrative dispersion and rivalry among various stakeholders, and a consequent overlapping of innovation efforts. Frequent changes in policy measures and instruments have rendered new policy initiatives less credible. The collaborative links between major stakeholders of innovation policy must therefore be upgraded and streamlined (OECD, 2011d and 2012d).

In recent years, the public R&D system and associated business support centres were made more responsive to the R&D demands of the business community. The authorities introduced a research voucher system, grants, tax incentives and various instruments to facilitate financing. Centres of excellence, competence centres and development centres that stimulate collaboration of public research with the business sector were also established (OECD, 2012c, 2012d). Public research has delivered some impressive results in terms of scientific output (Figure 25). Nevertheless, to facilitate further improvements, the governance of public research should be reformed so that universities and public research organisations are given more autonomy, while their accountability and performance should also be enhanced. International co-operation should be promoted further by expanding university programmes in foreign languages, opening up research programmes to foreign participation and opening the academic labour market internationally (OECD, 2012c, 2012d).

Figure 25. **Slovenia does well in terms of inputs into innovation process, but innovative activity is low**

Comparative performance of national science and innovation systems, 2014

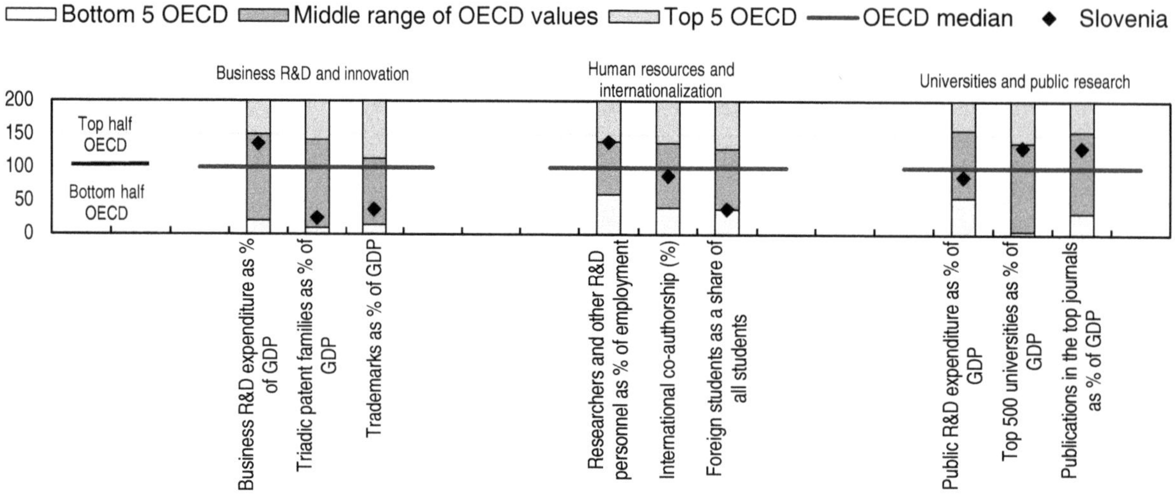

Note: Normalised index of performance relative to the median values in the OECD area (Index median = 100).

Source: based on *OECD Science, Technology and Industry Outlook 2014* and *OECD Main Science and Technology Indicators (MSTI) Database*, June 2014; USPTO Bulk Downloads: Trademark Application Text hosted by Reed Technology Information Services, *OHIM Community Trademark Database* CTM Download, *JPO Annual Reports 2001-13* and Graham, S., G. Hancock, A. Marco and A. Myers (2013), "The USPTO Trademark Case Files Dataset: Descriptions, Lessons, and Insights", *SSRN Working Paper*, *http://ssrn.com/abstract=2188621*; Elsevier B.V. (2014), *Elsevier Research Intelligence* (Scopus-Elsevier); *OECD Education Database*; and Academic Ranking of World Universities (ARWU) (2013), "Shanghai Ranking", *www.shanghairanking.com*.

StatLink http://dx.doi.org/10.1787/888933205012

Recommendations on innovation and R&D

Key recommendation

- Implement the government's unified innovation policy and monitor its progress. Improve collaborative links between major stakeholders of innovation policy.

Other recommendation

- Facilitate reform in universities and public research organisations, enhancing their autonomy, leadership and accountability. Further promote international co-operation.

Greening the economy

Transport sector is the most important contributor to air pollution, as measured by carbon dioxide emissions. Due to major investment in road construction in recent years, the transport system is locked into a highly carbon-intensive pattern, made worse by a high rate of international transit road traffic (OECD, 2014d). Together with wood-burning stoves for heating, this transportation pattern contributed to the emergence of air pollution hot-spots in some urban centres (Figure 26, Panel A) and steep increases in carbon dioxide emissions (Figure 26, Panel B). The share of emissions from road transport is much higher than its share in passengers and freight transport, and there is therefore potential to reduce emissions by improving and extending the railway system. The government plans to increase investments in railways using public private partnerships, but there are delays due to the slow design of projects and lengthy procedures to obtain various permits (OECD, 2012e).

Figure 26. **Air pollution indicators**

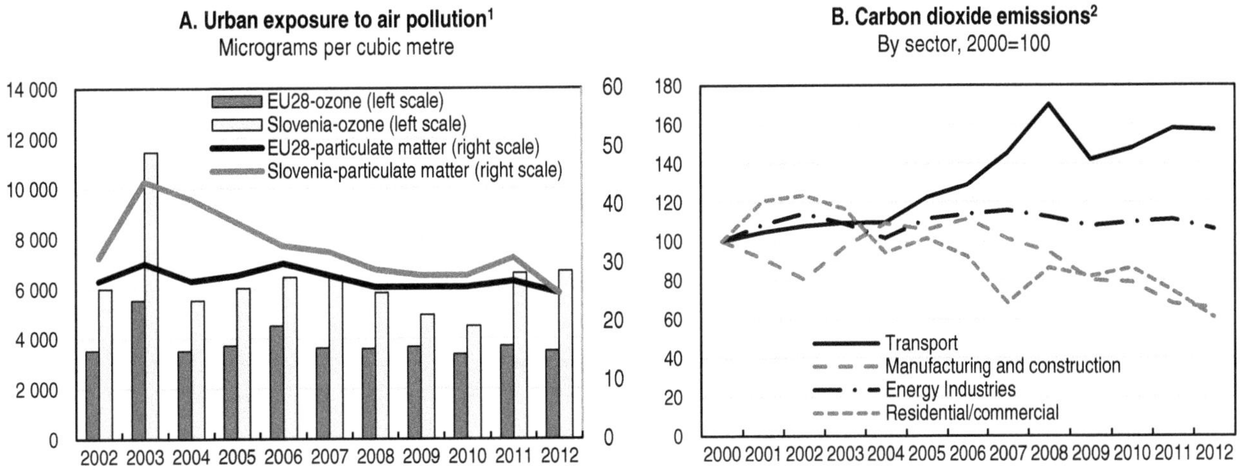

1. Population weighted data. For ozone (O_3) this covers the yearly sum of maximum daily 8-hour mean ozone concentrations above a threshold; for particulate matter (PM_{10}), it covers annual mean concentrations at background stations in agglomerations.
2. Excludes international marine and aviation bunkers; sectorial approach.

Source: CO_2 Emissions from *Fuel Combustion OECD Database*; Emissions of Greenhouse Gases and *Air Pollutants Eurostat Database*.

StatLink http://dx.doi.org/10.1787/888933205027

Revenues from environmental taxes amounted to 3.9% of GDP in 2013, one of the highest ratios among OECD countries (*OECD Environment Database*), which partly reflects high fuel consumption associated with transit traffic (OECD, 2013c). However, effective tax rates vary across different forms of energy. Tax rates on transport fuel are significantly higher than those on heating and process use and on electricity; and those on diesel are about 20% below those on gasoline in terms of carbon dioxide (CO_2) emissions (OECD, 2013c; Ministry of Finance). The differential between diesel and gasoline has been reduced recently due to reduced differential in excise duties on the two fuels. In addition, effective from January 2015, there was an increase in tax rate on CO_2 emissions by 20% per each kg of CO_2 for all energy products. Slovenia could improve the environmental effectiveness of these taxes by linking them further to emissions. It should also remove exemptions in the case of commercial use of diesel fuel and increase taxes on heavy fuel oil and gas oil used for heating.

Recommendations on the environment

- Upgrade the railway system and improve efficiency of railways, especially in the freight sector.
- Further align effective tax rates on different forms of energy to reflect environmental damage.

Bibliography

Arnold, J., B. Brys, C. Heady, Å. Johansson, C. Schwellnus and L. Vartia (2011), "Tax Policy for Economic Recovery and Growth", *The Economic Journal*, Vol. 121, No. 550.

Ayuso-i-Casals, J. (2012), "National Expenditure Rules: Why, How and When, European Economy", *Economic Papers*, 473, December.

Bijsterbosch, M. and M. Kolasa (2009), "FDI and Productivity Convergence in Central and Eastern Europe: An Industry-Level Investigation", *Working Paper Series*, No. 992, European Central Bank, Frankfurt-am-Main.

BAMC (2014), *Annual Report 2013*, Bank Assets Management Company.

Bank of Slovenia (2014a), *Policy Strategy Paper for Slovenia*, Ljubljana, 17 July.

Bank of Slovenia (2014b), Macroeconomic Developments and Projections, October.

Bank of Slovenia (2014c), *Financial Stability Review*, May.

Bank of Slovenia (2013), "Report on Comprehensive Review of the Banking System and Associated Measures", *Press Release*, 12 December.

CPC (2014), *Annual Report 2013*, Commission for the Prevention of Corruption (in Slovenian).

CPC (2013), *State of Corruption in Slovenia*, 2013, Commission for the Prevention of Corruption (in Slovenian), *https://www.kpk-rs.si/upload/t_datoteke/Ocena_stanja_korupcije_v_RS.pdf*.

Clemens, J and M. Wither (2014), "The Minimum Wage and the Great Recession: Evidence of Effects on the Employment and Income Trajectories of Low-Skilled Workers", *Working Paper*, 20724, National Bureau of Economic Research.

Dall'Orso, J. and U. Sila (2015), "Trends in Productivity and Sources of Productivity Growth in Slovenia", *OECD Economics Department Working Papers*, OECD Publishing, forthcoming.

Damijan, J.P. (2014), "Corporate Financial Soundness and its Impact on Firm Performance: Implications for Corporate Debt Restructuring in Slovenia", *Working Paper*, No. 168, European Bank for Reconstruction and Development.

Damijan, J.P., M. Rojec, B. Majcen and M. Knell (2013), "Impact of Firm Heterogeneity on Direct and Spillover Effects of FDI: Micro-Evidence from Ten Transition Countries", *Journal of Comparative Economics*, Vol. 41 (3), pp. 895-922.

ECB (2014), *Aggregate Report* on the comprehensive assessment, October.

Eissa, N. and H.W. Hoynes (2006), "Behavioral Responses to Taxes: Lessons from the EITC and Labour Supply", in *Tax Policy and the Economy*, Vol. 20:73-110.

European Commission (2015a), "Country Report Slovenia 2015", *Commission Staff Working Document*, Brussels, 26 May.

European Commission (2015b), *The 2015 Ageing Report. Economic and Budgetary Projections for the EU28 Member States* (2013-2060).

European Commission (2014a), *Slovenia: Review of Progress on Policy Measures Relevant for the Correction of Macroeconomic Imbalances*, November.

European Commission (2014b), "Macroeconomic Imbalances, Slovenia 2014", *Occasional Papers*, 187, March.

European Commission (2014c), "Assessment of the 2014 National Reform Programme and Stability Programme for Slovenia", *Commission Staff Working Document*.

European Commission (2014d), "The 2015 Ageing Report. Underlying Assumptions and Projection Methodologies", *European Economy*, No. 8.

European Commission (2012), "Active Ageing", *Special Eurobarometer*, 378.

Georgieva, S. and D.M. Riquelme (2013), "Slovenia: State-Owned and State-Controlled Enterprises", *ECFIN Country Focus*, Vol. 10, Iss. 3.

Guner, N., M. Lopez-Daneri and G. Ventura (2014), "Heterogeneity and Government Revenues: Higher Taxes at the Top?", *IZA Discussion Paper*, No. 8335, July.

Hattie, J. (2009), *Visile Learning: A Synthesis of Over 800 Meta-Analyses Relating to Achievement*, Routledge, London.

Hribernik, M. and R. Kierzenkowski (2013), "Assessing the Efficiency of Welfare Spending in Slovenia with Data Envelopment Analysis", *OECD Economics Department Working Papers*, No. 1058.

IMAD (2014a), "Slovenian Economic Mirror", No. 12, Vol. XX, December.

IMAD (2014b), *Autumn Forecast of Economic Trends 2014*.

IMAD (2014c), "Indebtedness and Deleveraging of Slovenian Firms", *Economic Issues*, 2014.

IMAD (2014d), *Economic Issues* 2014, August, Institute of Macroeconomic Analysis and Development, Ljubljana.

IMF (2015a), "Republic of Slovenia: 2014 Article IV Consultation", *IMF Country Report*, No. 15/41, February.

IMF (2015b), "Legal and Institutional Challenges in Corporate Insolvency. Republic of Slovenia: Selected Issues", *IMF Country Report*, No. 15/42, February.

IMF (2014), "Republic of Slovenia: 2013 Article IV Consultation", *IMF Country Report*, No. 14/11.

Joumard, I., M. Pisu and D. Bloch (2012), "Less Income Inequality and More Growth – Are They Compatible? Part 3. Income Redistribution via Taxes and Transfers Across OECD Countries", *OECD Economics Department Working Papers*, No. 926, OECD Publishing.

Klingebiel, D. (2000) "The Use of Asset Management Companies in the Resolution of Banking Crises", *World Bank Policy Research Working Papers*, No. 2284, World Bank.

Laeven, L. and F. Valencia (2008), "Systemic Banking Crises: A New Database", *IMF Working Paper*, No. 08/224.

Majcen, B., M. Čok, J. Sambt, T. Turk, N. Stropnik, G. Dekkers, V. Prevolnik Rupel, V. Lavrac, N. Kump and M. Ogorevc (2012), "Izgradnja kombiniranega mikrosimulacijskega modela in modela generacijskih računov", *Inštitut za ekonomska raziskovanja*, Ljubljana.

MDDSZ (2014), "Učinki Pokojninske Reforme in Nadaljnji Koraki", Ministry of Labour, Family, Social Affairs and Equal Opportunities, Ljubljana.

OECD (2014a), "Growth Prospects and Fiscal Requirements Over the Long Term", in OECD Economic Outlook, Vol. 2014, Iss. 1, OECD Publishing, Paris, DOI: *http://dx.doi.org/10.1787/eco_outlook-v2014-1-44-en.*

OECD (2014b), OECD Pensions Outlook 2014, OECD Publishing, Paris, DOI: *http://dx.doi.org/10.1787/9789264222687-en.*

OECD (2014c), "The Crisis and its Aftermath: A Stress Test for Societies and for Social Policies", in Society at a Glance 2014: OECD Social Indicators, OECD Publishing, Paris, DOI: *http://dx.doi.org/10.1787/soc_glance-2014-5-en.*

OECD (2014d), "Slovenia: Reforms for a Strong and Sustainable Recovery", *Better Policies*, OECD Publishing, Paris, DOI: *http://dx.doi.org/10.1787/9789264215894-en.*

OECD (2014e), *OECD Science, Technology and Industry Outlook 2014*, OECD Publishing, Paris, DOI: *http://dx.doi.org/10.1787/sti_outlook-2014-en.*

OECD (2013a), *OECD Economic Surveys: Slovenia 2013*, OECD Publishing, Paris, DOI: *http://dx.doi.org/10.1787/eco_surveys-svn-2013-en.*

OECD (2013b), *Government at a Glance 2013*, OECD Publishing, Paris, DOI: *http://dx.doi.org/10.1787/gov_glance-2013-en.*

OECD (2013c), *Taxing Energy Use: A Graphical Analysis*, OECD Publishing, Paris, DOI: *http://dx.doi.org/10.1787/9789264183933-en.*

OECD (2012a), "Slovenia: Towards a Strategic and Efficient State", *OECD Public Governance Reviews*, OECD Publishing, Paris, DOI: *http://dx.doi.org/10.1787/9789264173262-en.*

OECD (2012b), "The Public Sector Salary System in Slovenia", *OECD Public Governance Reviews*, OECD Publishing, Paris, DOI: *http://dx.doi.org/10.1787/9789264167551-en.*

OECD (2012c), *OECD Science, Technology and Industry Outlook 2012*, OECD Publishing, Paris, DOI: *http://dx.doi.org/10.1787/sti_outlook-2012-en.*

OECD (2012d), *OECD Reviews of Innovation Policy: Slovenia 2012*, OECD Publishing, Paris, DOI: *http://dx.doi.org/10.1787/9789264167407-en.*

OECD (2012e), *OECD Environmental Performance Reviews: Slovenia 2012*, OECD Publishing, Paris, DOI: *http://dx.doi.org/10.1787/9789264169265-en.*

OECD (2011a), *OECD Territorial Reviews: Slovenia 2011*, OECD Publishing, Paris, DOI: *http://dx.doi.org/10.1787/9789264120587-en.*

OECD (2011b), "Taxation and Employment", *OECD Tax Policy Studies*, No. 21, OECD Publishing, Paris, DOI: *http://dx.doi.org/10.1787/9789264120808-en.*

OECD (2011c), *Pensions at a Glance 2011: Retirement-income Systems in OECD and G20 Countries*, OECD Publishing, Paris, DOI: *http://dx.doi.org/10.1787/pension_glance-2011-en.*

OECD (2011d), *OECD Economic Surveys: Slovenia 2011*, OECD Publishing, Paris, DOI: *http://dx.doi.org/10.1787/eco_surveys-svn-2011-en.*

OECD (2009), "Creating Effective Teaching and Learning Environments: First Results from TALIS", *TALIS*, OECD Publishing, Paris, DOI: *http://dx.doi.org/10.1787/9789264068780-en*.

OECD (2005), "OECD Guidelines on Corporate Governance of State-owned Enterprises", *in* OECD, Corporate Governance of State-Owned Enterprises: A Survey of OECD Countries, OECD Publishing, Paris, DOI: *http://dx.doi.org/10.1787/9789264009431-10-en*.

Oliveira Martins, J. and C. de la Maisonneuve (2014), "The Future of Health and Long-Term Care Spending", *OECD Journal: Economic Studies*, OECD Publishing.

Rojec, M., (2014), "A Snapshot of the Main Ownership Features of the Slovenian Corporate Sector", IB Revija 1/2014.

Simoneti, M., M. Rojec and M. Rems (2002), "Ownership Structure and Post-Privatisation Performance and Restructuring of the Slovenian Non-Financial Corporate Sector", *Journal of East-West Business*, Vol. 7, No. 2, Routledge.

Sutherland, D. and R. Price (2007), "Linkages Between Performance and Institutions in the Primary and Secondary Education Sector", *OECD Economics Department Working Papers*, No. 558.

Woo, D. (2000), "Two Approaches to Resolving Nonperforming Assets During Financial Crises", *IMF Working Paper*, No. 00/33.

World Bank (2015), *Doing Business Survey 2015*.

ANNEX 1

Progress in structural reform

The objective of this Annex is to review action taken since the previous Survey *(April 2013) on the main recommendations from previous* Surveys. *The recommendations that are new to this Survey are contained in the corresponding chapters.*

Restructuring and deleveraging of banks and companies

Cleaning-up banks' balance sheets

Main recent OECD recommendations	Actions taken since the 2013 *Survey*
Conduct and disclose the main results of new top-down and bottom-up ("due-diligence") stress tests of the banking sector, which should be conducted under conservative and transparent assumptions.	Comprehensive Stress tests and Asset Quality Review (AQR) of 8 Slovenian banks were undertaken by independent experts in collaboration with the European Commission and the ECB. The results were announced in December 2013. In 2014, the comprehensive assessment for systemically important banks was performed by the ECB. In case of Slovenia, three banks were included.
Strengthen the Bank Asset Management Company (BAMC) by providing it with its own capital and ensuring that all directors and members of the inter-ministerial committee fulfil professional requirements.	The Bank Asset Management Company (BAMC) was strengthened in December 2013 and is fully operational.
Recapitalise distressed but viable banks, preferably by issuing shares, and wind down non-viable banks. To reduce the fiscal costs of bank resolutions, holders of subordinated debt and lower-ranked hybrid capital instruments should absorb losses.	Two small insolvent private banks are in the process of controlled liquidation. The three largest state-owned banks (NLB, NKBM and Abanka) and another small bank were recapitalised, while the shareholders and holders of subordinated debt were wiped out.
Privatise state-owned banks and do not retain a blocking minority shareholding.	The authorities committed to fully privatise NKBM (by the end of 2016) and Abanka (and merging it with a smaller bank, by June 2019), and to reduce the state's share in NLB to 25% plus one share by the end of 2017. In January 2015, the SSH received binding offers for the purchase of the State's 100% shareholding in NKBM.
Ring-fenced assets should be fully disposed at the end of the mandate of the BAMC and not transferred as currently envisaged to the sovereign holding company to avoid a permanent postponement of the resolution of impaired assets.	No action taken.

Enhancing banking supervision

Main recent OECD recommendations	Actions taken since the 2013 *Survey*
Enhance transparency and data disclosure by the Bank of Slovenia and ensure that a complete set of credit information from its credit registry is shared with banks.	New legislation was adopted in March 2015 in line with EU directives, to introduce capital shock absorbers, enhanced risk management and bank governance requirements, and improved transparency of bank operations through additional disclosure and assessment of systemic risks. The Central Credit Registry is being upgraded to better support supervisory tasks.
Make banking supervision more conservative and forward-looking by adopting a much more prudent approach to large and related exposures.	Large exposures requirements approach taken by the Bank of Slovenia is fully in line with the EU requirements stemming from the new rules on capital requirements CRR/CRD IV, and all subsequent technical and implementing standards.
Further improve resolution powers of the Bank of Slovenia by providing it with additional tools (bridge bank and bail-in) and foreseeing a financing arrangement, such as a resolution fund.	In December 2012, the Banking Act was amended entrusting Bank of Slovenia with additional resolution powers. In December 2014, the National Assembly passed a law establishing a bank resolution fund that is to become operational in 2015.

Simplifying insolvency procedures

Main recent OECD recommendations	Actions taken
Encourage distressed firms to apply early for insolvency procedures by a better law enforcement concerning the liability of debtors that fail to apply for insolvency procedures in a timely manner, encouraging balance-sheet insolvent borrowers to apply, and distinguishing between honest and fraudulent bankruptcy.	No action taken.
Ease restructuring of distressed businesses via simplified fast track in-court reorganisation of small and medium-sised enterprises and establishment of a legal framework for out-of-court restructuring.	In 2013, important reforms to facilitate early restructuring of viable companies were introduced. The framework provides for preventive restructuring of large- and medium-sised companies. The overall procedure of court-mandated debt restructuring has been streamlined by broadening the scope of companies eligible for a "simplified procedure" – now besides micro companies applies also to small companies.
Enforce the existing legislation that limits duration of certain insolvency procedures. Ultimately, the objective is to end all insolvency procedures within one year.	No action taken.

Fiscal sustainability

Reforming the tax mix

Main recent OECD recommendations	Actions taken
Improve the composition of the fiscal adjustment by restructuring and further increasing recurrent taxes on residential property, and refraining from reducing taxes without adopting offsetting measures.	In 2014, the tax on bank balance sheets was abolished. At the same time, tax rates on financial services tax and insurance premiums tax were increased as an offsetting measure. The new Real Estate Tax Law from 2014 was proclaimed unconstitutional by the Constitutional Court.

Increasing efficiency of public expenditure

Main recent OECD recommendations	Actions taken
Continue to reduce high-income earners' eligibility for family benefits and strengthen means testing of education-related benefits.	No action taken.
Continue to gradually cut the combined generosity of unemployment benefits, social assistance and other transfers for the unemployed and inactive persons to increase work incentives and strengthen fiscal sustainability.	No action taken.
Raise pupil-teacher ratios in pre-primary and lower secondary education and class sizes in primary and lower secondary education to reduce costs. Introduce universal tuition fees along with means-tested grants and loans with income-contingent repayments to ensure to boost spending efficiency.	No action taken.

Fiscal framework

Main recent OECD recommendations	Actions taken
Bolster the credibility of the expenditure rule by transparently setting its parameters, defining escape clauses and adopting a corrective mechanism for deviations from the rule.	The government in December 2014 adopted legislation to implement a Constitutional fiscal rule that requires a balanced budget over the medium term, but it still needs to be passed in parliament.
Allow IMAD (Institute for Macroeconomic Analysis and Development) to take over the role of the fiscal council to strengthen the fiscal framework.	No action taken.

Tackling the economic consequences of ageing

Reforming the pensions system

Main recent OECD recommendations	Actions taken
Pursue pension reform by gradually raising the pension eligibility age and contributory periods, eventually indexing them to life expectancy.	No action taken.
Consider further cutting replacement rates by lowering effective accrual rates and calculating pension rights over lifetime contributions.	No action taken.

Health care and long-term care

Main recent OECD recommendations	Actions taken
Further rationalise the public health benefit basket and shift from inpatient to ambulatory care.	The system of medical model practices in the primary healthcare was introduced. The number of specialists in family medicine (through increased number of posts in post-graduate training) was increased.
Broaden the tax base of compulsory health insurance to working students and raise contribution rates for pensioners.	Healthcare and pension contributions for student work have been introduced.
Implement reform plans for long-term care financing by setting up a specific funding system levied on the working-age population and pensioners.	No action taken.
Promote home care development by creating a level playing field with institutional care for accessibility to health services and giving patients more freedom to organise their own care with a system of vouchers.	No action taken.

Product markets, labour markets and corporate governance

Product markets and business environment

Main recent OECD recommendations	Actions taken
As currently envisaged in Slovenia to ease the progress of economic reforms, tighten criteria to veto a law by referendum.	The constitution was amended to impose tighter conditions on the calling of referenda.
Reduce state ownership in the economy.	In 2013, the parliament approved a list of 15 SOEs to be privatised, including one state-owned bank and a major telecom provider. By early 2015, five companies had been privatised and six are in the process.
Ease regulation of professional services.	The number of regulated professions has been lowered from 323 to 242 in 2014.
Strengthen the Competition Protection Office.	In January 2013, a new, independent public agency, the Slovenian Competition Protection Agency (CPA), took over the responsibility for enforcing the competition law. In 2013, the budget of the CPA was increased to address resource issues to a certain degree.
Develop equity markets by eliminating political interference into management of listed companies, improved rights of minority shareholders and enhancing operational and financial independence of the Slovenian Securities Market Authorities.	No action taken.
Streamline processes for accessing business premises, land and building permits.	No action taken.

Labour markets

Main recent OECD recommendations	Actions taken
Further reduce labour market dualism by phasing out the preferential treatment of student work.	In February 2015, healthcare and pension contributions for student work were introduced and a minimum hourly gross wage rate was set. Students will now accumulate years of pensionable service from their work.
Broaden access of unemployed to active labour market policies by merging the Employment Service of Slovenia and the Centres for Social Work.	No action taken.

Boosting innovation and greening the economy

Main recent OECD recommendations	Actions taken
Use more extensively research vouchers, funded with EU funds, to promote green innovation.	No action taken.
Align tax rates for diesel and petrol and consider introducing congestion charges.	The differential between diesel and gasoline has been reduced recently due to reduced differential in excise duties on the two fuels. In addition, effective from January 2015, there was an increase in tax rate on CO_2 emissions by 20% per each kg of CO_2 for all energy products.

Thematic chapters

Chapter 1

Raising competitiveness and long-term growth of the Slovenian economy

The rapid growth after independence stopped in 2008, as the global crisis exposed important structural weaknesses. Large state involvement and rigid labour and product markets lowered productivity. Weak corporate governance and easy credit before the crisis led to high indebtedness and overinvestment. Slovenia was slow to deal with the underlying structural problems. Gradually, important reforms have been implemented which raised credibility of Slovenia in the financial markets and boosted confidence. But economic recovery has been sluggish, many people are unemployed and living standards still remain below the pre-crisis levels. Cost competitiveness and export market performance deteriorated, and there have been marked improvements only recently. Better corporate governance and management practices in the state owned sector and privatisations can attract FDI and raise efficiency. Low innovative activity could be boosted by more FDI, stronger framework for entrepreneurial activity and better start-up support. Relatively high minimum wage is potentially reducing employment opportunities of low-skilled workers. Limiting the minimum wage growth, and lowering the high tax wedge on labour income could boost employment. Efficiency should be raised in early and tertiary education to enhance skills. Despite generous public support, overall students' performance could be improved and there are marked differences between students from different socioeconomic backgrounds.

The statistical data for Israel are supplied by and under the responsibility of the relevant Israeli authorities. The use of such data by the OECD is without prejudice to the status of the Golan Heights, East Jerusalem and Israeli settlements in the West Bank under the terms of international law.

Trends in productivity and sources of productivity growth

Living standards have fallen since the crisis primarily due to lower labour utilisation

After independence upon the break-up of Yugoslavia in 1991, Slovenia experienced robust growth (Figure 1.1) and incomes rose steadily towards the EU average (Figure 1.2, Panel A). The catch-up was facilitated by a relatively skilled labour force and a relatively modern industrial base. Production was reoriented to new markets in Europe, while Slovenia remained a competitive provider of goods and capital to the countries in the Balkans. Significant structural reforms paved the way to European Union (EU) accession in 2004 and euro adoption in 2007.

However, in the run up to the 2008 crisis, easy and cheap wholesale credit raised by Slovenian banks abroad, overly optimistic growth expectations and mispriced risk taking led to an investment boom in construction and much of the corporate sector. In addition, the optimism facilitated highly leveraged management buyouts, where internal managers took out risky loans to buy ownership stakes in companies. The resulting high indebtedness made corporates and banks vulnerable to changes in market conditions. Adjustment was also complicated by rigidities in labour and product markets and weak corporate governance, amid widespread state ownership. The subsequent drop in output was one of the largest in the OECD and the living standards still remain below the pre-crisis levels (Figure 1.2, Panel B). GDP per capita in purchasing power parity in 2014 was still more than 8% lower than in 2008. Recovery has been slow, and despite some recent reforms many of the structural problems remain un-addressed.

Figure 1.1. **Growth was strong after independence**

GDP in volume

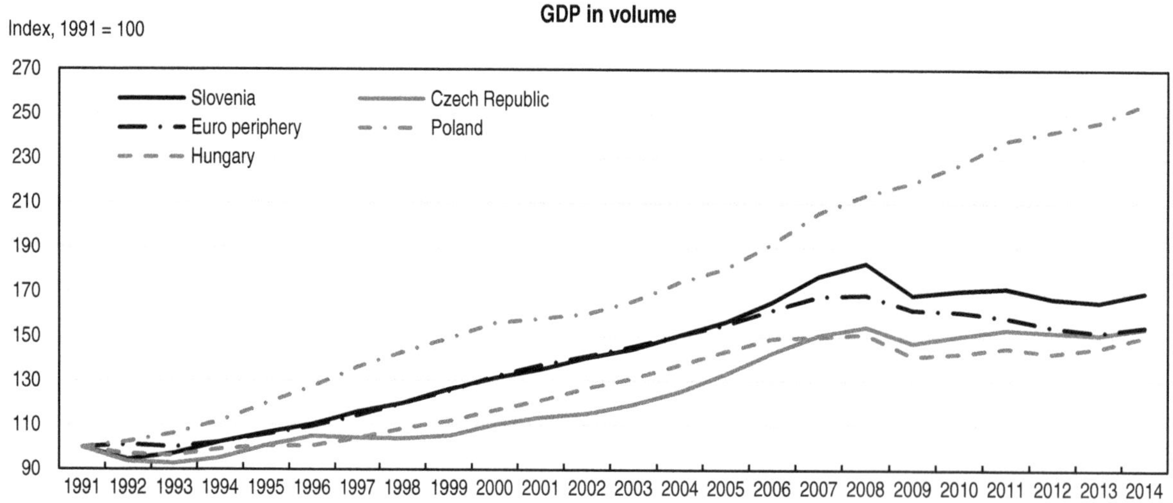

Source: OECD Economic Outlook 96 Database.

StatLink http://dx.doi.org/10.1787/888933205033

Figure 1.2. **Rapid catch-up stalled after the crisis**

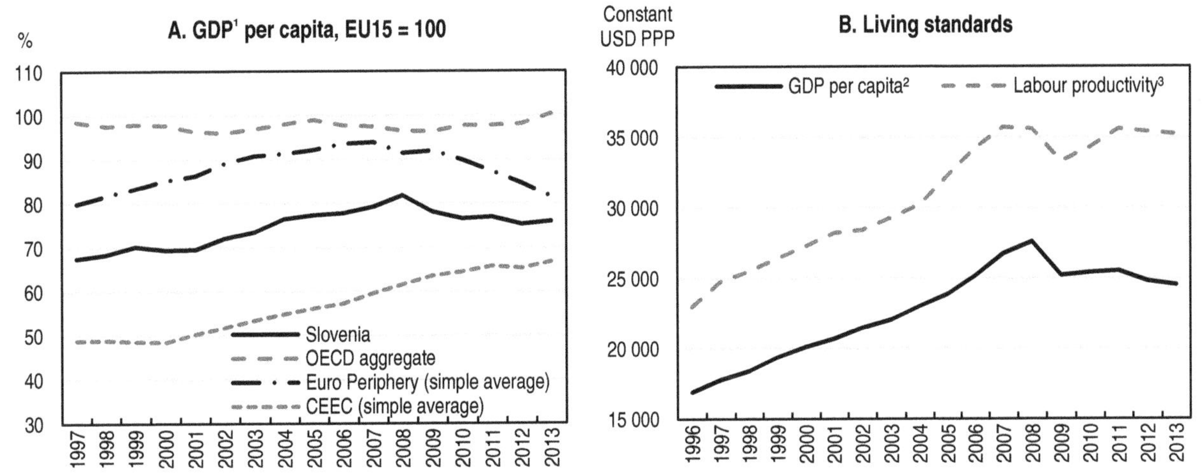

Note: CEECs include Poland, Hungary, Slovak Republic and Czech Republic; Euro Periphery includes Spain, Portugal, Greece and Ireland.

1. GDP in million USD, current prices, current PPP per thousand persons/thousand hours worked.
2. GDP in USD constant prices, constant PPP (base year 2005).
3. Labour Productivity measured as GDP per thousand hours.

Source: *OECD Productivity Database.*

StatLink http://dx.doi.org/10.1787/888933204789

Labour productivity – measured in GDP per hour worked – also grew strongly before the crisis and dropped substantially in 2008. It has, however, by now recovered to the pre-crisis levels. These positive developments reflect large adjustments in the use of labour. After the crisis, there was a rise in the unemployment rate, but also a sizeable fall in the labour force participation and adjustments in hours worked by the employed workers (Figure 1.3). To turn around the negative trend in living standards it will be therefore important to revive growth in labour utilisation, while sustaining productivity growth.

Figure 1.3. **There has been large adjustment in labour utilisation after the crisis**

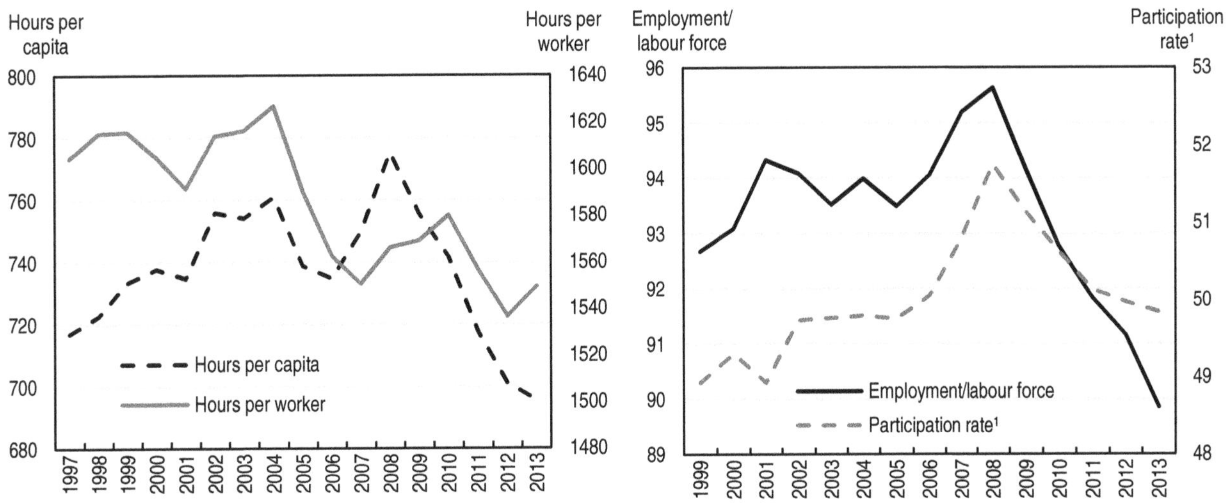

Note: Hours per capita can be decomposed into hours per worker (total hours/total employment), participation rate (labour force/population) and employment/labour force. The last term is equivalent to (1 – unemployment rate).

1. The participation rate refers to the ratio of the total labour force (aged 15 and over) to the total population.

Source: OECD Level of GDP per capita and *Productivity Database*, for Panel A; and OECD *Short-Term Labour Market Statistics Database*, for Panel B.

StatLink http://dx.doi.org/10.1787/888933205040

Prior to the crisis productivity in terms of value added per labour input grew in most sectors of the Slovenian economy (Figure 1.4, Panel A). However, productivity is strikingly low compared to the EU15 average in some specific sectors such as agriculture, mining and utilities (Figure 1.5). Productivity is also low in financial and insurance services, and professional services (especially in administrative and support service activities). After the crisis in 2008, all sectors except manufacturing, and mining and utilities turned to a negative productivity growth, measured as gross value added (GVA) per worker. Yet, in terms of GVA per hour, most sectors, except construction, for example, still experience positive productivity growth, reflecting more extensive use of labour (Figure 1.4, Panel B).

Figure 1.4. **Growth in value added per worker turned negative in most sectors, while value added per hour continued growing**

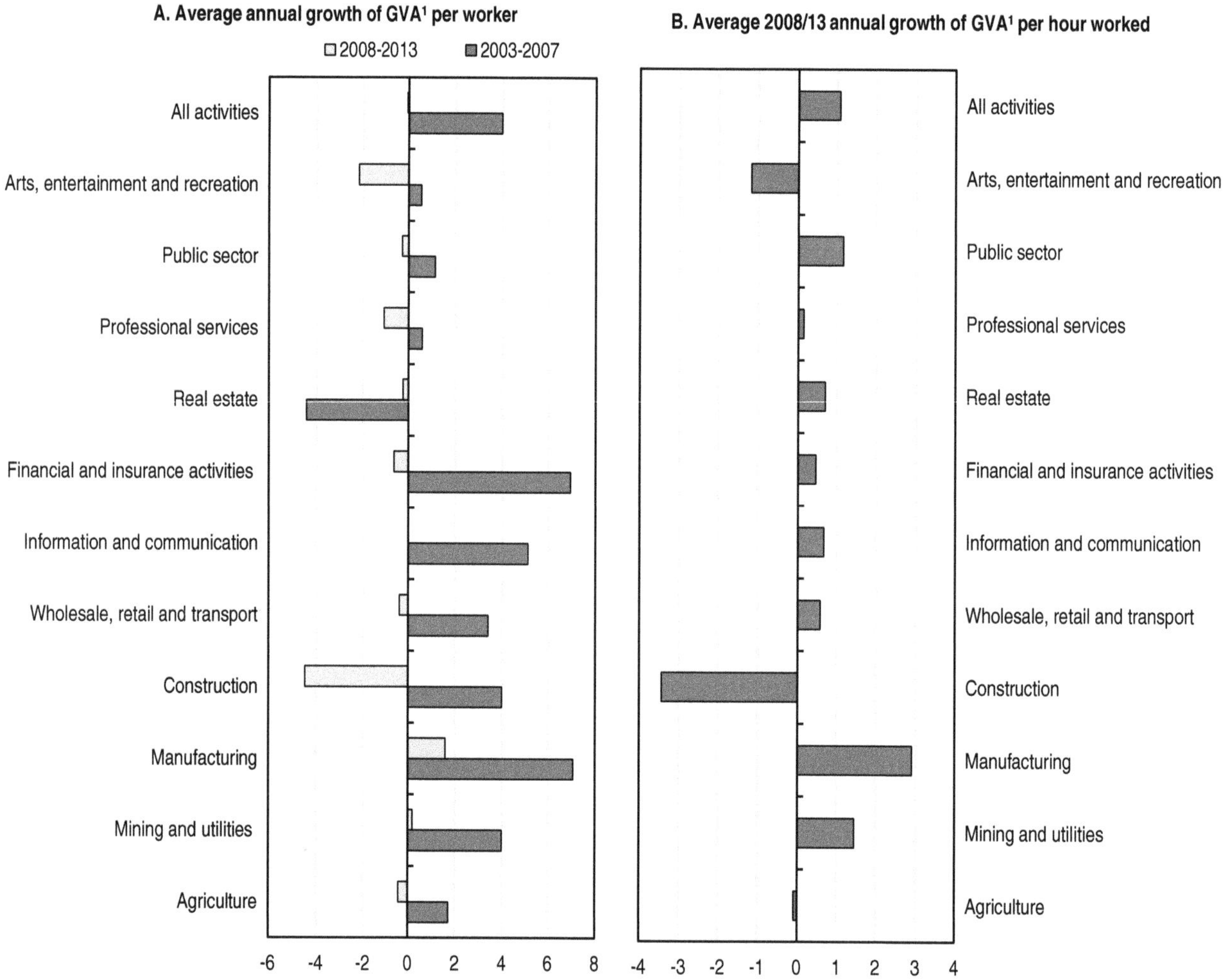

1. GVA in volume terms in million euros per thousand workers (reference year 2005).
Source: Eurostat *National Accounts* detailed breakdowns.

StatLink http://dx.doi.org/10.1787/888933205058

Factors contributing to growth

GDP growth can be decomposed into contributions from various factors of production: capital deepening, growth in the quantity of labour input, labour quality (human capital) and the residual – total factor productivity (TFP) growth [see Dall'Orso and Sila (2015) for a more detailed description of the methodology].

Figure 1.5. **There is scope to improve labour productivity in several sectors**

Gap from the EU15, in % (2013)

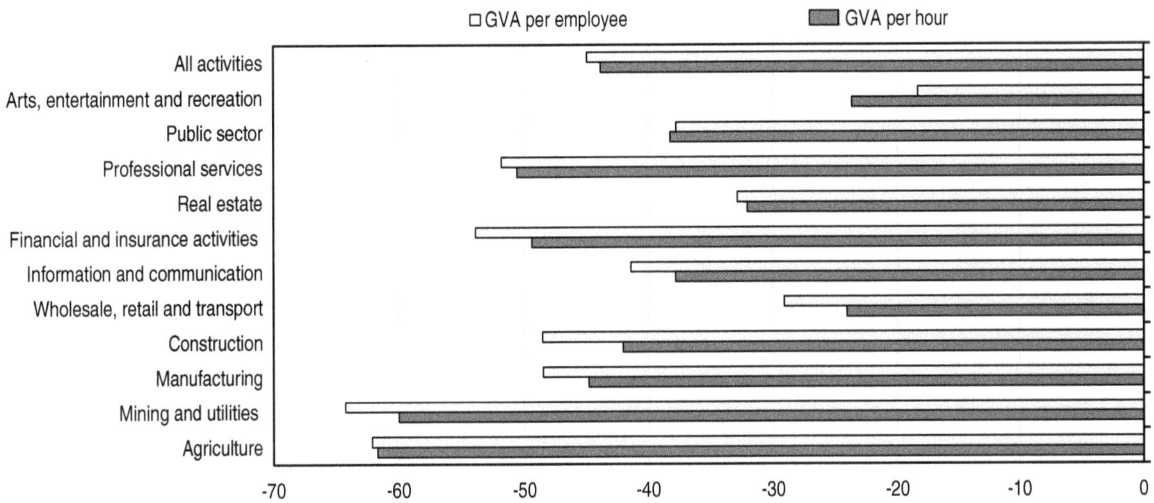

Note: Gross value added (GVA) per employee measured as GVA in current prices, basic prices, million euros per worker (total employment). GVA per hours measured as GVA in current prices, basic prices, million euros per thousand hours. Note that there is a sizeable difference in the productivity gap between this measure and the GDP per capita measure in the previous section. The difference stems from two factors – one is that GDP per capita is measured in PPP. The other one is that GVA is measured at basic prices, thus excluding indirect taxes but including subsidies on products.

Source: Eurostat *National Accounts* detailed breakdowns.

StatLink http://dx.doi.org/10.1787/888933205062

The growth accounting exercise shows that capital deepening and total factor productivity were Slovenia's main sources of economic growth from 1997 to 2007. After 2008, the GDP growth rate became negative, mainly due to falling labour quantity and negative TFP growth (Figure 1.6 and Table 1.1), while capital services and human capital

Figure 1.6. **Contribution of factors[1] to GDP growth**

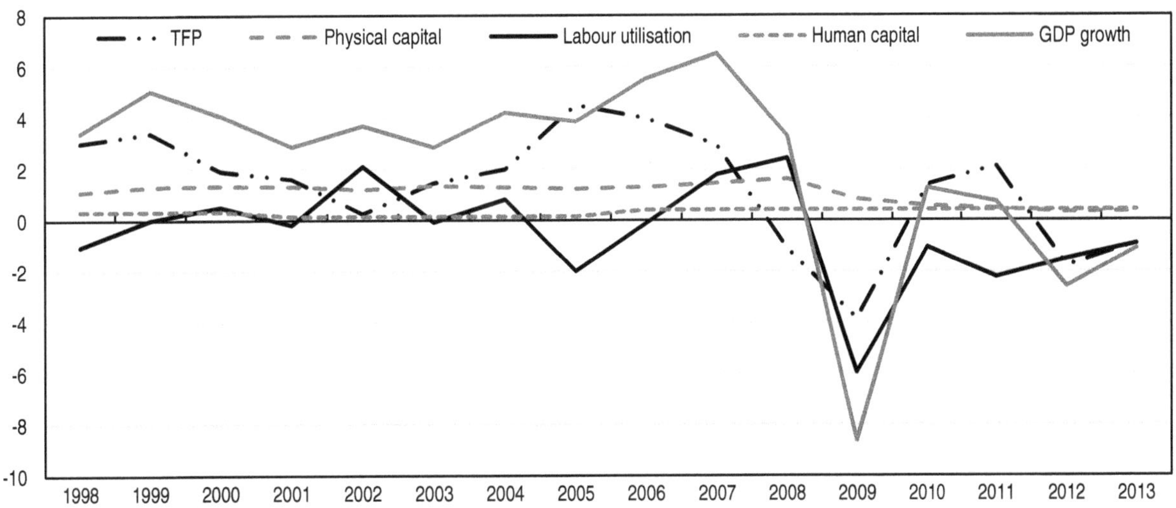

1. Human capital index is measured by average years of schooling; Labour quantity is measured in total hours worked; Physical capital is measured in volumes of capital stocks; TFP, Total Factor Productivity is calculated as a residual.

Source: *OECD National Accounts Statistics Database* and OECD calculations.

StatLink http://dx.doi.org/10.1787/888933205078

Table 1.1. **1997/2007 Growth accounting in CEECs,[1] Euro Periphery[2] and EU3[3]**

Average annual growth in percent[4]

	1997/2007				2008/2013			
	Slovenia[5]	CEEC[6]	EU3[6]	Euro periphery[6]	Slovenia[5]	CEEC[6]	EU3[6]	Euro periphery[6]
GDP growth	4.395	4.078	2.421	4.267	-1.107	1.076	0.194	-1.968
Human capital	0.25	0.374	0.858	0.614	0.398	0.264	0.81	0.392
Labour utilisation	0.184	0.014	0.275	1.258	-1.481	-0.209	0.149	-1.625
Physical capital	1.339	1.83	0.694	1.959	0.693	1.545	0.509	0.802
TFP	2.621	1.861	0.595	0.436	-0.717	-0.523	-1.274	-1.536

1. CEECs include Poland, Hungary, Slovakia and Czech Republic.
2. Euro periphery includes Spain, Portugal, Greece and Ireland.
3. EU3 includes France, Germany and United Kingdom.
4. Geometric average.
5. Average of 1998/2007 because of missing values for 1996.
6. CEEC, EU3 and Euro periphery values are simple averages.

Source: *OECD National Accounts Statistics* and own calculations.

contribution to GDP growth remained positive, albeit lower than before. Interestingly, TFP contribution started declining already in the year 2005, 3 years before the crisis, at the time of a steep rise in labour utilisation. This corroborates the argument put forward in the *2009 Economic Survey* that the Slovenian economy was showing signs of overheating. In particular, after the euro area entry in 2007, inflation peaked at the highest level within the euro area and unemployment fell significantly below the natural rate.

Among all countries included, the contribution from human capital before the crisis was the lowest in Slovenia (Table 1.1), pointing to potential weaknesses in the education and training systems. Since 2008, the GDP growth rate is lower in Slovenia compared to other Central and Eastern European countries (CEECs) mainly due to a dramatic fall in labour quantity contribution. The contribution from capital deepening in Slovenia has also dropped, reflecting lower investment. The drop in the TFP contribution to growth was sizeable in Slovenia, although its contribution is less negative than in the euro periphery countries. Thus, to return to growth, Slovenia needs to regain the TFP growth, together with higher labour participation and renewed investment cycle into physical capital. In the longer term, growth could also be better supported with increases in human capital.

Before the crisis, Slovenia experienced growth in productivity (both TFP and labour productivity), while in the last quarters of 2008, the country suffered from an unprecedented productivity drop and Slovenia remained in recession for a prolonged period. The interesting question is whether the crisis led to structural changes that undermine productivity growth in the future. If productivity growth has indeed shifted down permanently, this would have important consequences for long-term economic performance. Dall'Orso and Sila (2015) test this (see also Annex 2) using time series analysis and stability diagnosis techniques to detect potential structural breaks, but evidence is inconclusive. The analysis identifies four or five break dates in the 1997-2013 period. In addition, there is weak evidence that in 2011 Q4 there was another structural break in productivity, bringing average productivity growth down again. Nevertheless, it cannot be concluded that the break identified in 2011 Q4 and the lower average growth thereafter imply that productivity growth has come down more permanently.

External sector, global value chains and competitiveness

Slovenia is an export oriented economy with exports representing more than 70% of GDP. The most important export articles are machinery, road vehicles and pharmaceutical products. In the pre-crisis period (2004-07) Slovenia's exports grew rapidly at an average rate of 12% per year in volume terms (Figure 1.7). The crisis hit hard, with exports falling by

Figure 1.7. **Slovenia's exports have been growing steadily**

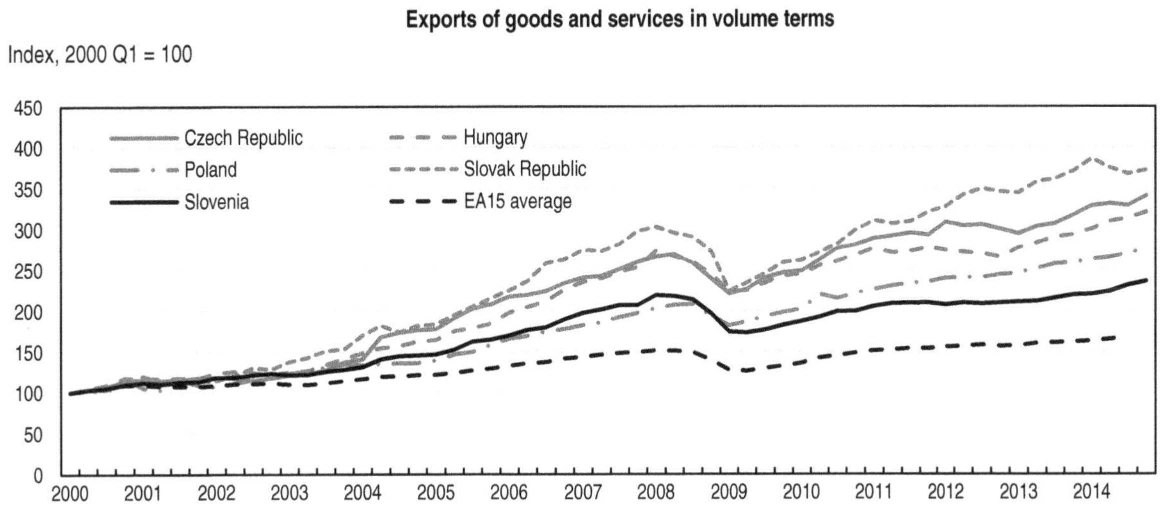

Source: *OECD Economic Outlook 96 Database.*

StatLink http://dx.doi.org/10.1787/888933205086

20% from 2008 Q1 to 2009 Q2 (peak to trough number), partly due to the country's export specialisation in cyclically sensitive goods, such as automotive components (OECD, 2011a). There has been a recovery in exports since then, but the recovery has been slow in comparison to benchmark economies (Figure 1.8). Slovenia's cost competitiveness and

Figure 1.8. **In the post-crisis period, Slovenian exports have under-performed**

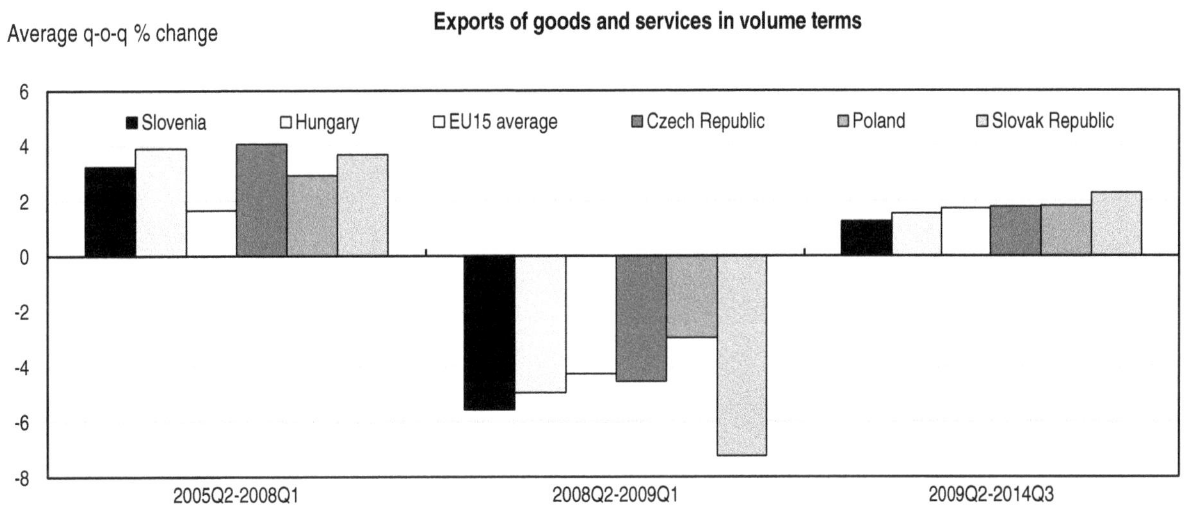

Source: *OECD Economic Outlook 96 Database.*

StatLink http://dx.doi.org/10.1787/888933205093

export market performance deteriorated and still lag behind peers (Figures 1.9 and 1.10). In the second half of 2014, however, competitiveness started improving and Slovenia has gained market shares. The tradable part of the economy, and manufacturing in particular, has made considerable unit labour cost (ULC) adjustments since 2010. And while in previous years cost competitiveness improved mainly owing to the adjustments in employment and earnings, in 2014 improvements have been mostly due to rises in value added (IMAD, 2014a).

Figure 1.9. **Slovenia's improvements in cost competitiveness lag some peers**

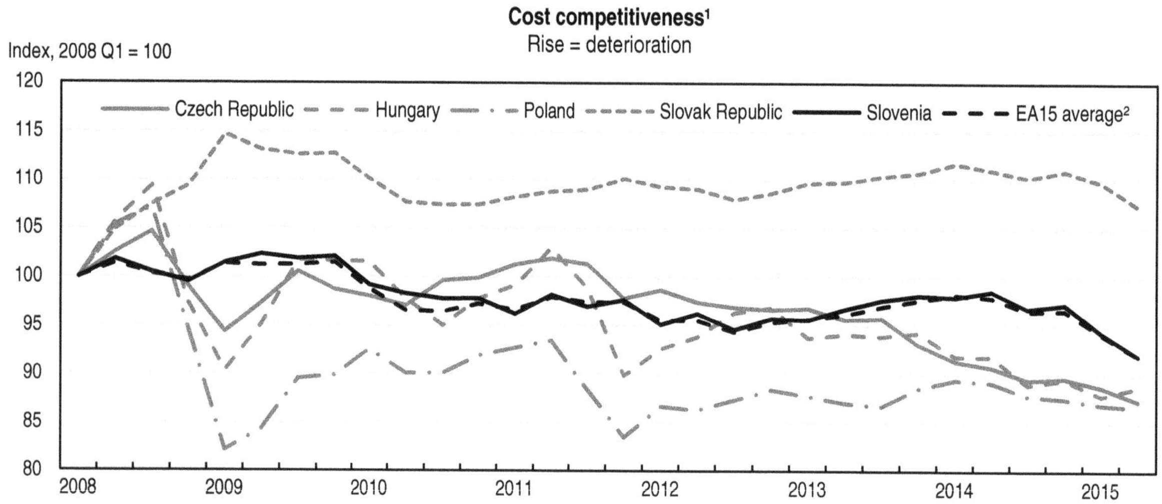

1. Real effective exchange rates based on unit labour costs for total economy.
2. Data refer to the weighted unconsolidated average across the EA15 countries.

Source: OECD Economic Outlook 96 Database.

StatLink http://dx.doi.org/10.1787/888933205103

Figure 1.10. **Export market performance stagnated, but there have been improvements recently**

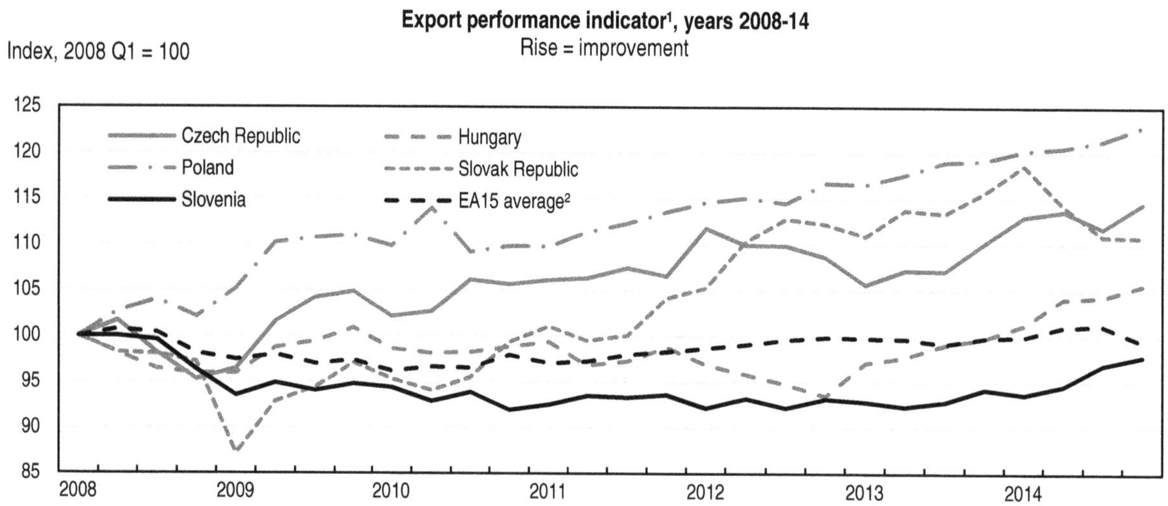

1. Export performance is measured as actual growth in exports relative to the growth of the country's export market, which represents the potential export growth for a country assuming that its market shares remain unchanged.
2. Data refer to the weighted unconsolidated average across the EA15 countries.

Source: OECD Economic Outlook 96 Database.

StatLink http://dx.doi.org/10.1787/888933205112

Slovenia has increased slightly the share of domestic value added incorporated in gross exports, indicating that it now benefits more from trade, but the share remains relatively low compared to most advanced economies (Figure 1.11). As many other small economies, Slovenia has a high participation in global value chains (GVCs) (Figure 1.12), primarily driven by the use of foreign intermediates (backward participation) in Slovenia's exports (OECD, 2013a). High backward participation is typical in the manufacturing sector, while services typically show a higher forward participation.

Figure 1.11. **The share of domestic value added in gross exports is still low**

Percentage od domestic value added embodied in gross exports

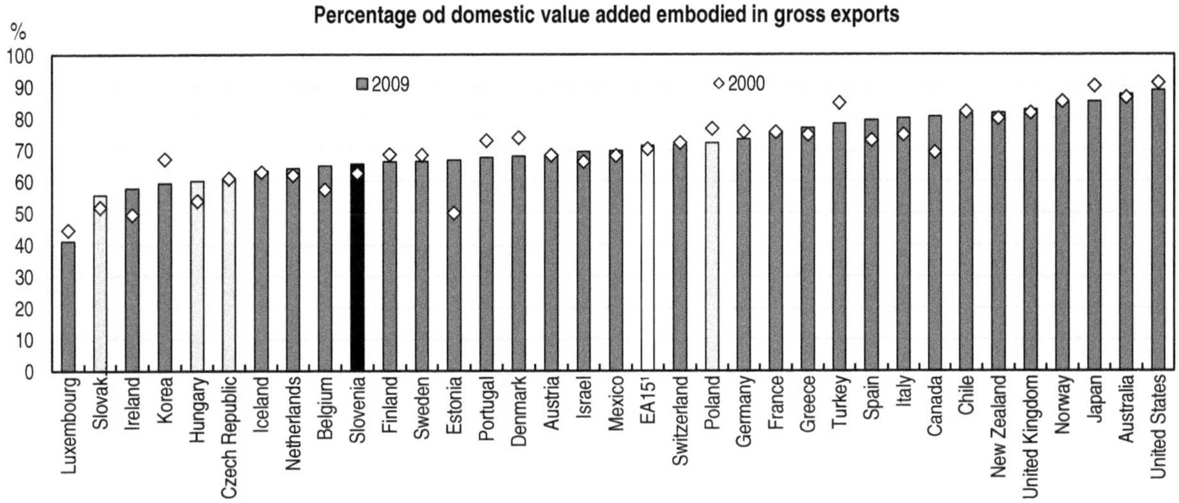

1. Data refer to the weighted unconsolidated average across the EA15 countries.

Source: OECD-WTO Trade in Value Added (TiVA) Database.

StatLink http://dx.doi.org/10.1787/888933205128

Figure 1.12. **Slovenia has a high GVC participation index due to high backward participation**

GVC participation across countries, 2009

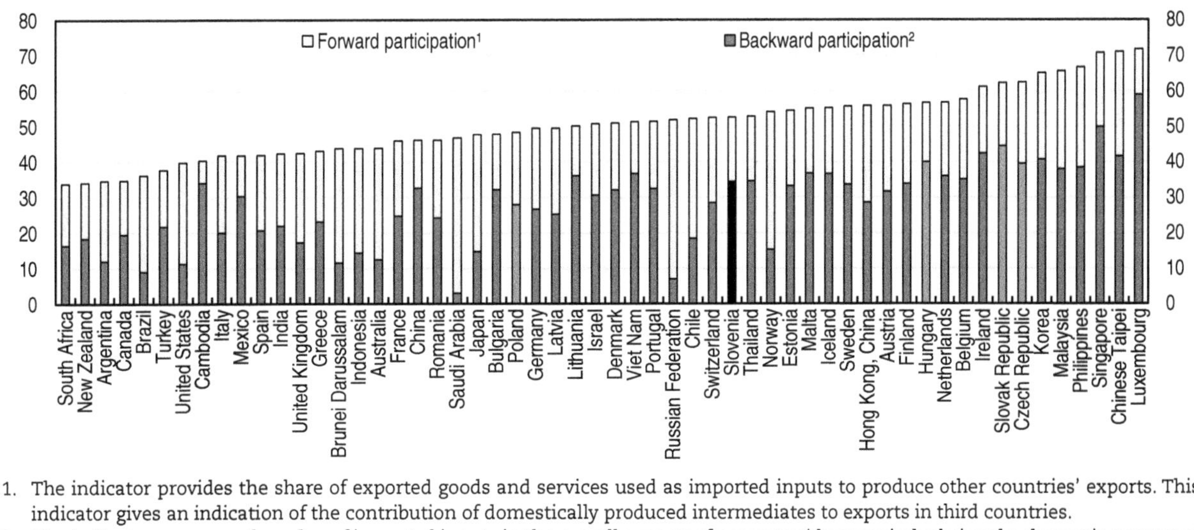

1. The indicator provides the share of exported goods and services used as imported inputs to produce other countries' exports. This indicator gives an indication of the contribution of domestically produced intermediates to exports in third countries.
2. The indicator measures the value of imported inputs in the overall exports of a country (the remainder being the domestic content of exports). This indicator provides an indication of the contribution of foreign industries to the exports of a country by looking at the foreign value added embodied in the gross exports.

Source: OECD Global Value Chains Indicators – May 2013.

StatLink http://dx.doi.org/10.1787/888933205131

The share of services in total exports is high compared to other CEECs, and has been increasing, but remains below the EA15 average. According to the OECD Services Trade Restrictiveness Index (STRI), Slovenia is open to services trade (Figure 1.13). In most of the services sectors Slovenia shows lower restrictions to trade than OECD and EA15 averages. This is good as services normally bring higher value added in trade compared to manufactured goods. In Slovenia, services account for about 20% of gross exports, but they represent 42% of value-added exports.

Figure 1.13. **Slovenia is open to services trade**

Services Trade Restrictiveness Index (STRI)

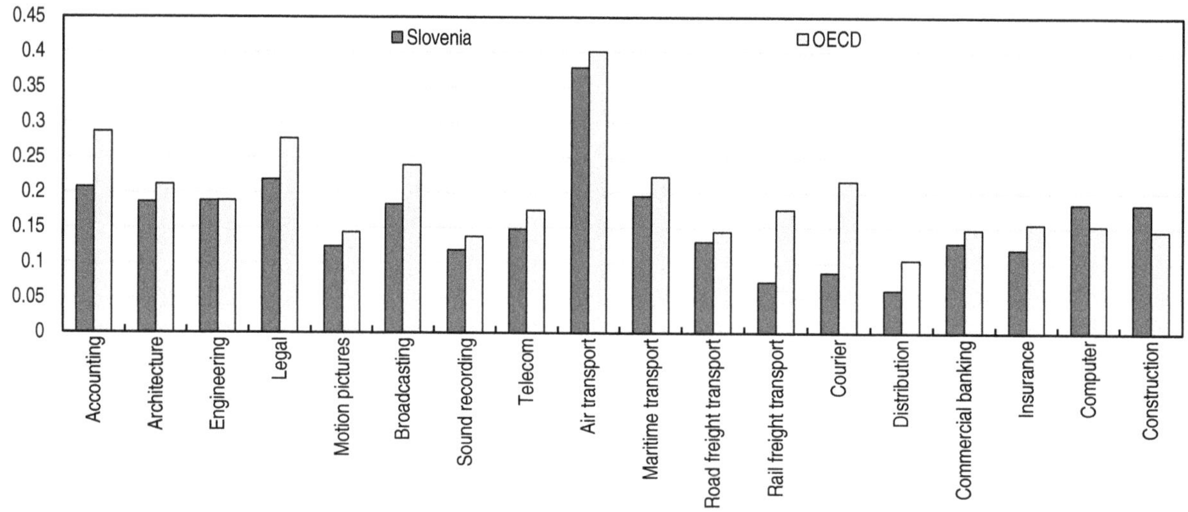

Note: The STRI takes the value from 0 to 1, where 0 is completely open and 1 is completely closed. It is calculated on the basis of information in the *STRI Database* which reports regulation currently in force.

Source: OECD *Services Trade Restrictiveness Index Database.*

StatLink http://dx.doi.org/10.1787/888933205142

Exports of goods are mainly concentrated in medium-high and medium-low technology industries (Figure 1.14), with biggest part of exports being intermediate goods.

Figure 1.14. **High-technology goods have increased their weight in export**

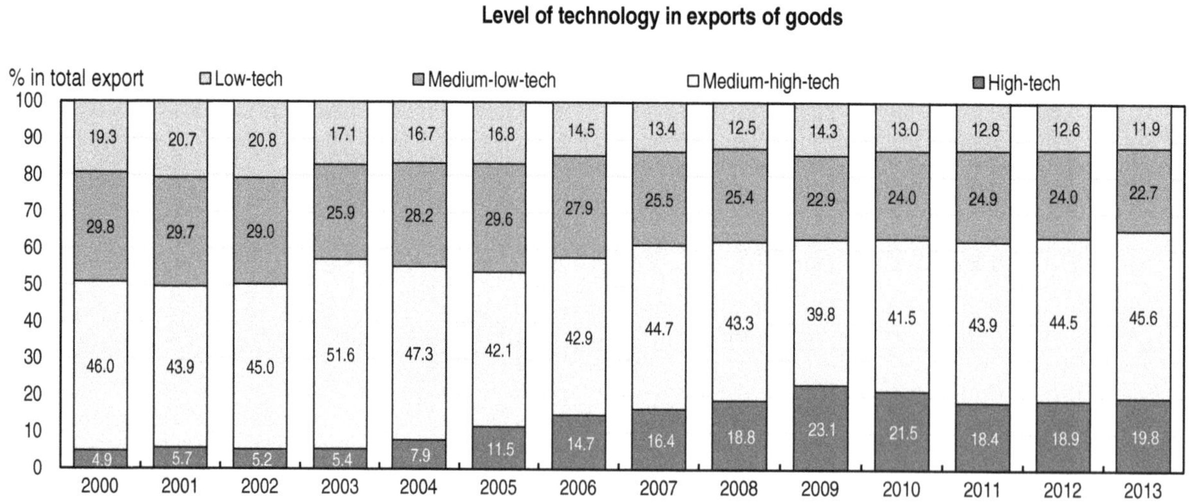

Source: OECD STAN *Bilateral Trade in Goods by Industry and End-Use Database.*

StatLink http://dx.doi.org/10.1787/888933205152

Slovenia evolved from being a net exporter of low and medium-low technology goods to a net exporter of high and medium-high technology goods (see Box 1.1). High-tech exports represent an important channel for learning by exporting and several studies show that starting to export helps boost innovation (Lovea and Ganotakisb, 2013; Hausmann et al., 2011). Moreover, high-tech firms tend to attract more FDI and at the same time, in presence of FDI, they grow faster (Damijan, Kostevc and Rojec, 2013). Further increases of high-tech exports would therefore help future growth.

Box 1.1. **High-technology manufacturing in Slovenia**

Share of the high- and medium-high technology manufacturing in total manufacturing GVA has risen from about 30% of total GVA in manufacturing in 1996 to 45% in 2012, which is higher than in some other CEEC peers, but lagging behind high performers such as Ireland and Germany (Figure 1.15). The rise can be explained by a growth in value added by pharmaceutical companies and a decrease in the contribution of low-technology industries, especially textile, wearing apparel, leather and furniture, due to bankruptcies.

Figure 1.15. **Share of high and medium technology manufacturing is relatively high**

% in total manufacturing GVA (2012)

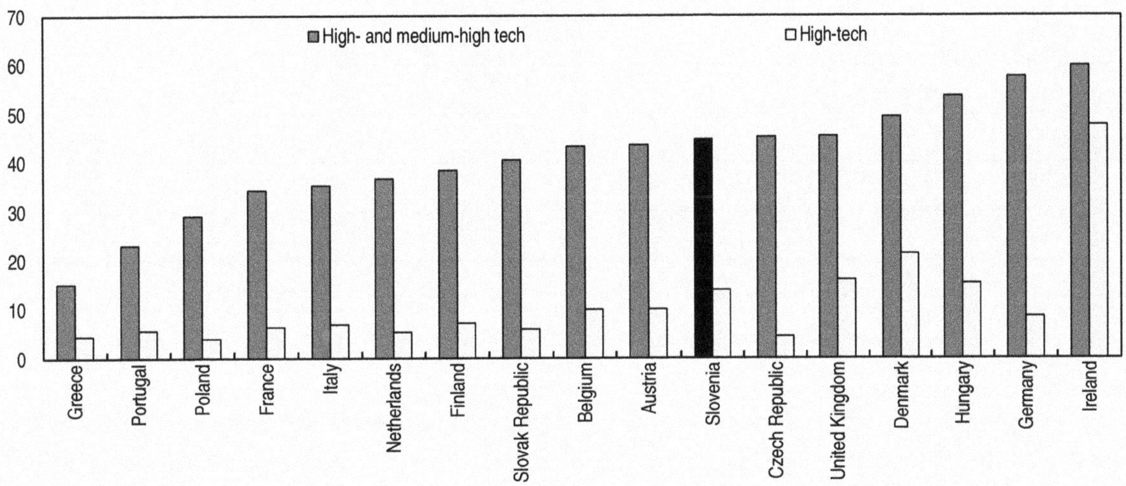

Note: GVA in basic prices and in current prices. Based on Eurostat aggregation of the manufacturing industry according to technological intensity, based on NACE Rev. 2, 2 digit level. For countries where data is not available for 2012, 2011 numbers are used.
Source: Eurostat and OECD calculations.

StatLink http://dx.doi.org/10.1787/888933205161

Improvement in overall business environment can contribute to increasing further the role of high-tech manufacturing, and thereby increase productivity and growth in Slovenia. In the last two decades productivity growth has been fastest in the high-technology manufacturing by a high margin (Table 1.2) and the level of productivity in the high-technology sectors is the highest too – about 2.6 times the level in the low-tech manufacturing (Figure 1.16, Panel A). High productivity also brings higher wages; in the high-tech manufacturing wages are about 2 times higher than in low-tech manufacturing (Figure 1.16, Panel B).

Box 1.1. **High-technology manufacturing in Slovenia** *(cont.)*

Table 1.2. **Productivity growth has been fastest in high-technology manufacturing**

Annual % change in GVA[1] per worker

	High technology	Medium-high technology	Medium-low technology	Low technology
1997-2007	11.6	7.6	1.4	5.3
2008-2012	6.5	0.9	-0.2	0.9

1. Gross value added at basic prices, in chain linked volumes, reference year 2005.

Source: Eurostat.and OECD calculations.

Figure 1.16. **Labour productivity and wages are higher in high technology manufacturing**

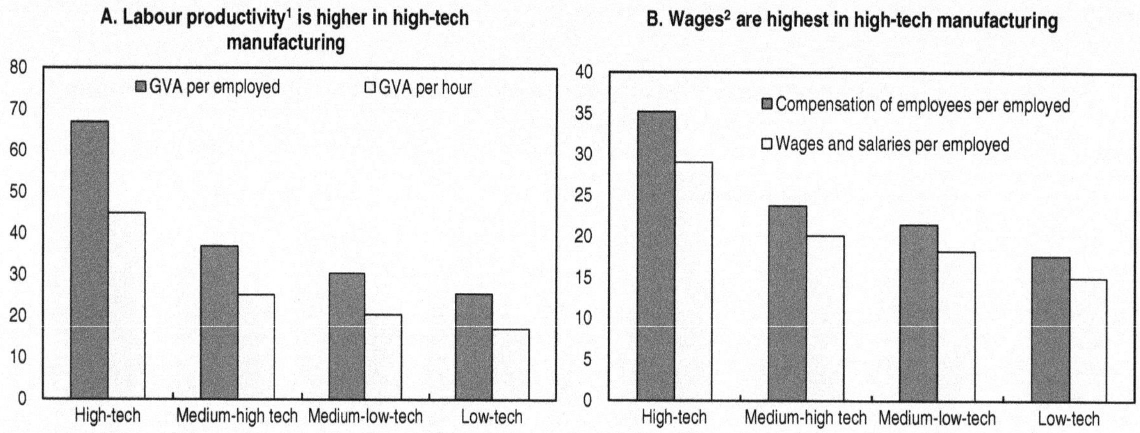

Note: Based on Eurostat aggregation of the manufacturing industry according to technological intensity, based on NACE Rev. 2, 2 digit level. GVA in basic prices and in current prices.

1. In 1 000 euros per person employed/1 000 hours, 2012.
2. In 1 000 euros per person employed, 2012.

Source: Eurostat and OECD calculations.

StatLink http://dx.doi.org/10.1787/888933205178

Slovenia is relatively competitive in high and medium high technology products as indicated by the high contribution of these products in the trade balance. In 2011, these products contributed 6% to the trade balance, as compared to 4.2% in the EU or 1.93% in the US (European Commission, 2013). Furthermore, the contribution has been increasing steadily in recent years.

Innovation, R&D and entrepreneurship

Increasing innovative activity

Expenditure on R&D and human resources in science and technology occupations in Slovenia is above the OECD average (Figure 1.17), with most of expenditure done by businesses (OECD, 2014a). Business enterprise expenditure on R&D (BERD) has increased rapidly, to the level of Austria's and Denmark's in terms of GDP, and it is higher than in many advanced OECD countries. However, the share of industry-financed BERD has dropped in recent years, while the share of government-financed BERD has increased. Slovenia is also strong in human resources in science and technology occupations. The number of researchers and R&D personnel has been on the rise and measured as % of all employees it is one of the highest among the OECD countries (OECD 2014f and 2013f; SORS, 2012).

Figure 1.17. **Slovenia does well in terms of inputs into innovation process, but innovative activity is low**

Comparative performance of national science and innovation systems, 2014

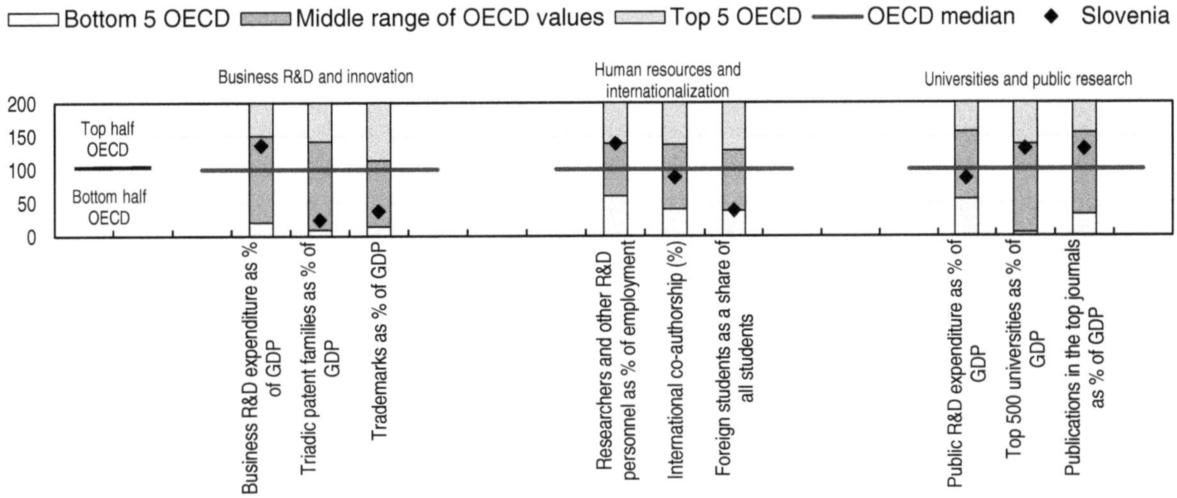

Note: Normalised index of performance relative to the median values in the OECD area (Index median = 100).

Source: based on *OECD Science, Technology and Industry Outlook 2014* and *OECD Main Science and Technology Indicators (MSTI) Database*, June 2014; *USPTO Bulk Downloads: Trademark Application Text* hosted by Reed Technology Information Services, *OHIM Community Trademark Database* CTM Download, *JPO Annual Reports 2001-2013* and Graham, S., G. Hancock, A. Marco and A. Myers (2013), "The USPTO Trademark Case Files Dataset: Descriptions, Lessons, and Insights", *SSRN Working Paper*, *http://ssrn.com/abstract=2188621*; Elsevier B.V. (2014), *Elsevier Research Intelligence* (Scopus-Elsevier); *OECD Education Database*; and Academic Ranking of World Universities (ARWU) (2013), "Shanghai Ranking", *www.shanghairanking.com*.

StatLink http://dx.doi.org/10.1787/888933205012

Compared to high R&D expenditure, a number of innovation outcomes are low as indicated by a low number of patents, trademarks, services' share of business R&D and a low number of innovative firms (Figure 1.17). The number of patents and the number of trademarks per GDP are below the OECD median. The bulk of R&D expenditure goes to technological innovations and majority of business R&D spending is undertaken only by a few large firms (e.g. two pharmaceutical firms account for a large share) (OECD, 2012c). Services' share of business R&D in 2011 (26%) was low compared to their value added share (67%). R&D intensity in services is much lower than the OECD average. This indicates a weak drive to develop non-technological innovation (OECD, 2011a, 2013f), which should be given more focus within R&D expenditure. The share of knowledge intensive services (e.g. financial intermediation and high-tech services) in total services exports is also small – roughly half of the share of the EU average (European Commission, 2014b).

Innovative activity could be increased by higher inflows of FDI and by improvement in the overall business environment. Inflows of FDI are currently small relative to other central and eastern European countries. There are three major constraints in overall business environment hindering innovation: a lack of entrepreneurial dynamism, barriers to doing business and the overly complex and opaque national innovation policy (OECD, 2011a). Improvement in the overall business environment that would better support innovation therefore involves strengthening entrepreneurship education in schools, improvement in the support environment for enterprises, investing in the national innovation system and strengthening links between universities and business.

Improving entrepreneurial dynamism

Birth and death rate of companies are low compared to other OECD countries and firms have a high survival rate (OECD, 2014c). This may be related to stigma in the case of failure, since Slovenia has the lowest number of adults who think that entrepreneurs who fail deserve a second chance (OECD, 2013h), as well as to protracted insolvency procedures. The legacy of the previous economic system may have left some generations without entrepreneurial culture. Prior to the transition to the market economy in 1990, policy makers' systematically shut out entrepreneurial considerations in policy making (EIU, 2009), which may have affected attitudes. Even today, less than 40% of Slovenian adults consider image of entrepreneurs as broadly favourable, one of the lowest among the 33 surveyed countries (OECD, 2013h, European Commission, 2013). Additionally, the share of adults who recognise business opportunities was only 17% in 2014, which ranks Slovenia to 68th place out of 70 countries (Global Entrepreneurship Monitor, 2015a).

The lack of entrepreneurship education may also affect entrepreneurial activity. Almost half of adults consider that school education did not help in developing sense of initiative and entrepreneurial attitude. Moreover, almost 60% think that schooling did not provide the skills and know-how needed to start a business (OECD, 2013h, European Commission, 2013). Opportunities for receiving entrepreneurship education in schools, universities and research institutions are still sparse, despite the gradual phasing-in of entrepreneurship studies into the school system through pilot projects since 2008 (OECD, 2011a). Entrepreneurial dynamism could be fostered by strengthening entrepreneurship education in schools and reforming the education system so that it encourages creativity and entrepreneurial drive.

Start-up entrepreneurship is rising

Start-up companies can play an important role in supporting innovation and business creation. They tend to be closely connected to knowledge institutions (e.g. universities) and therefore promote knowledge flows. The number of start-up companies in Slovenia is increasing faster than the average of all companies in the economy and is creating new jobs with high value added. According to *Global Entrepreneurship Monitor 2014* (2015b) Slovenia ranks 7th among 44 countries by innovativeness of early-stage entrepreneurs. In recent years support environment has improved and a large number of new measures have helped start-up entrepreneurs, including the reduction of administrative burdens to establish a start-up, subsidies for the start-up of innovative companies, a voucher system of training for potential entrepreneurs and rising enterprises, business incubators, technology parks and business accelerators with financial, mentoring, consulting and infrastructural products in one place (Ministry of Higher Education, Science and Technology, 2010; OECD, 2011a; Initiative start:up Slovenia, 2014). In the period 2013-14, the government contributed around EUR 10 million (0.03% of GDP) in the form of subsidies for start-ups and to improve innovative support environment.

To increase growth in the number of start-ups, further improvement in the support environment is needed. The entrepreneurship support in Slovenia does not differentiate between support for start-ups and other companies. This prevents the creation of a suitable and successful entrepreneurship policy and support mechanisms targeting start-up companies. In order to develop start-up ecosystem, Slovenia needs more support activities, a higher quality of already established support services and better networking with support institutions located internationally (Initiative start:up Slovenia, 2014).

Access to finance is another barrier for innovative start-ups and small- and medium-sized enterprises (SMEs). These companies tend to lack collateral, cash flow and a track record (OECD, 2013g). SMEs in Slovenia primarily depend on bank financing and since Slovenian capital market is shallow and illiquid, their sources of financing are even more limited. In line with trends elsewhere in the OECD, EU and Slovenia offer additional funds to these companies. The Slovene Enterprise Fund (SEF) and SID bank (the Slovenian development bank) offer financing for SMEs in conjunction with the commercial banks. Additional funds and instruments dedicated to financing via venture capital funds and business angels are offered by European Investment Fund and the COSME programme. However, the latter are at present unutilised (Bank of Slovenia, 2014a), possibly because firms are not familiar with their existence or lack business ideas.

Improving national innovation policy and public R&D

The lack of planning, implementation and co-ordination in national innovation policy also holds back innovation. The current public research system is marked by ingrained, administrative dispersion, by rivalry among various stakeholders and a consequent overlapping of innovation efforts. There is also a lack of transparency of support at the inter-ministerial and inter-agency level. The system of business support services (business incubators, technology parks, platforms and centres, etc.) would need to be more in touch with business demands, tailored to specific phases of a firm's life cycle. The institutional dispersion at the planning stage has undermined the delivery of government support services for business R&D and innovation activities. Frequent changes in policy measures and instruments have rendered the innovation framework unstable and unpredictable, making new policy initiatives less credible.

In pursuit of targets of innovation policies, Slovenia established an interdisciplinary research council that is in charge of evaluation and public budget allocation. This upgrades collaborative links between major stakeholders of innovation policy, which should be improved further. The *Research and Innovation Strategy of Slovenia 2011-20* (RISS) and the *National Higher Education Programme 2011-20* (NHEP) also propose measures for necessary reforms of the national innovation system and measureable implementation targets (OECD, 2014e). These aim towards a unifying innovation policy and should be implemented. An additional planned document within the EU framework is Smart Specialisation Strategy, with a goal to enable Slovenia to become a technology leader in its priority areas.

To enhance the efficiency of public R&D and to meet demands of the business community a research voucher system was introduced to encourage companies to hire public research organisations to do research for them (OECD, 2013b). Additionally, to foster business R&D and innovation Slovenia offers grants, R&D tax incentives, loan guarantees, mezzanine capital and equity (Figure 1.18). Centres of excellence (CoE), competence centres (CCs) and development centres that stimulate collaboration of public research with the business sector were also established (OECD, 2012b, 2012c, 2014e). CoE are aimed at promoting the concentration of knowledge at priority technological areas and horizontal linking along the entire chain of knowledge development, based on strategic partnerships between the private sector and academia. The CCs are defined as development and research centres that are managed by partners from industrial sector and link partners from the industry and public research sector. They focus on the promotion of the development capability and the application of new technologies (Ministry of higher education, science and technology, 2014). Development centres are linking private sector, research institutions and local authorities with the aim to concentrate knowledge and infrastructure in the priority sectors or at the regional level.

Slovenian government needs to reform universities and public research organisations (PROs) to facilitate further improvements in public research. Public research has delivered some impressive results in terms of scientific output (Figure 1.17), despite the low funding – Slovenia spends 0.3% of GDP on total higher education spending on R&D (HERD), compared to the OECD average of 0.4% of GDP (OECD, 2013f, 2013g). To facilitate further improvements, the governance of public research should be reformed so that universities and PROs are given more autonomy,

Figure 1.18. **Most relevant instruments of public funding of business R&D, 2014**

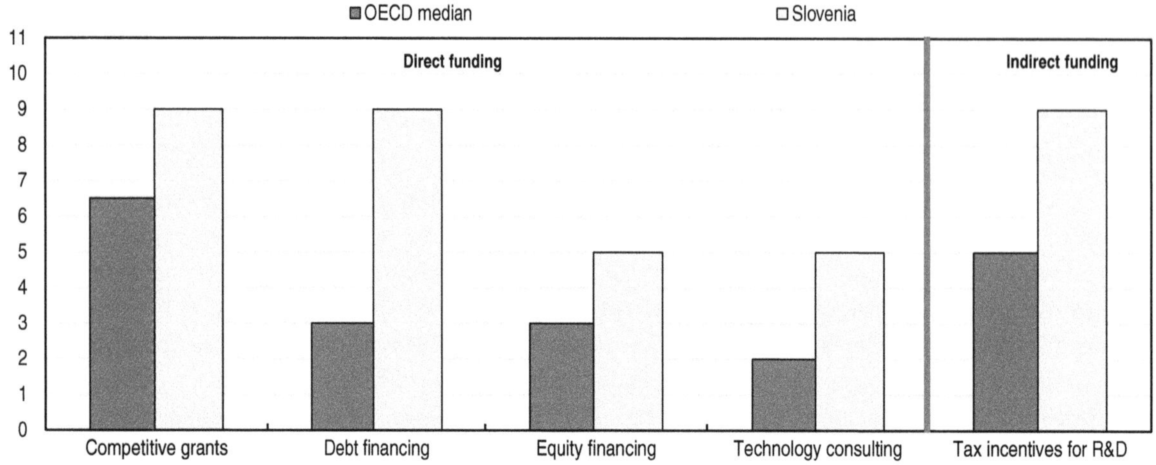

Note: The chart depicts the responses to questions on the principal instruments of public funding of business R&D and innovation and how their relevance has changed. The answers run from 0 (not used) to 9 (high and increasing relevance).
Source: OECD, based on country responses to the *OECD Science, Technology and Industry Outlook* policy questionnaire 2014.
StatLink http://dx.doi.org/10.1787/888933205187

firmly tied to accountability and performance. Such autonomy requires a strong and clear governance model. Universities will require strong leadership and the possibility to build critical mass, with active international recruiting and modern career models. Funding of science should support change through appropriate incentives. For PROs, a similar reform agenda is needed, after agreeing on the main strategic objectives of each major institute (OECD, 2012c, 2014a).

Slovenia's R&D system is highly internationalised in some respects (e.g. participation in European R&D programmes), but much less so in others (e.g. attracting foreign researchers and students), limiting the talent pool. Slovenia's lack of attractiveness is due to the fact that a majority of subjects are taught in Slovenian language, opaque or overly restrictive selection procedures, unattractive career models and salary regulations. Several measures aim to make Slovenia more attractive internationally, such as university programmes in foreign languages, payment of European funds to foreign researchers and opening of research programmes to foreign participation (e.g. in the Young Researcher Programme) (OECD, 2012b, 2012c). The government should also encourage businesses, universities and PROs to upgrade their strategic capabilities and become more ambitious in the choice of their participation in international, especially EU programmes. To extend the limited talent pool, the academic labour market should be opened further and attract top researchers and students from all over the world (OECD, 2012c).

Recommendations on innovation and R&D

Key recommendations

- Implement the government's unified innovation policy and monitor its progress. Improve collaborative links between major stakeholders of innovation policy.

Other recommendations

- Strengthen entrepreneurship education in schools and reform the education system so that it encourages creativity and entrepreneurship drive.
- Facilitate reform in universities and public research organisations, enhancing their autonomy, leadership and accountability. Further promote international co-operation.

Education, skills and human capital

Education is an important determinant of long-term growth and productivity performance in OECD countries (Sala-i-Martin et al., 2004; Hanushek and Wößmann, 2008 and 2011, OECD, 2013d). Not only does the accumulation of human capital boost labour productivity, but cognitive skills improve individual earning potential, ability to deal with change and the distribution of income (OECD, 2013d).

Slovenia has slightly higher expenditure on pre-primary education per student than the OECD average, also due to low pupil-teacher ratio (OECD, 2014b). The Kindergarten Act 2008 and the Exercise of Rights to Public Funds Act 2012 made early childhood education more affordable, and enrolment rates are above OECD average (OECD, 2013e, 2015). Children above 3 years spend 35 hours per week in kindergarten, compared to less than 30 hours on average in EU (European Commission et al., 2014), which is an additional cost driver. This measure, however, supports female labour market participation. Nevertheless, efficiency of spending could be improved to rationalise higher costs. Child-teacher ratios – currently the ratio is one of the lowest among the OECD countries (OECD, 2014b) – should be allowed to rise, and excess capacity could be transferred to locations that face particularly strong demand (e.g. Ljubljana) (OECD, 2011a).

Slovenia also has high expenditure per student in primary education, partly due to low average class size (OECD, 2014b). This is a consequence of a deliberately balanced development across all regions. Individual small settlements have schools where only a few pupils are enrolled, but equally require an adequate number of teaching and support staff, raising costs (OECD, 2011a). As in the case of pre-primary education, primary education likewise offers free optional extended primary school programme, organised as morning and after school care. There is room for efficiency gains in reorganising schools with low number of pupils in remote areas and reallocating funds to schools where classes are already big enough. Average class size can be increased as evidence shows that employing better qualified teachers, with good working conditions, is more important for student performance than the number of teachers (Sutherland and Price, 2007; Hattie, 2009; OECD, 2009b).

Judging by PISA, Slovenian 15-year-olds perform well compared to OECD average, but variation in performance between schools and programmes is large. Slovenian 15-year-olds in PISA 2012 were above OECD average in mathematics and science but below in reading. Performance has decreased in recent years, especially in reading (OECD, 2013c). Schools/programmes with students from a disadvantaged socio-economic background perform worse in PISA (Figure 1.19) and exhibit much worse disciplinary climate (Figure 1.20) (OECD, 2007, 2010a and 2013c). This can be partly explained by the fact that in Slovenia, the primary sampling is based on study programmes rather than different schools, hence the between-school variation captures the difference between different tracks that can be organised within the same school. Nevertheless, Slovenia still shows higher differences than countries – Austria, Czech Republic, Italy and Turkey – that use similar sampling. To address the inequality issues, the government has introduced measures targeting students from a disadvantaged socio-economic background, by offering intensive teacher education and training and introducing initiatives that help students with learning difficulties (Ministry of education, science and sport, 2014; OECD, 2015). However, the measures should be better targeted at socio-economically disadvantaged schools/programmes.

Figure 1.19. **Slovenia has one of the highest variations in mathematics performance between schools**

Percentage of explained variance by PISA index of economic, social and cultural status of students and schools

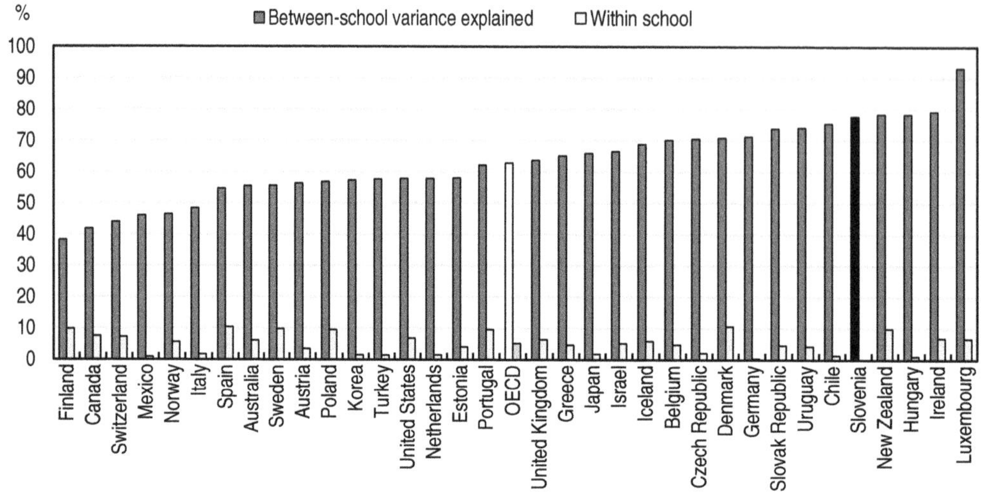

Note: In Slovenia, the primary sampling unit is defined as a group of students who follow the same study programme within a school (an educational track within a school). So in the case when various programmes are organised within the same school, the between-school variation captures the difference between tracks within a school. Similar sampling based on programmes is also done in Austria, Czech Republic, Italy and Turkey. The statistical data for Israel are supplied by and under the responsibility of the relevant Israeli authorities. The use of such data by the OECD is without prejudice to the status of the Golan Heights, East Jerusalem and Israeli settlements in the West Bank under the terms of international law.

Source: OECD, *PISA 2012 Database*.

StatLink http://dx.doi.org/10.1787/888933205195

Figure 1.20. **Difference in disciplinary climate between advantaged and disadvantaged schools is the highest in Slovenia**

Difference in the index of disciplinary climate

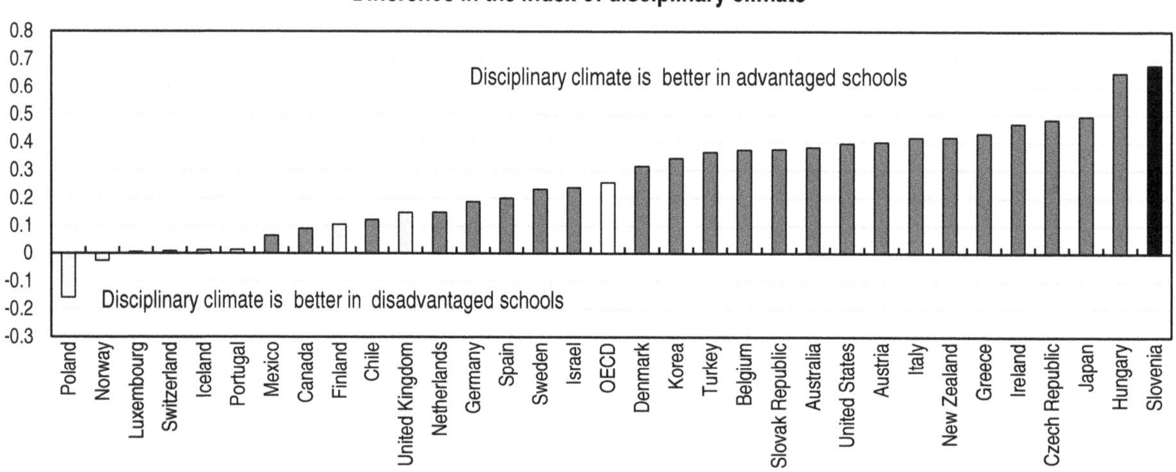

Note: In Slovenia, the primary sampling unit is defined as a group of students who follow the same study programme within a school (an educational track within a school). So in the case when various programmes are organised within the same school, the between-school variation captures the difference between tracks within a school. Similar sampling based on programmes is also done in Austria, Czech Republic, Italy and Turkey. The statistical data for Israel are supplied by and under the responsibility of the relevant Israeli authorities. The use of such data by the OECD is without prejudice to the status of the Golan Heights, East Jerusalem and Israeli settlements in the West Bank under the terms of international law.

Differences in the index of disciplinary climate between students in disadvantaged and advantaged schools that are not statistically significant are marked in grey.

Countries and economies are ranked in ascending order of the difference between disadvantaged and advantaged schools.

Source: OECD, *PISA 2012 Database*.

StatLink http://dx.doi.org/10.1787/888933205200

Students' interest in upper-secondary vocational education and training (VET) was on a decreasing trend, but there have been improvements in most recent years. The relatively long lasted decrease has created supply shortages in low-skilled manual jobs (OECD, 2014a). To sustain recent progress, additional effort should be put in fostering interest in VET programmes, highlighting good job prospects of such educational choice. Introduction of scholarships to further foster the interest in VET programmes in the school year 2015/16 is the move in the right direction. In international comparison the involvement of stakeholders in the Slovenian VET system remains limited, although there has been some progress following the reform of vocational education (2008-11). Practical training in the work place increased, and 20% of the curriculum is now designed in co-operation with social partners, particularly local companies (OECD, 2014a and 2015). A major challenge is to reform the VET system in a way that equips people with the skills needed by the fast-changing labour market and helps students to develop both foundation skills and acquire more technical capabilities (OECD, 2010b).

Participation in adult education programmes is relatively high, but is concentrated in the best-educated and prime-age workers (OECD, 2014a). Adults with low educational attainment show considerably less interest in adult learning activities and difference between individuals with high and low educational attainment in adult education participation is the highest in the EU (IMAD, 2010). Measures should be taken to bridge the gap by making adult education more affordable, boost participation in lifelong learning and reduce differences in participation between individuals with low and high education. To improve accessibility of adult education, targeted subsidies could be introduced to reduce adult education costs for those with low educational attainment (OECD, 2011a). Additionally, adult education should provide skills that are demanded by employers, raising also productivity (OECD, 2014a).

There is scope to increase tertiary education attainment of students whose parents have low education. In 2012, Slovenia had one of the highest entry rates to universities, but the proportion of students whose parents have low education levels was one of the lowest among the OECD countries (Figure 1.21). Despite generous public support for tertiary

Figure 1.21. **Probability of students whose parents have low levels of education attending tertiary education, 2009**

Likelihood ratio

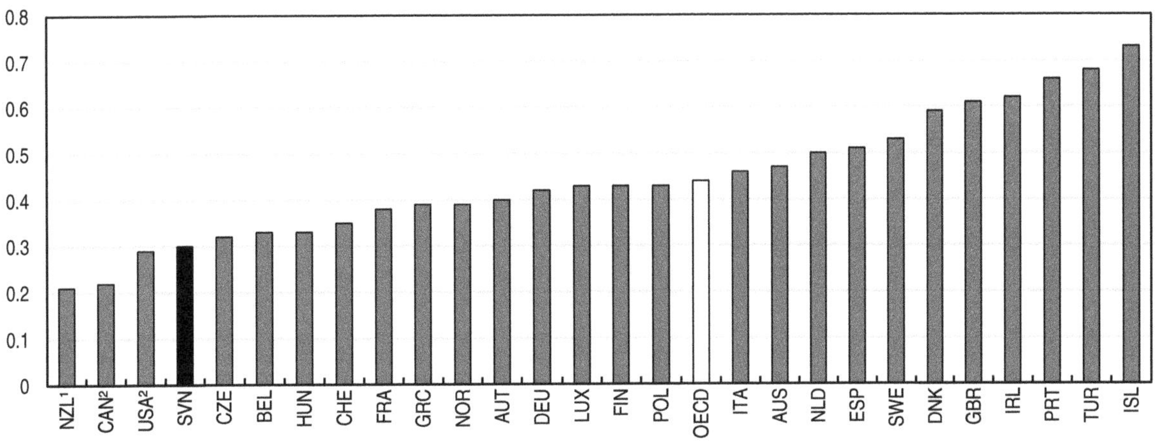

Note: The number of students attending higher education are under-reported for Australia, Canada, New Zealand and the United States compared to the other countries as they include only students who attained ISCED 5A, while the other countries include students who attained ISCED 5A and/or 5B. This may understate intergenerational mobility in these countries.

1. Data from Adult Literacy and Lifeskills Survey (ALL) of 2006.
2. Data from Adult Literacy and Lifeskills Survey (ALL) of 2003.

Source: OECD, *Education at a Glance 2012*; Table A6.1.

StatLink http://dx.doi.org/10.1787/888933205217

Figure 1.22. **Private costs of attaining tertiary education, 2010**

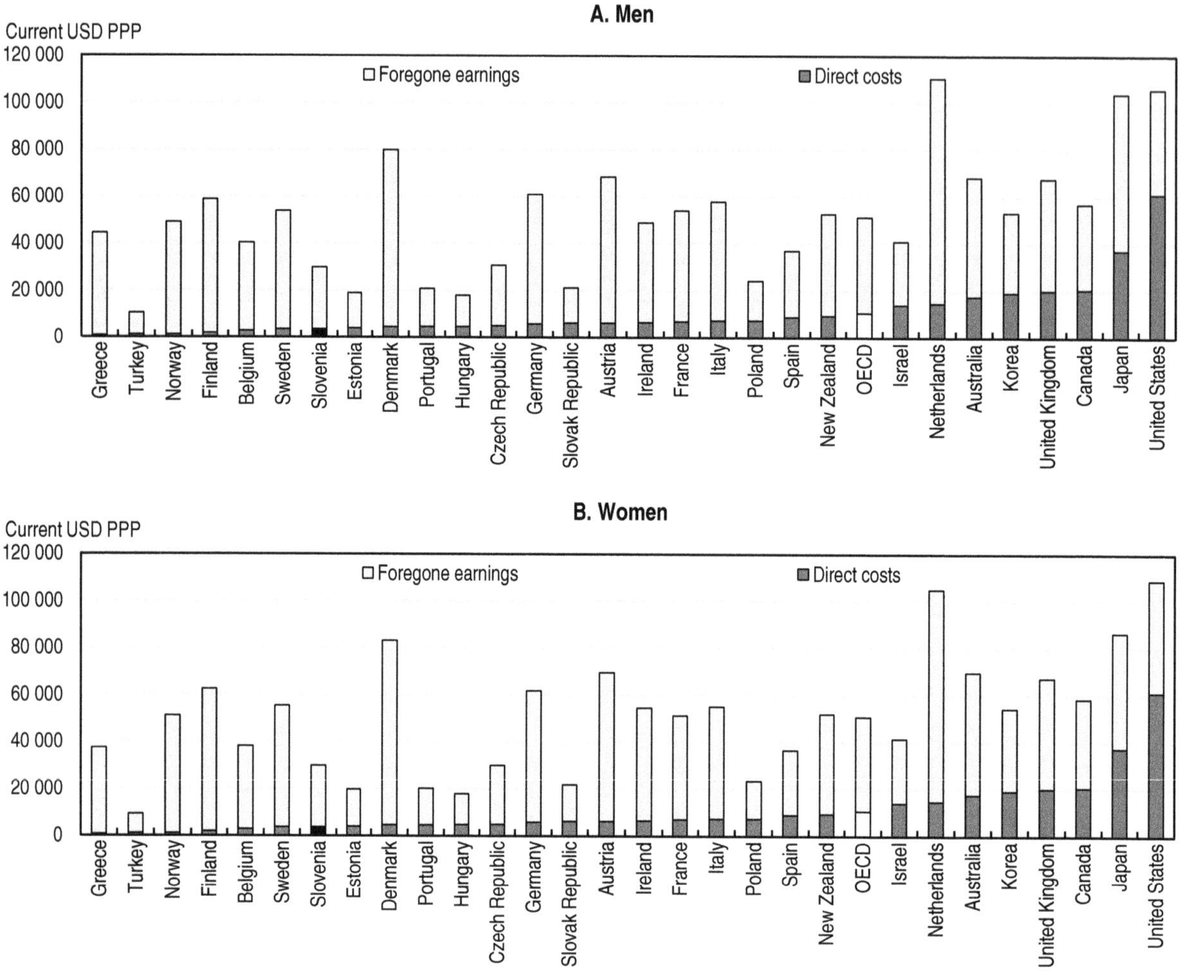

Note: Values are based on the difference between individuals who attained a tertiary education compared with those that attained an upper secondary or post-secondary non-tertiary education.
Source: OECD (2014b), *Education at a Glance 2014: OECD Indicators.*

StatLink http://dx.doi.org/10.1787/888933205222

education and one of the lowest direct private costs of studying (Figure 1.22), public support is regressive and not well targeted to the weakest. 35% of tertiary education expenditure goes to the top quintile of the income distribution and only 9% to the lowest one (OECD, 2013b). The government has offered scholarships to disadvantaged students to attend tertiary education (Eurydice, 2011). It could introduce better means testing of education-related allowances (transportation, student meals in tertiary education) and institute stricter eligibility criteria (accommodation subsidies, state scholarships). Important progress in means testing of benefits has been made with the implementation of a comprehensive electronic system in 2012, however, the eligibility criteria could be tightened further with carefully defined new thresholds (OECD, 2013b).

The tertiary system does not produce workers with the skills in demand. Mismatches between the output of the tertiary level education system and the need of the labour market are on the rise (Figure 1.23). Farčnik and Domadenik (2009) find that graduates in health, computing, engineering, manufacturing and construction have the highest likelihood of getting employed in the six months following their graduation. Despite recent improvements

Figure 1.23. **Mismatches on the labour market have increased for highly educated people**

Skill mismatch indicator by skill group, 4-period moving average

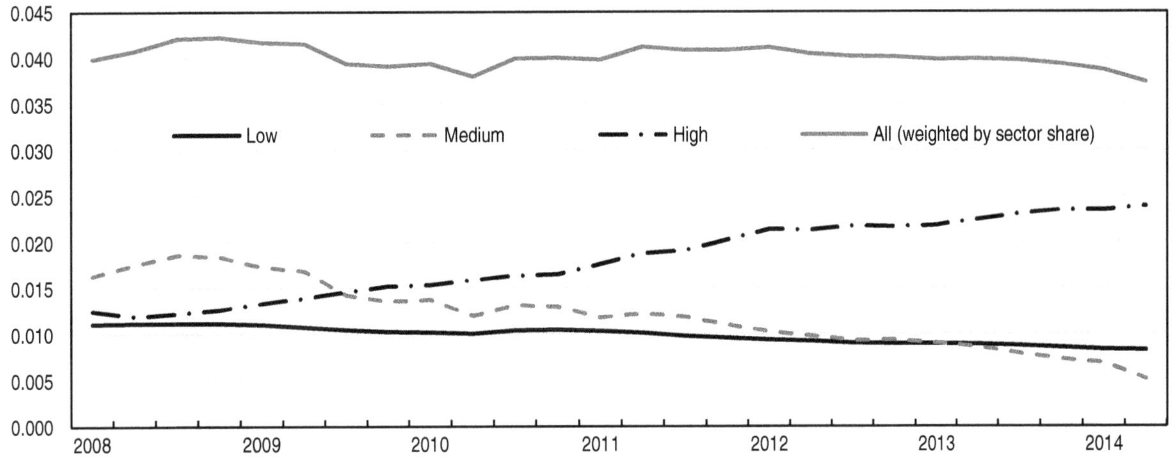

Note: The skill mismatch indicator is defined as the average absolute deviation between the share of education groups in employment and their share in the working age population. For details on the estimation of the skill mismatch indicator, see European Commission (2013), *Labour Market Developments in Europe 2013*, Brussels.
Source: Eurostat, calculations by IMAD.

StatLink http://dx.doi.org/10.1787/888933205231

the share of science and engineering graduates in Slovenia is low in international comparison (SORS, 2012), while the share of those in humanities and social sciences is high, contributing to the high unemployment among youth (IMAD, 2014b; OECD, 2011a). A greater share of engineering and science graduates is associated not only with a greater innovative and technology absorption capacity of the economy but also with human capital spill-overs and economy-wide productivity gains (OECD, 2011a). Furthermore, the proportion of dissatisfied employers with generic skills of tertiary graduates was the 2nd highest (18% compared to EU average of 8%) among the EU countries (European Commission, 2010), which may have contributed to higher mismatch. It is therefore important to boost the number of quality graduates from technical fields by improving demand via highlighting good job prospects of these professions and by providing sufficient institutional capacity via allocation of appropriate resources to these programmes. Entry rates in fields with poor labour market prospects should be reduced (IMAD, 2014b).

Per-student expenditure on core services at the tertiary level in Slovenia is low (OECD, 2014b; Figure 1.24), but it could be used more efficiently. Funding should be more dependent on students' progress and graduation rates by raising variable part of financing, which currently only amounts to 3% of total funding (OECD, 2013b). Faculties are also constrained by the Public Sector Act in determining salaries, which are lower than in the private sector, making it harder to compete for hiring and retaining most talented staff (OECD, 2011a). As should be the way forward in other parts of the public sector, individual faculties could be given more freedom in determining salaries, including performance related pay, which would also increase the quality of instruction and research output.

Efficiency of tertiary education system could be further increased by limiting tuition fee waivers and other in-study benefits to a normal study length. Currently, students have many benefits, including state-funded tuition fee waivers for over 80% of students (Eurydice, 2011), subsidies for living expenses (meals, accommodation, transportation and cultural activities), state scholarships and the flexibility of student work. The in-study benefits that are not tied

Figure 1.24. **Annual expenditure per student by educational institutions for all services by level of education, 2011**

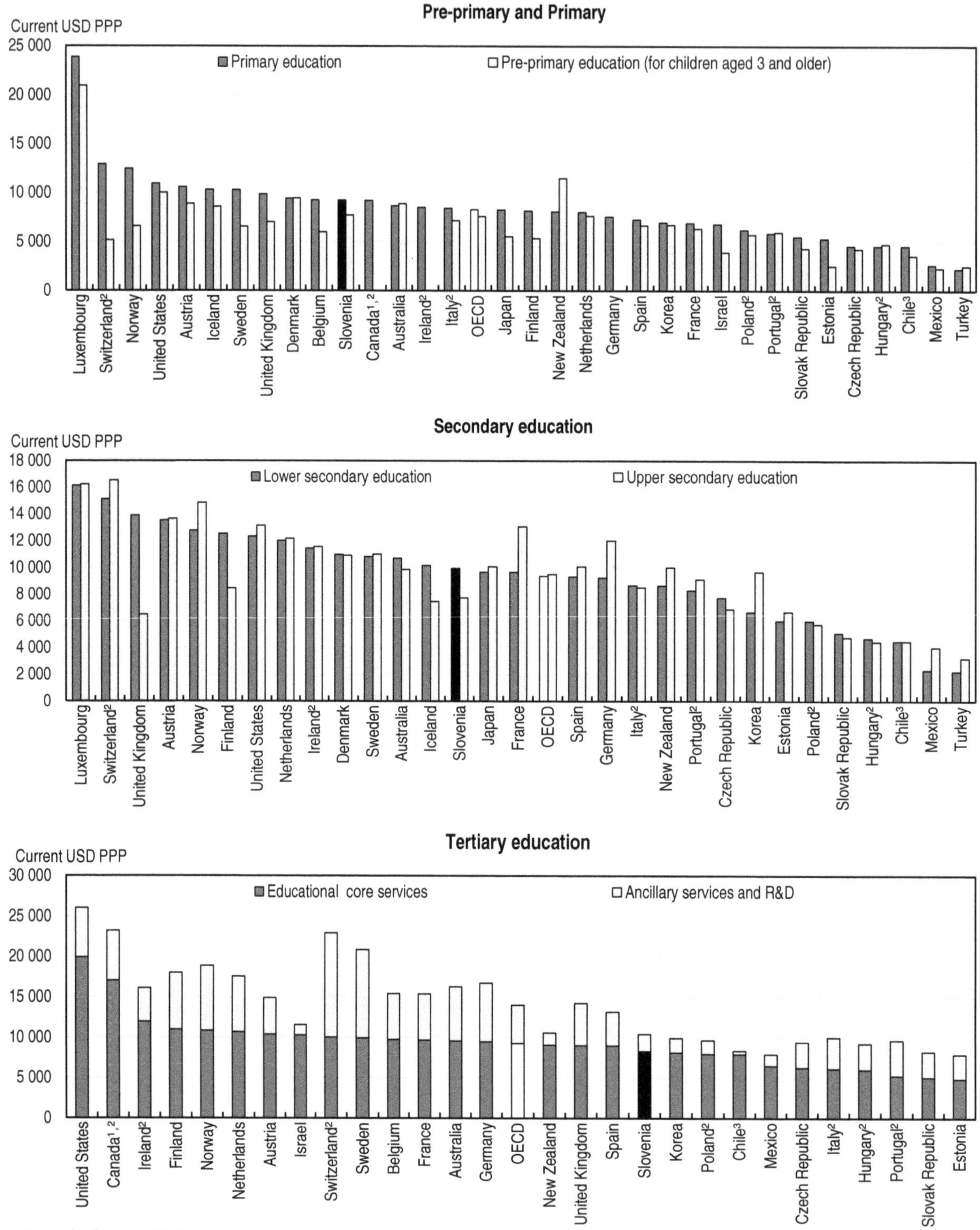

1. Year of reference 2010.
2. Public institutions only (for Canada, in tertiary education only; for Italy, except in tertiary education).
3. Year of reference 2012.

Source: OECD (2014b), *Education at a Glance 2014: OECD Indicators*.

StatLink http://dx.doi.org/10.1787/888933205245

to progress of studies and the shortage of workplaces for youth attract "fake students", who would not normally go into tertiary education. They are estimated to be as high as one third of tertiary students (Šušteršič et al., 2010). Such system does not provide incentives for the rapid completion of studies (OECD, 2011a; Čelebič, 2014). There is potential for improvement by tightening the eligibility of generous subsidies and in-study benefits to normal study length (OECD, 2011a). Finland, for example, has recently shortened the period during which students are eligible to receive financial support (OECD, 2014d). The new law on higher education is being prepared, according to which students who do not progress regularly, have to pay tuition fees. Its adoption is highly encouraged.

Recommendations on education and training

- Raise pupil-teacher ratios in pre-primary education and increase class size in primary education to reduce costs. Reorganise schools that serve too few students.
- Better target measures to upper secondary socio-economically disadvantaged schools and programmes.
- Improve the accessibility of adult education for individuals with low educational attainment levels introducing targeted subsidies. Evaluate how the outcome from adult education programmes is used by employers.
- Better target students from disadvantaged backgrounds to attain tertiary education. Further strengthen means testing of education-related benefits.
- Improve incentives to boost further the number of tertiary graduates from the fields of mathematics, science and technology by highlighting good job prospects and by providing funding for sufficient institutional capacity. Reduce entry rates in fields with poor labour market prospects.
- Give faculties more freedom in determining their salaries.
- Tie tuition fee waivers and other in-study benefits to adequate progress in studies.

Labour market policies for more jobs

The unemployment rate rose by 6 percentage points since the start of the crisis to approach 11% in the beginning of 2013, but has since decreased amid improving economic environment. More than 50% of the unemployed have been out of work for one year or more (Figure 1.25, Panel A), a 10 percentage point increase from 2007. Youth unemployment is also high and doubled from 2007 to over 20% in the first half of 2014 (Figure 1.25, Panel B). In addition, youth participation rate has decreased by almost 10 percentage points from 2007, to 34% in 2013.

High incidence of long-term unemployment is partly caused by institutional factors. The combined generosity of unemployment benefits, social assistance and other transfers, together with taxes, act as disincentives for the unemployed or the inactive to return to work (OECD, 2013b) (Table 1.3). For instance, a principal earner of a one-earner married couple with two children (at 67% of average wage) has one of the highest average effective tax rates (AETR). He loses 81% of the increase in gross income due to taxes and reduced benefits when moving from inactivity to employment. The average effective tax rates in Slovenia are significantly above 50% for all but two-earner married couples, and above the OECD average in all groups. Reform could boost work incentives if, at low income levels,

Figure 1.25. **Long-term unemployment is high and youth unemployment has risen**

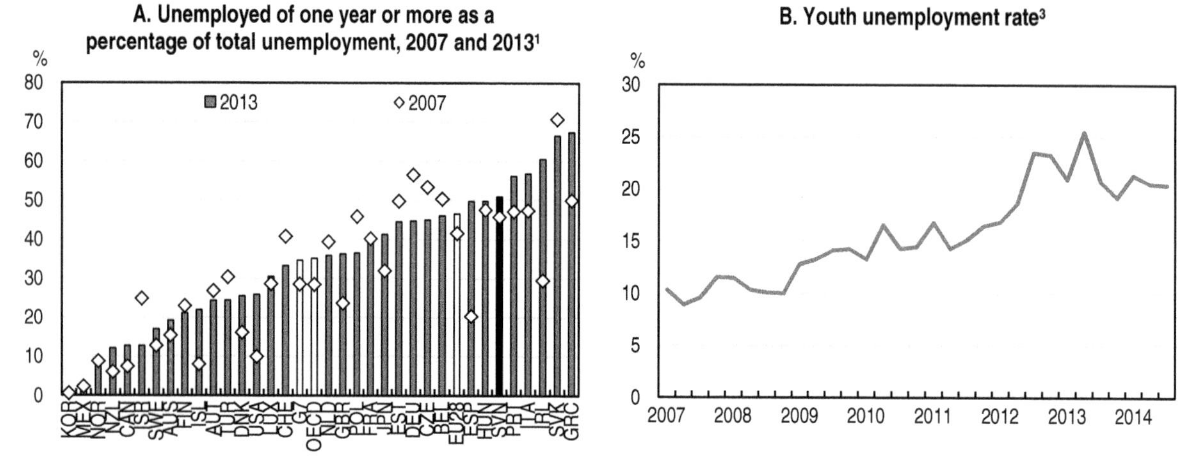

1. Countries are shown in ascending order of the incidence of long-term unemployment in 2013. Data are not seasonally adjusted but smoothed using three-quarter moving averages. OECD is the weighted average of 33 OECD countries excluding Chile.
2. Data are seasonally adjusted and refer to the unemployment rate of individuals aged 15-24.

Source: OECD calculations based on quarterly national labour force surveys, for Panel A; and *OECD Short-Term Labour Market Statistics Database*, for Panel B.

StatLink http://dx.doi.org/10.1787/888933204966

Table 1.3. **Inactivity traps and unemployment traps are high in international comparison**

Average effective tax rate when moving from unemployment/inactivity into work, per cent, 2012

	Wage level (% of average worker)	Inactivity trap[1]			Unemployment trap[2]		
		Slovenia	Other CEEC	OECD a verage	Slovenia	Other CEEC	OECD average
	67	**65**	55	63	**88**	62	70
One-earner married couple	100	**63**	46	54	**76**	57	65
	150	**56**	43	48	**65**	51	59
	67	**71**	43	56	**84**	66	69
Lone parent with two children	100	**63**	48	55	**78**	68	68
	150	**64**	44	51	**69**	58	62
	67	**81**	57	66	**88**	59	69
One-earner married couple with two children	100	**64**	50	60	**75**	55	67
	150	**65**	46	54	**66**	50	61
	67	**45**	35	35	**93**	68	70
Two-earner married couple with two children	100	**49**	34	36	**80**	63	66
	150	**48**	33	37	**68**	55	60

Note: Participation tax rates measure the extent to which taxes and benefits reduce the financial gain of moving into work.
1. Average effective tax rate when moving from inactivity into work for selected family types and earnings levels. The estimates here relate to the situation of a person who is not entitled to unemployment benefits (e.g. because they entitlements have expired). Instead, social assistance and other means-tested benefits are assumed to be available subject to relevant income conditions.
2. Average effective tax rate for a transition into full-time work for persons receiving unemployment benefits at the initial level, for selected family types and earnings levels (same in new job as in previous).

Source: OECD, *Tax-Benefit Models.*

benefits would be withdrawn at a lower rate than the after-tax increase in earnings, to allow a more generous net increase in income.

At the same time, in 2014, only 22% of registered unemployed received unemployment benefits, and almost 50% have not received any income in 2014 (Institut RS za socialno varstvo, 2014). To insure workers against labour market risks higher number of the unemployed should be covered and the duration of benefits could be increased. Currently, unemployment benefits are a strongly increasing function of previous work experience, with up to 25 months of insurance provided for older workers, but only two months for younger workers. Longer benefits should be targeted to vulnerable groups such as the young and the low-skilled (Chetty, 2008).

The government has tried to address the issue of high youth unemployment by several measures. Employers are partly exempt of paying income taxes and employers' contributions for employing youth permanently. Furthermore, within the framework of active labour market policies (ALMP) co-financing of corporate scholarships, employment subsidies, the education and training and the programme promoting self-employment have been offered (Bank of Slovenia, 2013). At the European level, the Youth Guarantee programme aims at facilitating the transition of youth from education to employment. All these programmes should be closely monitored and evaluated from the perspective of effectiveness (IMAD, 2014b). IMAD (2014b) estimates that the percentage of youth (in the 15-29 age group) that left unemployment due to ALMP was around 14% in 2013. These programmes have, together with improved economic situation, led to stabilisation of youth unemployment but it remains high (Figure 1.25, Panel B).

Employment prospects of low-skilled workers are affected also by the relatively high minimum wage. Slovenia has one of the highest minimum wages relative to median among the OECD countries (Figure 1.26), and it was raised by 23% in 2010. According to the Bank of

Figure 1.26. **Slovenia is one of the countries with the highest minimum wage relative to the median wage, 2012**

Ratio of minimum to median wage of full-time dependent employees

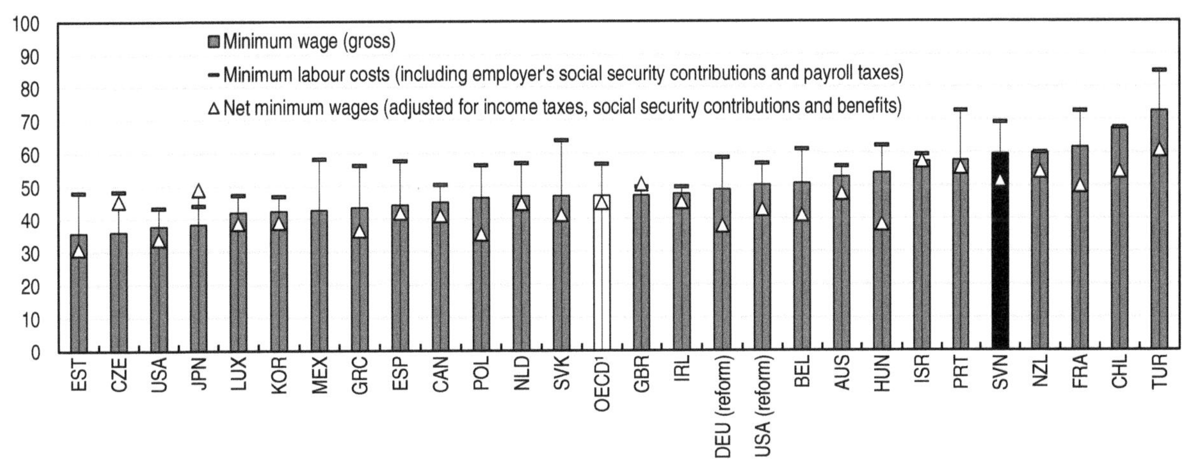

1. Median ratio for the countries shown.

Source: OECD *Minimum Wage Database*; and OECD *Tax-Benefit Models*.

StatLink http://dx.doi.org/10.1787/888933205252

Slovenia (2014a) survey, the minimum wage hike was the main reason for dismissals in 7% of firms (Figure 1.27), and prevented new hiring in close to a quarter of firms, making it a major barrier to employment. High minimum wage also exerts pressure on other wages and prices – over a fifth of the firms had to raise wages for all workers and around 13% of the firms raised prices (Bank of Slovenia, 2014a). The Law on Minimum Wage stipulates that minimum wage should be increased by at least the inflation rate each year, but cites other benchmarks for adjustment, such as wage trends, economic growth and employment trends. Evidence

Figure 1.27. **How did the firms react to change in minimum wage legislation**

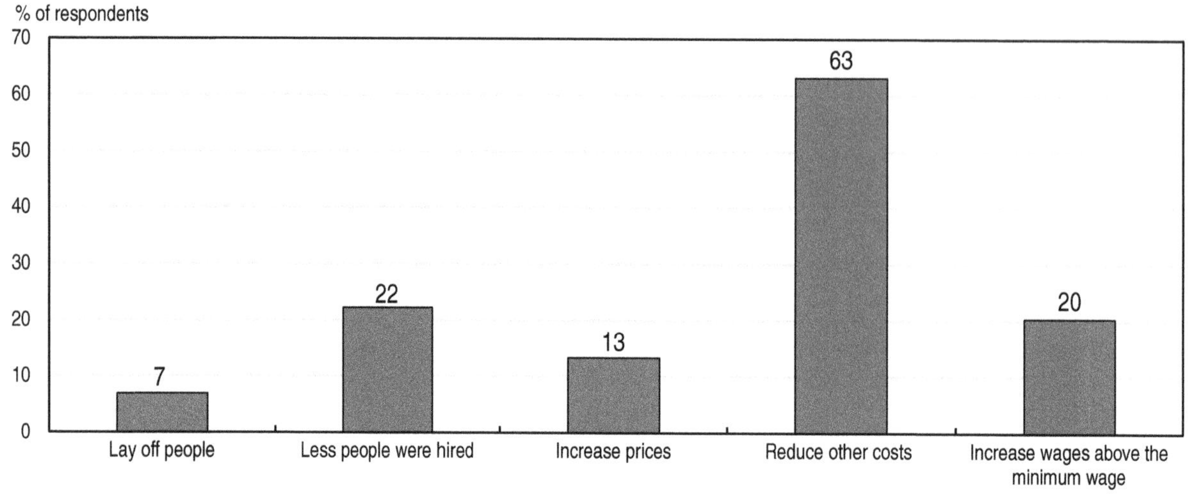

Note: Only answers of companies with minimum wage receivers are included.
Source: *Wage Dynamics Network Survey* 2014, Bank of Slovenia calculations.

StatLink http://dx.doi.org/10.1787/888933205265

shows that earned income tax credits, rather than minimum wage increases, have been successful in supporting the incomes and employment of lower-income families in the USA (Eissa and Hoynes, 2006; Clemens and Wither, 2014). Going forward, minimum wage growth should be moderated, with a view to restoring the link to productivity and boosting employment opportunities. Incomes of low-skilled workers can be better protected through social transfers and tax measures that incentivise employment.

Before the 2013 labour reform, Slovenia had one of the most restrictive employment protection (EPL) for permanent contracts and no direct cost for terminating fixed-term contracts (Figure 1.28) (OECD, 2014a). The aim of the reform was to increase labour market flexibility and decrease labour market duality. The reform increased flexibility (e.g. simplified administrative procedures related to hiring and firing and shorter notice periods) and lowered costs of permanent employment contracts (reduced severance payments). On the other hand, for fixed-term contracts, it introduced redundancy payments and limited to two years the maximum duration of a fixed-term employment for a given job (OECD, 2013b). In the case of dismissal, employers' costs are now the same across both contract types. Bank of Slovenia (2014a) survey shows that only 14% of companies reported a change in their human resources policy due to the new legislation, (Figure 1.29, Panel A). Evidence nevertheless confirms that the reform may have led to a slight reduction in duality as the share of permanent contracts among new hires indeed increased to 28% from 24% within a year (IMAD, 2014b; Figure 1.29, Panel B). The increase was especially pronounced among youth (IMAD, 2014b).

Student work was a major factor behind labour market duality, as it benefited from a preferential tax and regulatory treatment. Among youth, 74% of contracts are temporary, almost three times the OECD average (OECD, 2014a), and students account for the majority of those (IMAD, 2014b). For comparison, the incidence of temporary contracts among the total population is only marginally higher in Slovenia than the OECD average (17.5% compared to 13.5% in 2012). The reform of student work from February 2015 introduced a minimum hourly gross wage rate and healthcare and pension contributions. Students will

Figure 1.28. **The employment protection legislation index in Slovenia prior to and following the change in the year 2013**

A. Strictness of employment protection – individual and collective dismissals (regular contracts)[1]

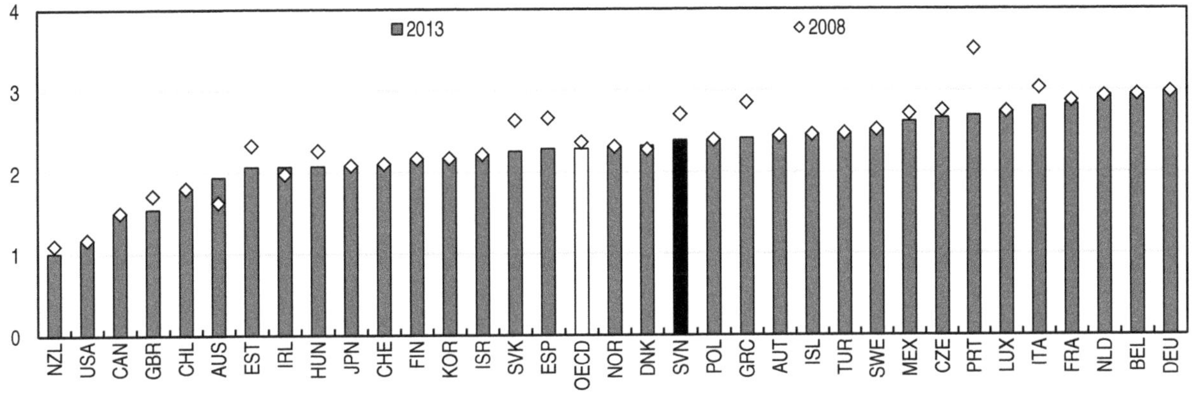

B. Strictness of employment protection – regulation on temporary contracts[2]

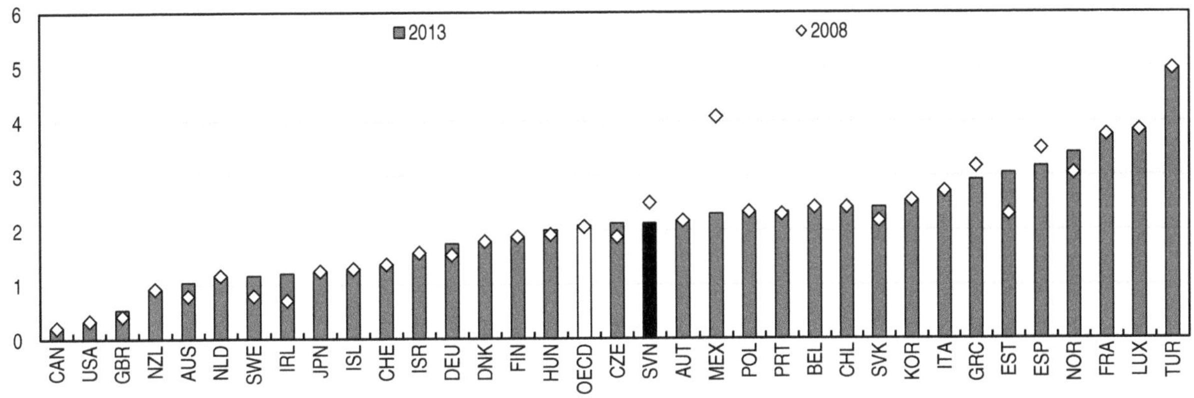

1. The OECD indicator of employment protection legislation (EPL) for regular employment measures the procedures and costs involved in dismissing individual regular employees. The indicator runs from 0 to 6, representing the least to most restrictive EPL.
2. The OECD indicator of regulation on temporary contract (EPT) measures the restrictions on the use of temporary employment by firms, with respect to the type of work for which these contracts are allowed and their duration.

Source: *OECD Employment Protection Database*, 2013 update.

StatLink http://dx.doi.org/10.1787/888933205274

now accumulate years of pensionable service from their work. These changes increase the cost of student labour, but it will remain more flexible than regular employment. Phasing out the preferential treatment of student work has been often recommended to Slovenia by the OECD and is a major step in the right direction.

In 2012, Slovenia spent only 0.3% of GDP on active labour market programmes (ALMP), half the OECD average (Figure 1.30; OECD, 2014a). Slovenia spends little on training, especially of older and low-skilled people. Given the high share of long-term unemployed and the at-risk-of-poverty rate among the unemployed it would be sensible to step up ALMPs. Resources devoted to training and job search services should be increased to support employment and ensure that the long-term unemployed remain attached to the labour market (OECD, 2014a; IMAD, 2014b). Additionally, further development of active labour market programmes targeting the long-term unemployed to find jobs or access

Figure 1.29. **The effects of the 2013 labour market reform on firms' employment decisions has been limited**

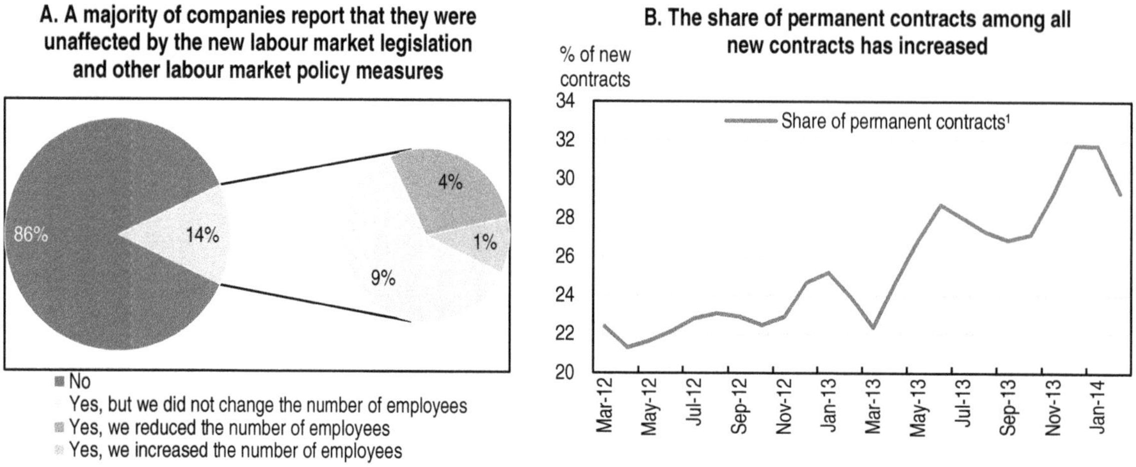

1. Data are smoothed using a moving average filter.
Source: For Panel A: *Wage Dynamics Network Survey 2014* and Bank of Slovenia calculation; for Panel B: SORS.

StatLink http://dx.doi.org/10.1787/888933205283

Figure 1.30. **Slovenia spends less on active labour market programmes than majority of other countries**

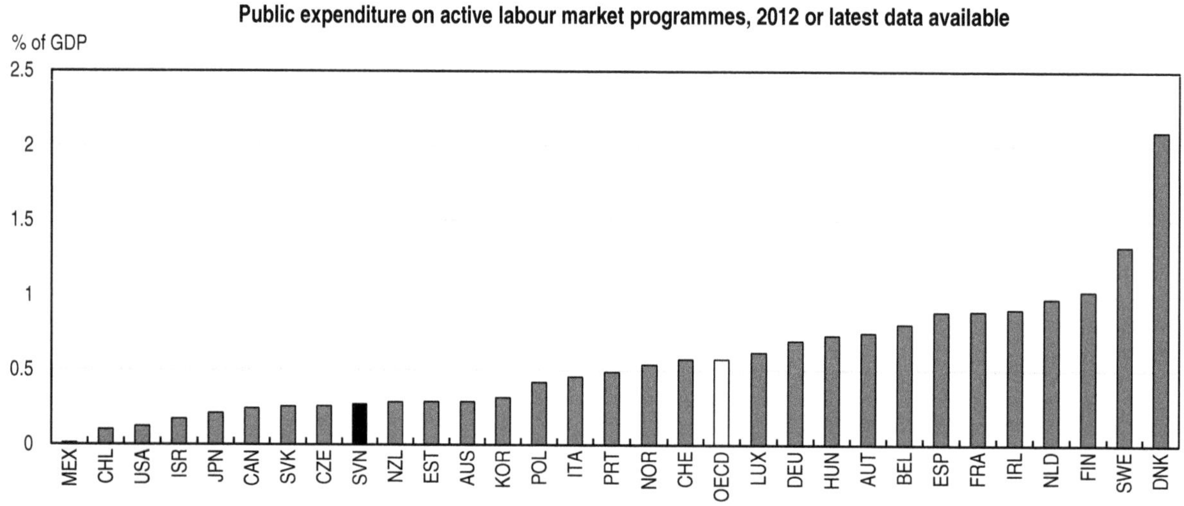

Source: OECD Social Expenditure Database.

StatLink http://dx.doi.org/10.1787/888933205298

training would be beneficial (OECD, 2014a). Job counselling and activation programmes [e.g. interviews with employment counsellors, independent search for job, applications for jobs, acceptance of suitable work (OECD, 2005)] are available to all unemployed, but, in practice, only less than 50% take part. Encouraging participation through increased awareness, and specifically targeting the least involved groups of unemployed should become a policy priority. It is also necessary to create a system of independent evaluations of the effects of individual ALMPs and act accordingly if changes to the implementation measures are warranted (IMAD, 2014b).

Recommendations on the labour market

Key recommendations

- Increase resources for active labour market policies and better target assistance to the long-term unemployed and the low-skilled, based on evaluation of individual programmes.

Other recommendations

- Restructure the combined effects of unemployment benefits, social assistance and taxes so that, at low income levels, benefits would be withdrawn at a lower rate than the after-tax increase in earnings, in order to increase work incentives for the unemployed and inactive persons.
- Increase coverage rates for unemployment benefits, making them less reliant on previous work experience.
- Moderate growth in the minimum wage, with a view to restoring the link to productivity and gradually increasing the gap between the minimum and median wage.

Lowering barriers to product market competition and improving the business environment

Regulatory settings should promote rather than inhibit competition

Slovenia's overall regulatory framework is among the most restrictive in the OECD as indicated by the OECD product market regulation (PMR) indicator (Figure 1.31, Panel A). The PMR score has improved since 2008, but is worse than for most of its Central and Eastern European country (CEEC) peers and other euro area countries. This underperformance stems largely from the pervasive state involvement in the economy, but there is room for further improvement also with the complexity of regulatory procedures and administrative burdens on start-ups (Figure 1.31, Panel B).

Product market regulation is essential for well-functioning market economies to protect market integrity, and to achieve environmental, health and safety objectives. Yet, regulations can also create unnecessary barriers to market entry, limit the ability of firms within a market to compete, or reduce the choices and information available to consumers. Many empirical studies have shown that competition can raise output per capita by increasing investment and employment as well as by encouraging companies to be more innovative and efficient (e.g. Bouis and Duval, 2011; Bourlès et al. 2010; Conway et al., 2006; Nicoletti and Scarpetta, 2005). Dall'Orso and Sila also show that a less restrictive business environment has a positive effect on productivity (see also Annex 3). In light of these economic gains, many countries have, step by step, removed obsolete or badly-designed regulations over the past decades. They have reduced state involvement in business sectors, made it easier for entrepreneurs to create firms and to expand them, and facilitated the entry of foreign products and firms.

Improving the business environment

The government stepped up efforts to simplify regulatory procedures and administrative burdens when opening a company. The number of regulated professions has decreased from 323 to 242 (European Commission, 2015) and a typical number of days to complete mandatory procedures to register a public limited company was reduced

Figure 1.31. **Product market regulation is overly strict**

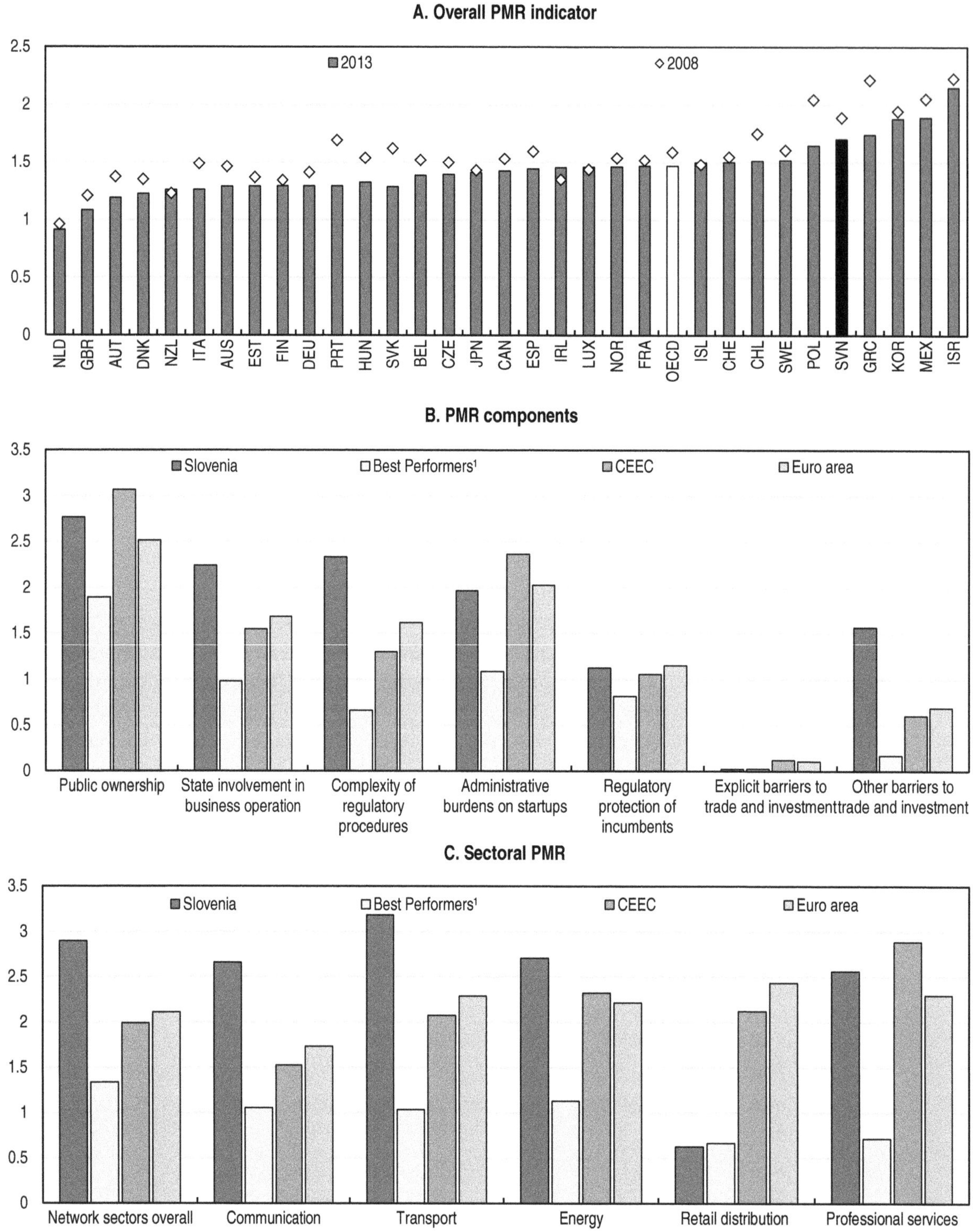

Note: The numerical PMR indicators represent the stringency of regulatory policy in specific areas on a scale of 0 to 6 with a higher number indicating a policy stance that is deemed less conducive to competition. In each case, it characterises the stance of regulation as it stood in early 2013 and does not reflect the reforms implemented since then.

1. Best performers are the five countries with the lowest scores.

Source: OECD PMR Indicators Database.

StatLink http://dx.doi.org/10.1787/888933204990

from 20 in 2008 to less than 4 in 2013. Administrative burdens for sole proprietors were reduced even further. In 2013, the government issued a "Single document to enable better regulation and business environment and increase competitiveness" to improve co-ordination in these efforts, and tasked the Ministry of Economic Development and Technology to implement it. The government is to be notified twice a year on progress (Government of Slovenia, 2013).

These reforms are welcome but more is needed. According to the PMR survey, although Slovenia set up single contact points for getting information on all notifications and licenses that are required to open up a business, they have not been sufficiently established at the local level. Furthermore, the single contact points do not issue or accept all notifications and licenses. When setting up a public limited company, entrepreneurs have to complete 13 administrative procedures and they typically need to contact five public (e.g. tax office, one-stop shop), or private (notary/lawyer, bank) bodies to register a company. In Canada for example this was reduced to a single visit to a one-stop shop. Slovenia could introduce the "silence is consent" rule for issuing licences required to open up a business, as they have been successfully implemented in Portugal and the Slovak Republic.

Dealing with construction permits and registering property takes a long time, despite reduced red tape for setting-up new companies. In the *Doing Business Survey* (World Bank, 2015) Slovenia ranks 26 out of 31 high income OECD economies on registering property (Figure 1.32). Slovenia ranks at the very bottom among high income OECD countries on the length of time that it takes to register property; 109.5 days in Slovenia compared to one day in Portugal and New Zealand, or 2.5 days in the Netherlands. Time to obtain construction permits in Slovenia takes 212.5 days, more than three times the time in Finland or Denmark, and it is quite costly.

Figure 1.32. **Slovenia ranks low on a number on doing business indicators**

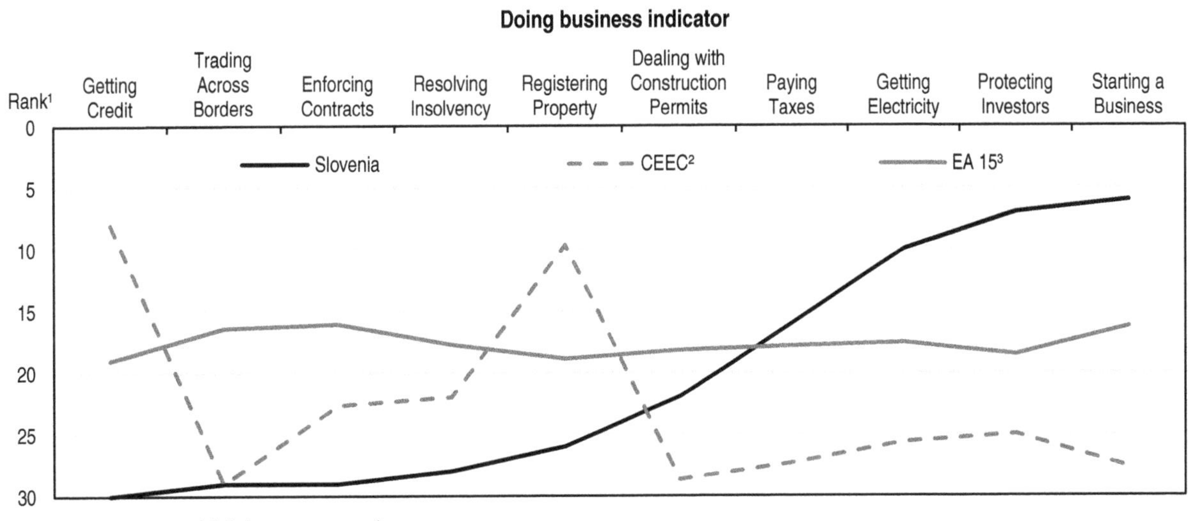

1. Rank among OECD high income countries.
2. Non-weighted average of Slovak Republic, Poland and Czech Republic.
3. Non-weighted average.

Source: World Bank, *Doing Business Indicator 2015*.

StatLink http://dx.doi.org/10.1787/888933205303

Slovenia should further ease regulation of professional services – accounting, legal, engineering and architecture services (Figure 1.31, Panel C). Education requirements to enter a profession are excessively high in Slovenia. According to the PMR survey, to enter fully each of these four professions requires a university degree, in many cases another specialised degree, and compulsory practice lasting up to 5 years. Each profession also requires compulsory membership in a chamber of the profession. Since services sectors are generally less exposed to foreign competition, regulation plays an important role in affecting the quality, variety and price of services through stronger competition. Analysis of productivity across sectors indeed shows that the gap in productivity from the EU15 is one of the biggest for professional services (Figure 1.5).

At the regulatory level, Slovenia has low restrictions to FDI, but there exist high non-tariff barriers to trade and investment (Figure 1.31, Panel B). For example, responses to the PMR questionnaire show that regulations are not systematically published to the international public in a foreign language. There is also evidence that in certain transactions foreign parties are at a disadvantage – e.g. foreign firms may not participate in tenders for government transport contracts. Furthermore, when business practices are perceived to restrict competition, foreign firms cannot seek redress through competition agencies or trade policy bodies, but only by pressing charges through courts.

Public ownership is widespread

Slovenia's unique pattern of firm ownership – low foreign direct investment and high share of state ownership – stems partly from the nature of transition from a socialist economy to a market based economy with private property. At the macro level, the monetary authorities resisted strong capital inflows to reduce appreciation pressures on the currency. Meanwhile, the privatisation process explicitly favoured internal buy-outs by managers and employees and was left incomplete, with the state directly and indirectly retaining large ownership shares in firms across the economy (Domadenik and Prašnikar, 2004; OECD, 2002). Two state-owned funds – pension (KAD) and restitution (SOD) fund – kept controlling stakes in many large "strategic" enterprises. Such structure provided the government with a strong mechanism to influence the boards and management of privatised firms. In part, this was motivated by a desire to manage the extent to which foreign firms gained control over domestic economy (OECD, 2011b).

High and widely dispersed internal (managers and employees) ownership and ineffective external ownership provided management with insufficient incentives to restructure enterprises. Internal owners were concerned with keeping their jobs, rather than with maximising profitability, and external owners had insufficient power and incentives to change and monitor management practices (OECD, 2002; OECD, 2011b). There is evidence that productivity growth in transition economies were higher in privatised firms than state-owned firms, as private firms had greater incentives and flexibility to restructure, absorb new technologies and innovate. In particular, privatised firms to outside owners showed significantly better performance than firms with insiders as owners (Frydman et al., 1999; OECD, 2011b).

In Slovenia, enterprises directly owned (or indirectly controlled) by the state are most common in network industries, which often have a natural monopoly, but also in banking and insurance, and even manufacturing, where there is no clear public policy role for the state to have a controlling interest (OECD, 2011a). The PMR indicator for the network industries – energy, transport and communication – is high due to strong state dominance (Figure 1.31, Panel C). Government holds majority stakes in the largest company in most network sectors, in particular in telecommunications, postal services, rail transport and airlines. Furthermore, road transport has heavy entry barriers and in postal services the state-owned company plays a dominant role on the market.

The profitability and productivity of state-owned enterprises (SOEs) is lower than of privately and foreign-owned companies operating in same sectors (Rojec, 2014; European Commission, 2014a and 2015). Prices of electricity and telecommunications in Slovenia are relatively low, indicating that heavy state involvement does not lead to excessively high prices. Only in the land transportation sector were mark-ups high (Molnar, 2010). Also, in January 2015, the competition protection agency found that the biggest (state-controlled) supplier of natural gas violated its dominant position in the supply of gas to industrial users, which led to excessive prices. Productivity measured as GVA per employed in the electricity and gas sector in Slovenia is 55% lower than in the EU15, and significantly below Slovenia's average. Similarly, transportation sector and telecommunications exhibit large gaps in productivity to the EU15.

Apart from slowing growth, pervasive state ownership poses risks also to public finances as the losses and high debt levels increase recapitalisation needs, as recently showcased in the banking sector. SOEs are also the main beneficiaries of state guarantees, worth 18% of GDP in 2013, which constitute a contingent liability for the general government (European Commission, 2015; Georgieva and Riquelme, 2013). There is therefore scope to improve productivity, competition and reduce risks to public finances in these industries by reducing state dominance.

Rationalising public ownership, privatisations and corporate governance

Recently, the government has become more open to privatisation. In 2013, the parliament approved a list of 15 SOEs to be privatised, some in the manufacturing sector, but also an airport, an airline company, one state-owned bank and a major telecom provider. As of April 2015, four companies have been privatised and seven are in the process. Reducing public ownership, ensuring efficient regulation for privatised monopolies and simplifying administrative procedures will attract more foreign direct investment (FDI), improve corporate governance as well as boost competitiveness through direct technology transfers and spill-overs.

The government should continue with privatisation. As spelled out in the *2011 Economic Survey of Slovenia*, to get the best value for taxpayers, the government should undertake pre-privatisation valuations and make sure that share offerings are not under-priced or targeted to a specific investor group. Privatisation should be subject to independent oversight and high levels of transparency and accountability should be ensured (OECD, 2011a). Besides following through with privatisations, it is important to set up a solid framework for managing the assets that remain in state ownership. Governance problems and interconnectedness of banks with poorly performing public state enterprises also contributed to excessive debt build-up before the crisis.

Slovenia has taken significant steps to improve the governance of its SOEs. The 2009 OECD accession review recommended that Slovenia centralises the management of its ownership in the form of an ownership agency, and that the agency should "quickly develop policy instruments that will enable it to successfully execute its function". In 2010, the parliament set up the central ownership agency to manage state assets (OECD, 2011b). Nevertheless, the agency was later scrapped, and a setting up of new sovereign holding company was proposed. Finally, with new legislation enacted in April 2014, the new Slovenian Sovereign Holding (SSH) became fully operational. The role of the SSH is to consolidate and manage all state assets under one structure, and to execute privatisation of some of these assets. The new legislation also includes specific authorisation for SSH to decide on the disposal and voting of shares held by existing funds under state ownership, strengthening its capacity to manage and dispose of remaining state-owned assets (OECD, 2014a).

Effective implementation of the new SSH law is critical to ensure successful ownership oversight. Among the important next steps will be the appointment of professional SSH board members capable of acting with independent judgment in their companies' interests and the development of more detailed plans and policies for the SSH's future operations. The state should not be involved in the day to day management of SOEs and company boards should be composed of experts who can exercise independent and objective judgement; they should be professionals rather than political appointees (OECD, 2011a). It is also important to ensure high quality disclosure and transparency requirements for the remaining SOEs (OECD, 2014a). When setting up its own corporate governance framework for SOEs the SSH should closely follow the OECD's SOE Corporate Governance Guidelines (OECD, 2006). Following examples of Hungary and the Czech Republic, the SSH could also regularly conduct quantitative cost-benefit analyses of the merits of retaining the state's existing equity stake for all SOEs (OECD, 2011a).

Another priority is to develop an asset management strategy. According to the SSH law, assets are to be classified into three types: strategic, important and portfolio. The minimum share in strategic assets is 50% plus one vote, in important assets 25% plus one vote, while the SSH is permitted to freely dispose of portfolio assets. The government is yet to agree on an asset management strategy for assets that will remain under state control, eventually to be confirmed by parliament. It is critical that the strategy provides a rigorous rationale for why certain assets should be owned by the state. There should be a bias against owning assets that are in direct competition with private assets or in markets where there is potential for significant competition (OECD, 2011a).

Less public ownership and deeper capital markets would attract more FDI

FDI has been modest (Figure 1.33, Panel A), despite low direct regulatory restrictions (Figure 1.31, Panel B). Inward stock of FDI is just above 30% of GDP, less than half the share in

Figure 1.33. **FDI has remained low**

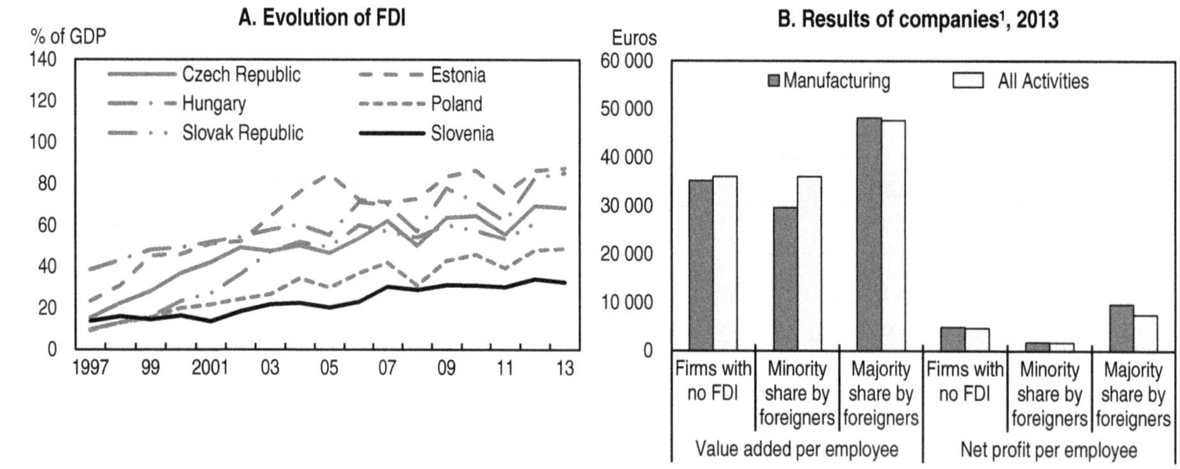

1. A firm is classified "Firms with no FDI" if less than 10% of its equity shares belong to foreign investors; a firm is classified "Minority share by foreigners" if more than 10% and less than 50% of its equity shares belong to foreign investors; a firm is classified "Majority share by foreigners" if more than 50% of its equity shares belong to foreign investors.

Source: OECD FDI series of BOP *and IIP Aggregates Database* for Panel A; and Bank of Slovenia for Panel B.

StatLink http://dx.doi.org/10.1787/888933205005

Estonia, Hungary or the Czech Republic. Ownership structure and FDI were discussed extensively in the *2011 Economic Survey of Slovenia*. The reason for such low FDI, despite the efforts of government to create a friendly regulatory and tax environment, lies in pervasive state ownership and political unwillingness for large privatisations. Analysis in Dall'Orso and Sila (2015) confirms that better business environment has a positive impact on inward FDI and, in particular, lowering state control of the economy is an important factor facilitating FDI (see also Annex 3). At a time when deleveraging in the corporate sector is dragging down investment and activity, opening up more to FDI can attract needed fresh capital.

There are a number of channels through which FDI boosts productivity performance. Efficiency gains can come from technology transfers through supply chains, better management practices, better integration with foreign markets, and better human capital formation (OECD, 2011a). A large body of empirical evidence supports this. For example, Bijsterbosch and Kolasa (2009) analyse the experience of central and eastern European countries and find that foreign investment has been an important factor in productivity growth. They also report that productivity benefits have been largest in countries with the greatest absorption capacity for new technologies, either because productivity differential *vis-à-vis* the euro area was not too big or that there were higher levels of human capital. Damijan, Rojec, Majcen and Knell (2013) compare cohorts of similar foreign and domestic owned firms over time, and find that foreign owned firms persistently outperform domestic firms in terms of TFP growth in the Czech Republic and Slovenia. Our own analysis also shows that FDI has a positive effect on productivity and on R&D activity (Dall'Orso and Sila, 2015; and Annex 3).

Companies with FDI perform better than domestically owned ones. Data from the Bank of Slovenia (2014b) show that about 4.5% of all non-financial companies have FDI, but they account for 19% of capital, 23% of assets and 22% of employees in the entire corporate sector. Companies with a majority share held by foreigners – representing 82% of all firms with FDI – have significantly higher productivity and higher profit per employees than domestically owned companies (Figure 1.34, Panel B). Firms with FDI also offer on average about 12% higher wages. Comparing raw data however, may exert a bias as foreign investors may be cherry-picking firms in better condition and better growth potential. Yet, even after controlling for this, Simoneti et al. (2002) find evidence that foreign owned companies in Slovenia experienced more rapid asset, sales, exports, value added and employment growth than domestic enterprises in mid 1990s.

A consequence of state dominance is that the legal and regulatory architecture of private capital markets are not well developed (OECD, 2011b). Slovenia is characterised by a shallow and relatively illiquid capital market. Total equity capitalisation and average monthly turnover are both low in comparison to other EU countries (Figure 1.34). The legal framework in Slovenia provides a relatively high degree of protection for shareholders, but in practice minority shareholders are widely dispersed and have limited economic interests in companies. To exercise their rights, shareholders must have a threshold level of voting interest (either 5 or 10%), meaning that often only the larger shareholders have the practical means to seek some form of redress. The extent to which duties of directors in companies can be enforced has been limited. This is reflected in the very low number of cases that have been heard for breach of directors' duties and their low rates of success (OECD, 2011b).

A number of questionable buyout and takeover transactions in the past suggest that there have been difficulties in appropriately regulating the capital markets. Legislative amendments improved operational independence of the Securities Market Agency (SMA)

Figure 1.34. **Equity market capitalisation and turnover – 2013**[1]

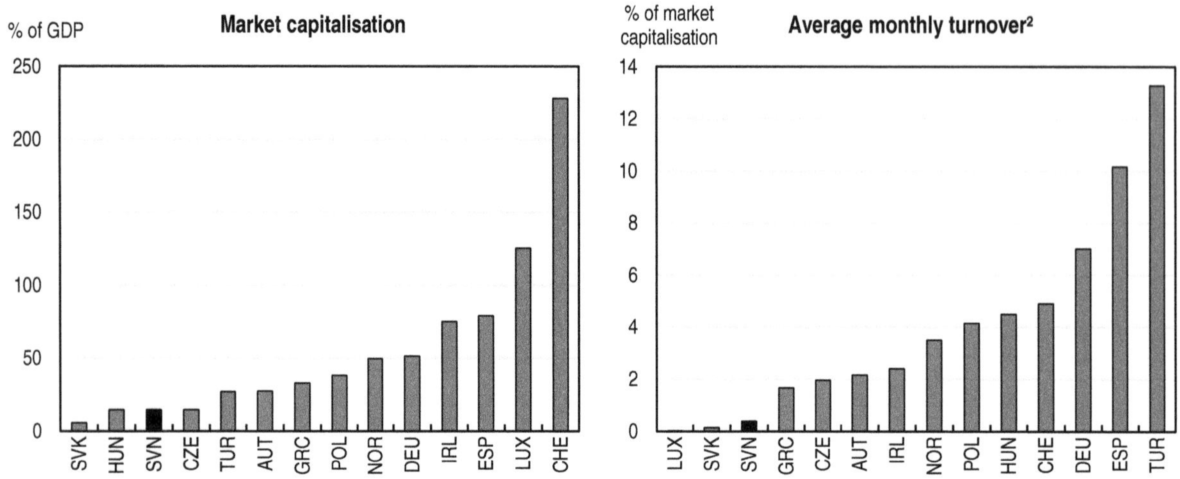

1. December 2013 for market capitalisation.
2. Value of equity trading in the year to December 2013.
Source: Federation of European Securities Exchanges.

StatLink http://dx.doi.org/10.1787/888933205311

and there have been improvements in the quality of enforcement. However, annual budget plans of the SMA are subject to government approval, and its employees remain subject to public employment regulations that prevent them from receiving market based salaries (OECD, 2013b). It remains important to ensure the Securities Market Agency has the financial and operational independence to adequately exercise its function.

The competition framework could be strengthened

With respect to anticompetitive agreements, Slovenia's law largely tracks the EU's competition law. However, its approach with respect to abuse of a dominant position may result in an overabundance of cases in which there is no competition problem from the perspective of effects-based economic analysis (OECD, 2014a). There were also recurrent complaints that resources of the competition authority have been inadequate, which has limited its potential to recruit and retain experienced and well-trained staff. The Competition Protection Agency's (CPA) annual budget must be negotiated with the competent ministry and approved by the government, limiting its financial and operational independence.

Progress has been made in improving budgetary autonomy for the Competition Protection Agency and in maintaining its independence (European Commission, 2015). Slovenia implemented several amendments to its competition law in 2012 and 2013. In January 2013, a new, independent public agency, the Slovenian Competition Protection Agency (CPA), took over the responsibility for enforcing the competition law. In 2013, the budget of the CPA was increased to address resource issues, and CPA was able to recruit more people. Nevertheless, with 27 full time equivalent employees covering competition enforcement, CPA is the smallest in the European Union, and far below the EU average of 116 people.

Recommendations on product market regulation and business environment

Key recommendations

- Continue privatising state-owned enterprises and do not hold controlling interests in firms operating in competitive markets.
- Introduce the "silence is consent" rule for issuing licences required to open up a business and make obtaining construction permits and registering property faster.

Other recommendations

- Prepare an asset management strategy for assets in public ownership and strengthen the corporate governance of SOEs by appointing professional board members.
- Reduce entry barriers in professional services (accounting, legal, engineering and architecture).

Tax system that better supports growth

Relatively high tax burden is primarily levied on consumption and labour

Slovenia relies to a large extent on the taxation of labour (personal income tax and social security contributions) and consumption while capital and property are relatively lightly taxed. The total tax take – 37% of GDP in 2013 – is relatively high; above the OECD average of 34%, close to levels in countries with higher level of development such as Iceland, Germany or Luxembourg. In 2013, almost 80% of tax revenues were collected from social security contributions and from taxes on goods and services while revenues from personal income tax amounted to about 14% and from corporate income to about 3% (Figure 1.35).

Figure 1.35. **Relatively high tax burden is primarily levied on consumption and labour**

Year 2013 or latest data available

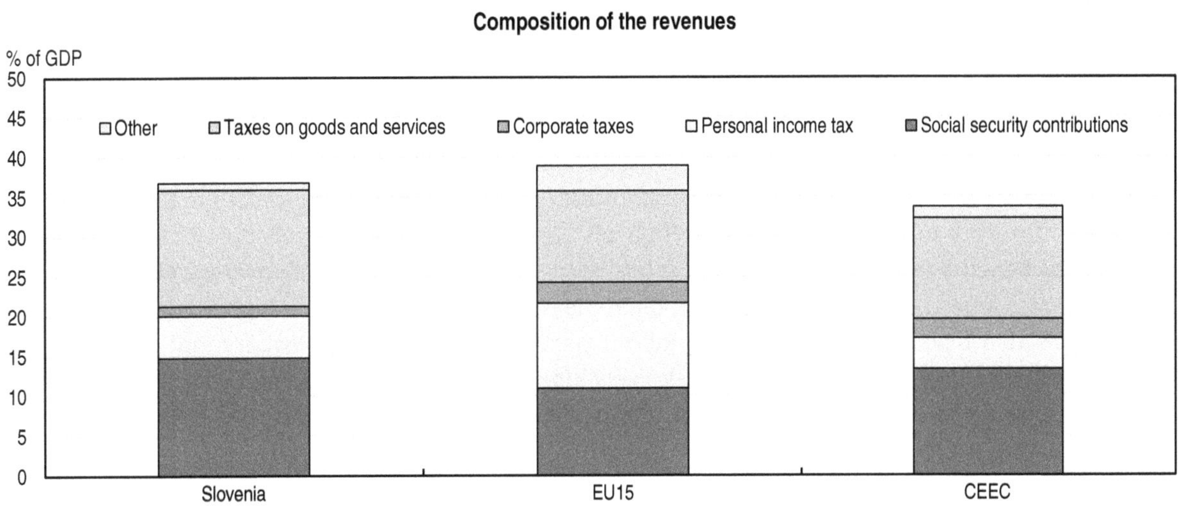

Source: OECD Public Sector, *Taxation and Market Regulation Database.*

StatLink http://dx.doi.org/10.1787/888933205324

Slovenia could reform its tax system in a revenue-neutral manner to better support inclusive and sustainable growth. Arnold et al. (2011) find that recurrent taxes on immovable property are least harmful to growth, followed by consumption taxes (and other property taxes). Taxes on production factors labour and capital (personal income taxes and corporate income taxes) are most harmful to growth. Therefore, Slovenia has room to reduce taxes on labour, and compensate with increases in property taxes and changes in indirect consumption taxes.

To attract investment Slovenia has been cutting the corporate income tax rate over the last 10 years, from 25% in 2005 to 17% in 2013, the second lowest in the OECD (OECD, 2014a). Measures have been taken to broaden the tax base, although tax incentives for investment have been introduced which narrow the tax base, for example via research and development (R&D) and investment tax allowances (*2009* and *2013 Economic Surveys*). While low rates of corporate income tax support investment – also from abroad – and total factor productivity growth in the medium term, another issue worth considering is that lowering the corporate tax rate too much below the top personal income tax rate can prompt high-income individuals to shelter their savings within corporations (Arnold et al., 2011). Therefore, given the current fiscal position and the fact that intake from the current tax is already quite low there is no room for further cuts in the corporate income tax rate.

Reducing tax rates on labour income

The tax on labour is relatively high due to high social security contributions and a progressive personal income tax. Reducing marginal tax rates on labour income should be Slovenia's top priority for tax reform to increase incentives to work. The marginal tax wedge – the share of an extra euro of labour costs that is kept by the government through personal income taxes and employee and employer social security contributions – is high across the income distribution (Figure 1.36). At 67% of average earnings for a person with no children it stands at 43.6%, above the OECD average, while it stands at 60.4% for a person earning 167% of average earnings, one of the highest in the OECD. After introducing the additional 50% tax bracket for those earning more than 5 times the average wage – a temporary measure introduced in 2013 to help fiscal consolidation – the marginal tax wedge for top earners stands at 66% (OECD, 2014a). Yet, Guner et al. (2014) find that increasing progressivity of the personal income tax brings very little in terms of additional government revenue.

Certain groups of workers are especially sensitive to changes in taxation on labour. The tax wedge on low wages increases labour costs of employing low-skilled and young workers, reducing their employment opportunities. The situation is aggravated in Slovenia with the very high minimum wage. High tax wedges can also induce people to stay on social benefits rather than work, and it has been shown that in Slovenia average effective tax rates when returning to work from unemployment and inactivity are high. High labour taxes also have adverse effects on labour participation of older workers and add to incentives for early retirement. The relatively high labour tax wedge on high wage earners also bears the risk of brain drain of highly qualified workers or prevents firms from attracting talent from abroad.

Reducing the tax wedge on labour would therefore encourage hiring, labour force participation and investment in skills (OECD, 2011c). This could be achieved by reducing the top marginal income tax. This can be reformed in a consistent manner together with reducing eligibility of high earners for various social benefits not to increase inequality. The progressivity of cash transfers is relatively low in Slovenia (Joumard et al., 2012; OECD, 2014g). With the 2012 reform, the eligibility of high-income earners for cash transfers was reduced

Figure 1.36. **Marginal tax wedge is high**

% of total earnings of a single person with no children

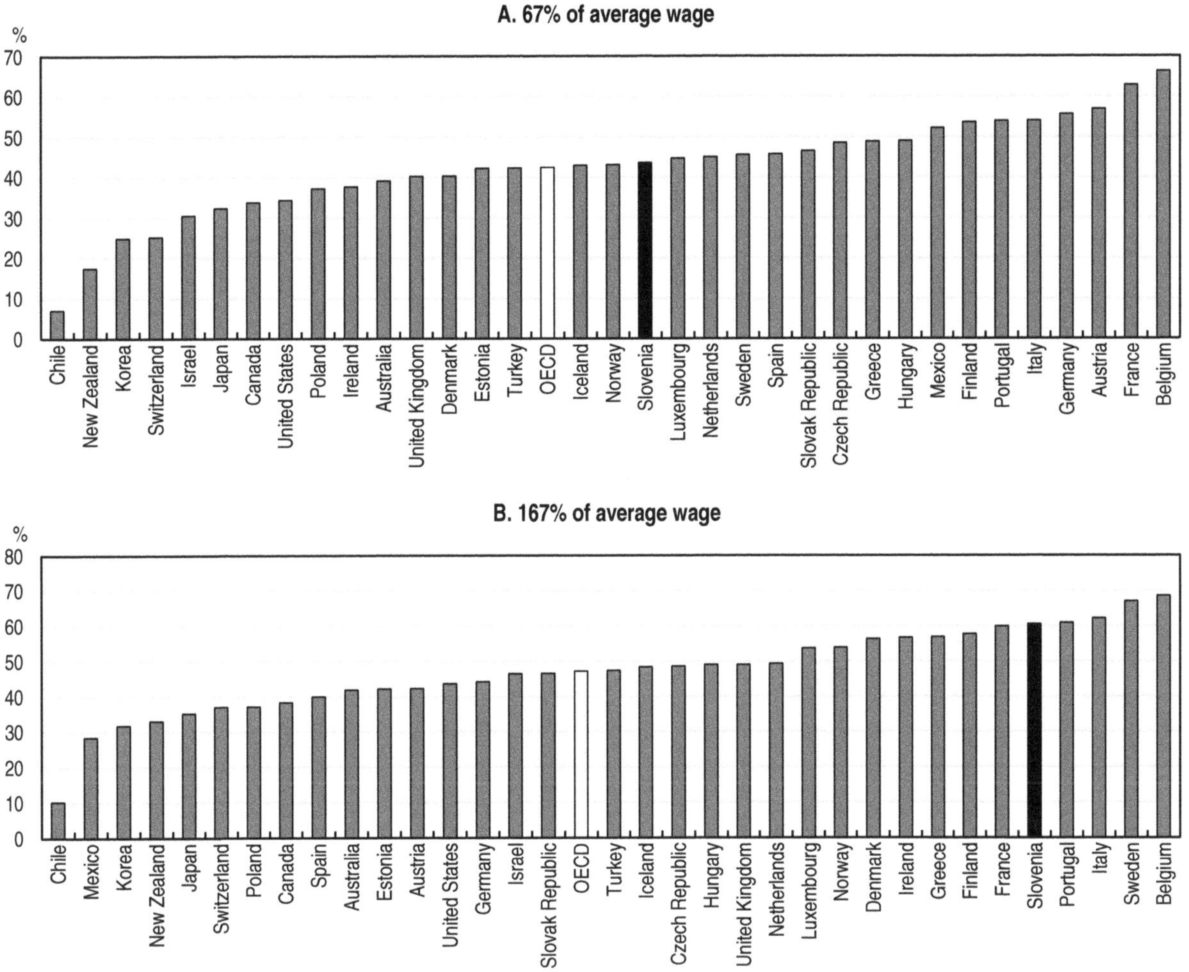

Source: OECD *Taxing Wages* (2014).

StatLink http://dx.doi.org/10.1787/888933205338

by taking into account all income and also property of individuals and families. But better means testing could further reduce the share of high-income earners eligible for support.

Increasing the reduced VAT rates and making tax expenditures fairer

The reductions in marginal tax rates on labour could be financed by raising taxes on consumption and reducing various tax expenditures, while preserving the equity-friendly nature of the tax system. As discussed in OECD (2014a), Slovenia could convert some personal income tax deductions (e.g. for social security contributions and for dependent children) into tax credits, to reduce the financial benefit of tax expenditures on individuals in high income brackets. It could remove exemptions and other tax preferences for certain forms of income (e.g. severance pay, pensions and capital gains on long-held assets), and consider shifting from flat-rate taxation of personal capital income to more progressive rates.

There is also room for increases in indirect taxes on consumption. At 22%, the standard value-added tax (VAT) rate is already high, but Slovenia applies a reduced VAT rate (9.5%) to quite a wide range of goods and services. For goods and services that are disproportionately consumed by higher-income households such as books, cultural services, hotels and restaurant meals, the reduced VAT rate could be removed and the standard VAT rate applied instead.

Improvements in tax compliance and mitigation of the shadow economy are also important to sustain tax revenues. The European Commission (2014c) assesses that Slovenia has made progress on this front and there are indications that the government programme, introduced in 2013, has yielded positive results. Undeclared employment has been addressed through the introduction of special online voucher register and tax fraud has been checked through stricter rules for using cash-register software. The government has also devoted attention to improving the tax culture and encouraging the voluntary, correct and prompt payment of taxes (Government of Slovenia, 2014).

Increasing taxes on real estate

The recurrent taxation of residential and other real estate is a key element of a tax system that supports inclusive and sustainable growth. This form of taxation has been found to have relatively limited negative effects on economic growth (Arnold et al., 2011). The tax revenues from taxes on property in 2013 were a mere 0.7% of GDP, about one third of the 2012 OECD average (Figure 1.37), so there is ample room to increase this tax. In fact, Slovenia had enacted a Real Estate Tax Law in 2014, but this law was proclaimed unconstitutional by the Constitutional Court. Slovenian government plans to prepare an alternative property tax reform with the same policy objectives while satisfying legal requirements, which we see as a positive step.

Figure 1.37. **There is room to raise recurrent taxes on real estate**

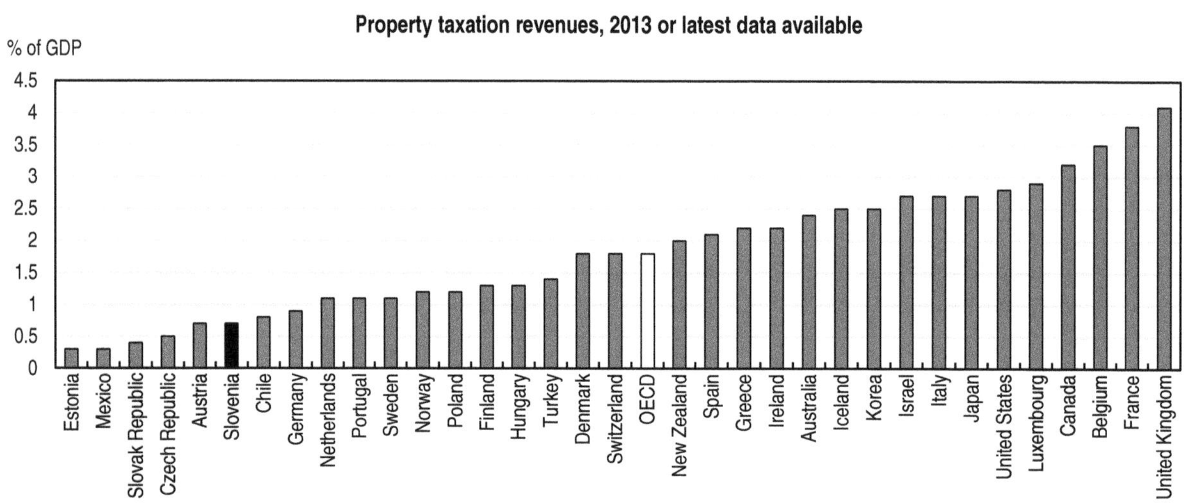

Source: Public Sector, *Taxation and Market Regulation Database.*

StatLink http://dx.doi.org/10.1787/888933204911

Aligning tax rates on different forms of energy

Revenues from environmental taxes amounted to 3.9% of GDP in 2013, one of the highest ratios among the OECD countries (OECD Environment Database). While overall effective tax rates on energy are at or above the OECD average, high revenues stem also from high fuel consumption associated with transit traffic (OECD, 2013i). Nevertheless, effective tax rates vary across different forms of energy. Tax rates on transport fuel are significantly higher than those on heating and process use and on electricity, and those on diesel are about 20% below those on gasoline in terms of energy content and carbon dioxide (CO_2) emissions, respectively (OECD, 2013i; Ministry of Finance). The differential between diesel and gasoline has been reduced recently due to reduced differential in excise duties on the two fuels. In addition, effective from January 2015, there was an increase in tax rate on CO_2 emissions by 20% per each kg of CO_2 for all energy products. Slovenia could therefore improve the environmental effectiveness of these taxes by linking them further to emissions. It should also for example remove exemptions in the case of commercial use of diesel fuel and increase taxes on heavy fuel oil and gas oil used for heating.

Recommendations on the tax system

- Reduce top tax rates on labour income. Better target family benefits and strengthen means testing of education-related benefits.
- Reduce tax expenditures and the use of reduced VAT rates in an equity-friendly manner.
- Increase recurrent taxes on real estate.
- Further align effective tax rates on different forms of energy to reflect environmental damage.

Bibliography

Arnold, J., B. Brys, C. Heady, Å. Johansson, C. Schwellnus and L. Vartia (2011), "Tax Policy for Economic Recovery and Growth", *The Economic Journal*, Vol. 121, No. 550.

Bai, J. and P. Perron (1998) "Estimating and Testing Linear Models with Multiple Structural Changes", Econometrica, Vol. 66, No. 1.

Bank of Slovenia (2014a), *Macroeconomic Developments and Projections*, October.

Bank of Slovenia (2014b), *Direct Investment 2013*, Ljubljana.

Bank of Slovenia (2013), *Macroeconomic Developments and Projections*, October.

Bijsterbosch, M. and M. Kolasa (2009), "FDI and Productivity Convergence in Central and Eastern Europe: An Industry-Level Investigation", *Working Paper Series*, No. 992, European Central Bank, Frankfurt-am-Main.

Bouis, R. and R. Duval (2011), "Raising Potential Growth After the Crisis: A Quantitative Assessment of the Potential Gains from Various Structural Reforms in the OECD Area and Beyond", *OECD Economics DepartmentWorking Papers*, No. 835, OECD Publishing, Paris.

Bourlès, R., G. Cette, J. Lopez, J. Mairesse and G. Nicoletti (2010), "Do Product Market Regulations in Upstream Sectors Curb Productivity Growth: Panel Data Evidence for OECD Countries", *OECD Economics DepartmentWorking Papers*, No. 791, OECD Publishing, Paris.

Chetty, R. (2008), "Moral Hazard vs. Liquidity and Optimal Unemployment Insurance", *Journal of Political Economy*, University of Chicago Press, Vol. 116(2), pp. 173-234, 04.

Clemens, J. and M. Wither (2014), "The Minimum Wage and the Great Recession: Evidence of Effects on the Employment and Income Trajectories of Low-Skilled Workers", National Bureau of Economic Research, *Working Paper*, 20724.

Conway, P., D. de Rosa, G. Nicoletti, and F. Steiner (2006), "Regulation, Competition and Productivity Convergence", *OECD Economics DepartmentWorking Papers*, No. 509, OECD Publishing, Paris.

Čelebič, T. (2014), "Tertiary Education in Slovenia – Participation, Efficiency, Quality, Financing and Employability", *Working Paper*, 4/2014, Vol. XXIII.

Dall'Orso, J. and U. Sila (2015), "Trends in Productivity and Sources of Productivity Growth in Slovenia", *OECD Economics Department Working Papers*, OECD Publishing, forthcoming.

Damijan, J., Č. Kostevc and M. Rojec (2013), "FDI, Structural Change and Productivity Growth: Global Supply Chains at Work in Central and Eastern European Countries", *IRMO Occasional Papers*.

Damijan, J.P., M. Rojec, B. Majcen and M. Knell (2013), "Impact of Firm Heterogeneity on Direct and Spillover Effects of FDI: Micro-Evidence from Ten Transition Countries", *Journal of Comparative Economics*, Vol. 41 (3), pp. 895-922.

Domadenik, P. and J. Prašnikar (2004), "Enterprise Restructuring in the First Decade of Independence", in Mrak, M. et al. (eds.), *Slovenia: From Yugoslavia to European Union*, World Bank, Washington, DC.

Eissa, N. and H.W. Hoynes (2006), "Behavioral Responses to Taxes: Lessons from the EITC and Labour Supply", in *Tax Policy and the Economy*, Vol. 20:73-110.

EIU (Economist Intelligence Unit) (2009), "A New Ranking of the World's Most Innovative Countries", *The Economist*, London.

European Commission (2015), "Country Report Slovenia 2015", *Commission Staff Working Document*, Brussels, 26 May.

European Commission (2014a), "Macroeconomic Imbalances, Slovenia 2014", *Occasional Papers*, 187, March.

European Commission (2014b), *Innovation Union Scoreboard 2014*.

European Commission (2014c), "Assessment of the 2014 National Reform Programme and Stability Programme for Slovenia", *Commission Staff Working Document*.

European Commission (2013), "Research and Innovation performance in Slovenia", *Country Profile*.

European Commission (2010), "Employers' Perception of Graduate Employability", *Eurobarometer*.

European Commission/EACEA/Eurydice/Eurostat (2014), "Key Data on Early Childhood Education and Care in Europe, 2014 Edition", *Eurydice and Eurostat Report*, Luxembourg, Publications Office of the European Union.

Eurydice (2011), "Chapter 3: Student Fees and Support", *Modernisation of Higher Education in Europe 2011: Funding and the Social Dimension*.

Farčnik, D. and P. Domadenik (2009), "School to Work Transition: Evidence from a Matched Employer-Employee Dataset", *Paper presented at the European Economics and Finance Society conference*, University of Warsaw, 4-7 June.

Frydman, R., C. Gray, M. Hessel and A. Rapaczynski (1999), "When Does Privatization Work? The Impact of Private Ownership on Corporate Performance in the Transition Economies", *The Quarterly Journal of Economics*, 114, 1153-1191.

Georgieva, S. and D.M. Ruqielme (2013), "Slovenia: State-Owned and State-Controlled Enterprises", *ECFIN Country Focus*, Vol. 10, Iss. 3.

Global Entrepreneurship Monitor (2015a): *2014 Global Report*.

Global Entrepreneurship Monitor (2015b), *Leveraging Entrepreneurial Ambition and Innovation: A Global Perspective on Entrepreneurship, Competitiveness and Development*.

Government of the Republic of Slovenia (2014), *Stability Programme, Amendments 2014*, Ljubljana, April.

Government of Slovenia (2013), Single document to enable better regulation and business environment and increase competitiveness, No. 01005-2/2013/11.

Guner, N., M. Lopez-Daneri and G. Ventura (2014), "Heterogeneity and Government Revenues: Higher Taxes at the Top?", *IZA Discussion Paper*, No. 8335, July.

Hanushek, E. and L. Wößmann (2008), "The Role of Cognitive Skills in Economic Development", *Journal of Economic Literature*, Vol. 46, No. 3, pp. 607-68, September.

Hanushek, E. and L. Wößmann (2011), "How Much do Educational Outcomes Matter in OECD Countries?", *Economic Policy*, CEPR, CES, MSH, Vol. 26, No. 67, pp. 427-91.

Hattie, J. (2009), *Visile Learning: A synthesis of Over 800 Meta-Analyses Relating to Achievement*, Routledge, London.

Hausmann, R. and C.A. Hidalgo (2011), "The Network Structure of Economic Output", *Journal of Economic Growth*.

IMAD (2014a), *Slovenian Economic Mirror*, Vol. XX, no. 12, December.

IMAD (2014b), *Economic Issues 2014*, Institute of Macroeconomic Analysis and Development, Ljubljana, August.

IMAD (2010), *Development Report 2010*, Institute of Macroeconomic Analysis and Development, Ljubljana.

Initiative start:up Slovenia (2014), *Start:up Manifesto*.

Institut RS za socialno varstvo (2014), *Socialni polozaj v Sloveniji 2013-2014*.

Jimeno, J.F., E. Moral and L. Saiz (2006), "Structural Breaks in Labor Productivity Growth: The United States vs. the European Union", *Documentos de Trabajo*, Num. 0625, Banco de España.

Joumard, I., M. Pisu and D. Bloch (2012), "Less Income Inequality and More Growth – Are They Compatible? Part 3. Income Redistribution via Taxes and Transfers Across OECD Countries", *OECD Economics Department Working Papers*, No. 926, OECD Publishing.

Lovea, J. H. and P. Ganotakisb (2013), "Learning by Exporting: Lessons from High-Technology SMEs", *International Business Review*.

Ministry of Higher Education, Science and Technology (2014), website: *www.arhiv.mvzt.gov.si/en/areas_of_work/science_and_technology/centres_of_excellence_and_competence_centres*.

Ministry of Higher Education, Science and Technology (2010), *Resolution on Research and Innovation Strategy of Slovenia 2011-2020*, Republic of Slovenia.

Ministry of Education, Science and Sport (2014), Some Explanations and Comments to the Findings and Recommendations of *"OECD Better Policies Series: Slovenia, Reforms for a Strong and Sustainable Recovery, May 2014"*, mimeo.

Molnar, M. (2010), "Measuring Competition in Slovenian Industries – Estimation of Mark-ups", *OECD Economics Department Working Paper*, No. 787.

Nicoletti, G. and S. Scarpetta (2005), "Product Market Reforms and Employment in OECD Countries", *OECD Economics Department Working Papers*, No. 472, OECD Publishing, Paris.

OECD (2015), Education Policy Outlook 2015: Making Reforms Happen, OECD Publishing, Paris, DOI: *http://dx.doi.org/10.1787/9789264225442-en*.

OECD (2014a), Slovenia: Reforms for a Strong and Sustainable Recovery, Better Policies, OECD Publishing, Paris, DOI: *http://dx.doi.org/10.1787/9789264215894-en*.

OECD (2014b), Education at a Glance 2014: OECD Indicators, OECD Publishing, Paris, DOI: *http://dx.doi.org/10.1787/eag-2014-en*.

OECD (2014c), Entrepreneurship at a Glance 2014, OECD Publishing, Paris, DOI: *http://dx.doi.org/10.1787/entrepreneur_aag-2014-en*.

OECD (2014d), OECD Economic Surveys: Finland 2014, OECD Publishing, Paris, DOI: *http://dx.doi.org/10.1787/eco_surveys-fin-2014-en*.

OECD (2014e), OECD Science, Technology and Industry Outlook 2014, OECD Publishing, Paris, DOI: *http://dx.doi.org/10.1787/sti_outlook-2014-en*.

OECD (2014f), Main Science and Technology Indicators, Vol. 2014/1, OECD Publishing, Paris, DOI: *http://dx.doi.org/10.1787/msti-v2014-1-en*.

OECD (2014g), "The Crisis and its Aftermath: A Stress Test for Societies and for Social Policies", in OECD, Society at a Glance 2014: OECD Social Indicators, OECD Publishing, Paris, DOI: *http://dx.doi.org/10.1787/soc_glance-2014-5-en*.

OECD (2013a), Interconnected Economies: Benefiting from Global Value Chains, OECD Publishing, Paris, DOI: *http://dx.doi.org/10.1787/9789264189560-en*.

OECD (2013b), OECD Economic Surveys: Slovenia 2013, OECD Publishing, Paris, DOI: *http://dx.doi.org/10.1787/eco_surveys-svn-2013-en*.

OECD (2013c), PISA 2012 Results: Excellence through Equity (Vol. II): Giving Every Student the Chance to Succeed, PISA, OECD Publishing, Paris, DOI: *http://dx.doi.org/10.1787/9789264201132-en*.

OECD (2013d), OECD Economic Surveys: Switzerland 2013, OECD Publishing, Paris, DOI: *http://dx.doi.org/10.1787/eco_surveys-che-2013-en*.

OECD (2013e), "Slovenia", in OECD, Education at a Glance 2013: OECD Indicators, OECD Publishing, Paris, DOI: *http://dx.doi.org/10.1787/eag-2013-70-en*.

OECD (2013f), OECD Science, Technology and Industry Scoreboard 2013: Innovation for Growth, OECD Publishing, Paris, DOI: *http://dx.doi.org/10.1787/sti_scoreboard-2013-en*.

OECD (2013g), OECD Economic Surveys: Ireland 2013, OECD Publishing, Paris, DOI: *http://dx.doi.org/10.1787/eco_surveys-irl-2013-en.*

OECD (2013h), Entrepreneurship at a Glance 2013, OECD Publishing, Paris, DOI: *http://dx.doi.org/10.1787/entrepreneur_aag-2013-en.*

OECD (2013i), Taxing Energy Use: A Graphical Analysis, OECD Publishing, Paris, DOI: *http://dx.doi.org/10.1787/9789264183933-en.*

OECD (2012a), OECD Economic Surveys: Finland 2012, OECD Publishing, Paris, DOI: *http://dx.doi.org/10.1787/eco_surveys-fin-2012-en.*

OECD (2012b), OECD Science, Technology and Industry Outlook 2012, OECD Publishing, Paris, DOI: *http://dx.doi.org/10.1787/sti_outlook-2012-en.*

OECD (2012c), OECD Reviews of Innovation Policy: Slovenia 2012, OECD Publishing, Paris, DOI: *http://dx.doi.org/10.1787/9789264167407-en.*

OECD (2011a), OECD Economic Surveys: Slovenia 2011, OECD Publishing, Paris, DOI: *http://dx.doi.org/10.1787/eco_surveys-svn-2011-en.*

OECD (2011b), Corporate Governance in Slovenia 2011, Corporate Governance, OECD Publishing, Paris, DOI: *http://dx.doi.org/10.1787/9789264097704-en.*

OECD (2011c), "Taxation and Employment", *OECD Tax Policy Studies*, No. 21, OECD Publishing, Paris, DOI: *http://dx.doi.org/10.1787/9789264120808-en.*

OECD (2010a), PISA 2009 Results: Overcoming Social Background: Equity in Learning Opportunities and Outcomes (Vol. II), PISA, OECD Publishing, Paris, DOI: *http://dx.doi.org/10.1787/9789264091504-en.*

OECD (2010b), "Learning for Jobs", *OECD Reviews of Vocational Education and Training*, OECD Publishing, Paris, DOI: *http://dx.doi.org/10.1787/9789264087460-en.*

OECD (2009a), OECD Economic Surveys: Slovenia 2009, pp. 26-34 and 47-49, OECD Publishing, Paris, DOI: *http://dx.doi.org/10.1787/eco_surveys-svn-2009-en.*

OECD (2009b), "Creating Effective Teaching and Learning Environments: First Results from TALIS", TALIS, OECD Publishing, Paris, DOI: *http://dx.doi.org/10.1787/9789264068780-en.*

OECD (2007), PISA 2006: Science Competencies for Tomorrow's World: Vol. 1: Analysis, PISA, OECD Publishing, Paris, DOI: *http://dx.doi.org/10.1787/9789264040014-en.*

OECD (2006), "OECD Guidelines on Corporate Governance of State-owned Enterprises", *in* OECD, Corporate Governance of State-Owned Enterprises: A Survey of OECD Countries, OECD Publishing, Paris, DOI: *http://dx.doi.org/10.1787/9789264009431-10-en.*

OECD (2005), OECD Employment Outlook 2005, OECD Publishing, Paris, DOI: *http://dx.doi.org/10.1787/empl_outlook-2005-en.*

OECD (2002), OECD Investment Policy Reviews: Slovenia 2002, OECD Publishing, Paris, DOI: *http://dx.doi.org/10.1787/9789264196162-en.*

Rojec, M., (2014) "A Snapshot of the Main Ownership Features of the Slovenian Corporate Sector", *IB Revija*, 1/2014.

Sala-i-Martin, X., G. Doppelhofer and R. Miller (2004), "Determinants of Long-Term Growth: A Bayesian Averaging of Classical Estimates (BACE) Approach", *American Economic Review*, Vol. 94, No. 4, pp. 813-35, September.

Simoneti, M., M. Rojec and M. Rems (2002), "Ownership Structure and Post-Privatisation Performance and Restructuring of the Slovenian Non-Financial Corporate Sector", *Journal of East-West Business*, Vol. 7, No. 2, Routledge.

SORS (2012), Collection brochures: Education in Slovenia, September.

Sutherland, D. and R. Price (2007), "Linkages Between Performance and Institutions in the Primary and Secondary Education Sector", *OECD Economics Department Working Papers*, No. 558.

Šušteršič, J., B. Nastav and T. Kosi (2010), "Ekonomski vidiki študentskega dela" (Economic Aspects of Student Work), Faculty of Management Koper, University of Primorska.

World Bank (2015), *Doing Business* Survey 2015.

ANNEX 1

Naming of economic sectors

Following the Eurostat NACE (Rev. 2) decomposition, we named the sectors according to the table below.

Code	Name	Short name
A	Agriculture, forestry and fishing	Agriculture
BDE	Mining and utilities	Mining and utilities
C	Manufacturing	Manufacturing
F	Construction	Construction
G-I	Wholesale and retail trade, transport, accomodation and food service activities	Wholesale, retail and transport
J	Information and communication	Information and communication
K	Financial and insurance activities	Finance and insurance
L	Real estate activities	Real estate
M-N	Professional, scientific and technical activities; administrative and support service activities	Professional services
O-Q	Public administration, defence, education, human health and social work activities	Public sector
R-U	Arts, entertainment and recreation; other service activities; activities of household and extra-territorial organisations and bodies	Arts, entertainment and recreation
	TOTAL	All activities

ANNEX 2

Structural breaks in productivity growth

Before the crisis, Slovenia experienced a continuous growth in productivity, while in the last quarters of 2008 the country suffered from an unprecedented productivity drop (Figure A2.1). Even though productivity growth reached its pre-crisis levels soon thereafter,

Figure A2.1. **Structural breaks**

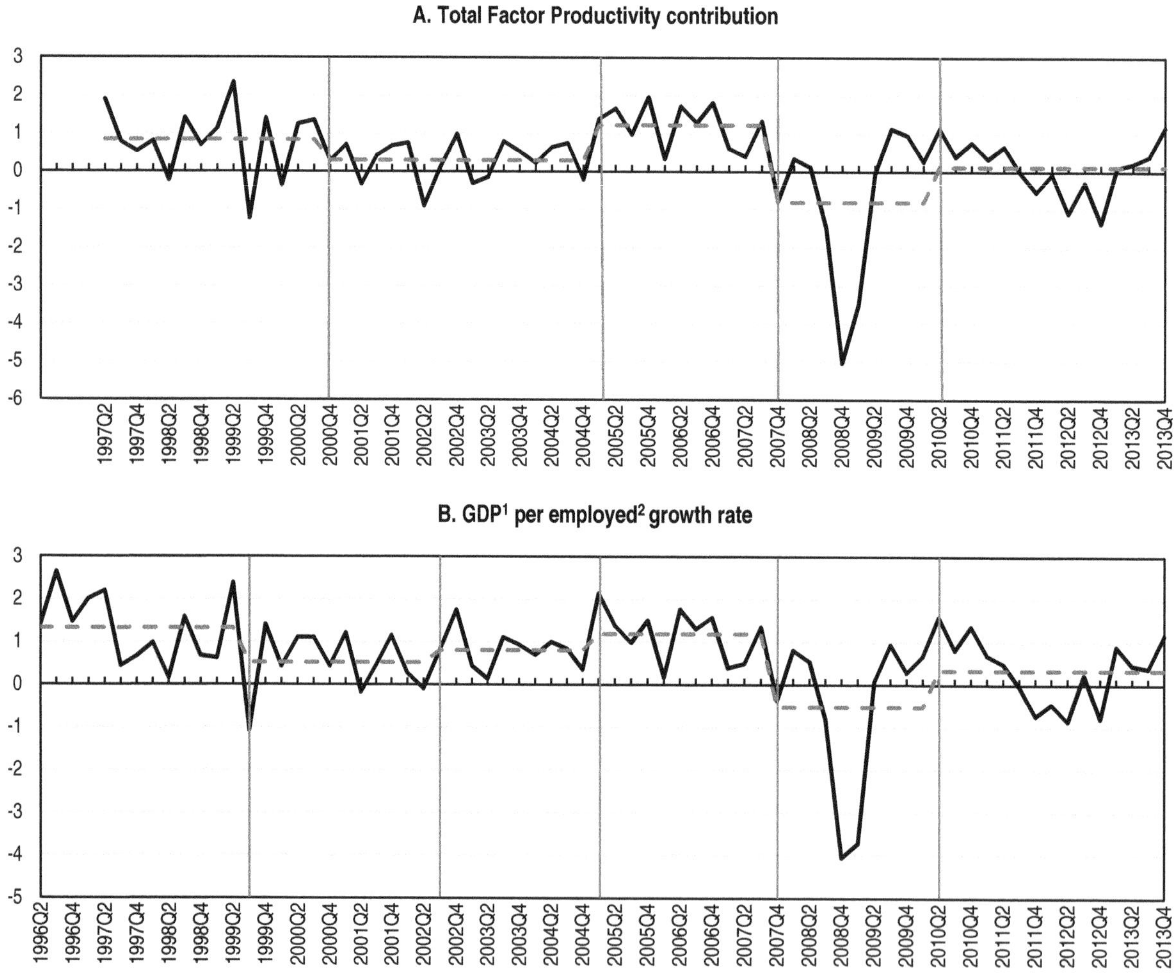

1. GDP at market prices measured in millions of euros, chain-linked volumes, reference year 2005 (at 2005 exchange rates).
2. Persons employed (total employment).

Source: Barro Lee educational attainment dataset, Eurostat and *OECD National Accounts Statistics*; OECD calculations.

StatLink http://dx.doi.org/10.1787/888933205344

from the end of 2011 it slowed down again, and Slovenia remained in recession for a prolonged period. The interesting question is, whether the crisis led to structural changes that undermine productivity growth in the future. If productivity growth has indeed shifted down permanently, this would have important consequences for long-term economic performance.

To test this, we use time series analysis and stability diagnosis techniques to detect potential structural breaks. Following the approach of Jimeno et al. (2006), the simultaneous estimation of breakpoints method developed by Bai and Perron (1998) is used. The method lets the data detect when breaks occur, but does not provide any structural explanations of why a break has occurred.

Structural breaks in productivity are explored using three series: quarterly growth rates of GDP per employed and GDP per hour, and total factor productivity contribution to growth. The GDP series and employment data is taken form Eurostat quarterly national accounts. Total hours worked are available on annual basis only and have been linearly interpolated. The TFP series is obtained from the growth accounting exercise performed using quarterly GDP (in volumes) series form the Eurostat quarterly national accounts, OECD quarterly series of productive capital stock and linearly interpolated OECD annual series of total hours worked. For more details see Dall'Orso and Sila (2015).

For each of the three series, four or five break dates are detected (Figure A2.1 and Table A2.1). For three of the identified breaks evidence is quite robust. In 2005 Q1, Slovenia entered a period of accelerated productivity growth, which was then reduced strongly between 2007 and 2008. Towards the end of 2009/beginning of 2010 productivity growth returned to pre-2005 levels. On top of that, there is also evidence of one or two breaks in productivity growth in the early 2000s. More interestingly, the GPD per hour series offers tentative evidence that in 2011 Q4 there was another structural break in productivity, bringing average productivity growth down again.

Table A2.1. **Structural break dates**

Bai and Perron global simultaneous estimation

GDP/workers growth rate	1999 Q3		2002 Q3	2005 Q1	2007 Q4	2010 Q2	
TFP contribution to growth		2000 Q4		2005 Q1	2007 Q4	2010 Q2	
GDP/hours growth rate		2000 Q4		2005 Q1	2007 Q2	2009 Q3	2011 Q4

Source: OECD calculations.

Given the numerous breaks identified by this analysis, it is too early to conclude that the break identified in 2011 Q4 and the lower average growth thereafter imply that productivity growth has come down more permanently. This is especially so, as in the most recent period productivity growth has recovered. Nevertheless, Slovenia should no doubt be cautious about its competitiveness and productivity growth and should implement policies to support them.

ANNEX 3

The impact of business environment on productivity and on FDI

This Annex (see also Dall'Orso and Sila, 2015) focuses on the impact of institutional setting and foreign direct investment (FDI) on labour productivity, measured by GDP per person employed. An unbalanced Panel of 34 OECD member countries is used, for the 1996-2013 period, from the OECD *National Accounts Database*. A fixed-effects model is estimated to control for unobserved heterogeneity across countries following Bijsterbosch and Kolasa (2009) and Box 1.3 in the *2012 Economic Survey of Finland*.

First, the logarithm of productivity is regressed on R&D intensity and expenditures on education (both measured as expenditures as a share of GDP), and capital intensity (measured as gross productive capital stock over employment). The capital intensity controls for variation in the industry mix and capital intensity. Table A3.1 column 1 shows that both the R&D and the education expenditure have a positive impact on productivity levels, while the capital intensity does not seem to have a statistically significant impact on productivity.

Table A3.1. **Determinants of productivity – Panel of OECD member countries**

	(1)	(2)	(3)
Dependent variable: log productivity			
Capital intensity	1.25e-09	1.35e-09	1.91e-09**
	(1.23e-09)	(8.25e-10)	(8.79e-10)
R&D intensity	0.0758***	-0.00941	-0.00636
	(0.0173)	(0.0170)	(0.0164)
Expenditures on education	0.0866***	0.0602***	0.0478***
	(0.0119)	(0.00890)	(0.00884)
Barriers to entrepreneurship		-0.0295**	-0.0231**
		(0.0119)	(0.0116)
Barriers to trade and invest		-0.0953***	-0.0912***
		(0.00868)	(0.00839)
State control		-0.0255**	-0.0216**
		(0.0108)	(0.0105)
FDI intensity			0.000698***
			(0.000215)
Observations	432	365	362
Number of countries	33	33	33

Note: Standard errors in parentheses (*** p<0.01, ** p<0.05, * p<0.1). All regressions are run using country fixed effects and include a constant term.

To determine the impact of the institutional setting on productivity levels, in column 2 we include the OECD PMR indicators on barriers to entrepreneurship, barriers to investment and trade, and the indicator of state control. Results show, as predicted, that all three barriers have a strong and statistically significant negative effect on productivity. For example, ceteris paribus, if Slovenia were to reduce its state control from 2.5 to 1.4 – the level of best performing country, the Netherlands – its productivity would be improved by 2.7%. The impact of barriers to trade and investment is especially strong. A drop of this indicator to the average level (from 0.8 to 0.5) could lead to a productivity increase of 2.6%. In column 3, we additionally include the measure of FDI penetration – the inward stock of the FDI as % of GDP. The coefficients of other institutional variables are not much changed. The results indicate that the FDI intensity (FDI as share of GDP) has a statistically significant positive effect on productivity.

Next, the role of institutional factors on the FDI is explored. High barriers to entrepreneurship and barriers to trade and investment are expected to have a deterring effect on investment. Regressing FDI intensity on the institutional factors (Table A3.2, column 1), it is confirmed that all three institutional variables have a negative impact on the FDI intensity. The state control, which is high in Slovenia, has a strong negative impact on inward FDI. Column 2 suggests, that higher FDI brings more R&D expenditure, and column 3 suggests that institutional factors are also important for the R&D expenditure, partly also through their effect on the FDI (including the FDI intensity together with the institutional variables would render its coefficient statistically not significant).

Table A3.2. **Influence of policy indicators on FDI intensity and R&D intensity**

	(1)	(2)	(3)
Dependent variable:	FDI intensity	R&D intensity	R&D intensity
Barriers to entrepreneurship	-11.96***		-0.171***
	(2.901)		(0.0442)
Barriers to trade and investment	-5.744**		-0.0900***
	(2.501)		(0.0330)
State control	-10.46***		-0.134***
	(2.618)		(0.0392)
FDI intensity		0.00464***	
		(0.000667)	
Observations	486	490	412
Number of countries	34	34	34

Note: Standard errors in parentheses (*** p<0.01, ** p<0.05, * p<0.1). All regressions are run using country fixed effects and include a constant term.

Replicating the analysis also using Slovenian cross-sector data yields results consistent with the above. The database covers the time period 1995-2012 and includes 21 sectors from the NACE Rev. 2 decomposition from the *OECD STAN Database*, together with sector data on 1995-2012 annual inward FDI stocks from the Bank of Slovenia. We exclude the sector "Public administration and defence, compulsory social security" in order to better capture the impact on productivity in the "business sector".

Table A3.3 column 1 reports the results from regressing the logarithm of sector productivity, measured as GVA in volumes per person employed, on R&D intensity (expenditure on R&D in GVA) and capital intensity (the ratio of gross capital formation in

Table A3.3. **The impact on Influence of R&D intensity, capital intensity and FDI intensity on sector productivity**

	Including financial/insurance sector		Excluding financial/insurance sector
	(1)	(2)	(3)
Dependent variable: log productivity			
R&D intensity	3.428***	2.489**	1.304
	(1.238)	(1.053)	(0.986)
Capital intensity	0.00183	0.00208*	0.00304***
	(0.00140)	(0.00118)	(0.00110)
FDI intensity		0.709***	1.904***
		(0.0947)	(0.212)
Observations	152	152	137
Number of sectors	13	13	12

Note: Standard errors in parentheses (*** p<0.01, ** p<0.05, * p<0.1). All regressions are run using sector fixed effects and include a constant term.

volumes over total employment). The R&D has a strongly positive impact on productivity, while capital intensity is not statistically significant. In column 2, we include the sector FDI intensity, and it confirms the result that sectors with higher FDI have higher productivity. For a robustness check, and because of a special position of the financial sector in the recent crisis, in column 3 we do the same analysis, but excluding the financial sector. The positive effect of the FDI intensity becomes even stronger.

Chapter 2

The economic consequences of an ageing population in Slovenia

Slovenia's population is set to age rapidly in the coming decades. This demographic trend will increasingly put pressure on already fragile public finances as age related expenditure is projected to rise by 3 percentage points of GDP by the year 2030. Ensuring debt sustainability and generational equity requires reforms of social support systems and necessitates adjustments in labour markets. Policy makers will thus need to act more strongly than in the past to rein in ageing-related outlays, pursue efficiency-enhancing restructurings of health and long-term care systems, and adopt measures to strengthen labour force participation. In particular, further increases in the relatively low pension age in line with the rise in life expectancy would reduce pension costs and the burden on the active population. Better utilisation of medical resources and co-ordinated purchasing of medical supplies would curb health care expenditure, while a dedicated funding mechanism for long-term care would enhance the sustainability of the system. Moreover, removing incentives for early retirement in combination with active labour market policies would increase the labour force participation rates of older workers from its currently very low levels.

The statistical data for Israel are supplied by and under the responsibility of the relevant Israeli authorities. The use of such data by the OECD is without prejudice to the status of the Golan Heights, East Jerusalem and Israeli settlements in the West Bank under the terms of international law.

As in many other OECD countries, declining fertility rates and higher life expectancy are progressively changing the demographic structure and leading to a rapid ageing of the population in Slovenia. With fewer children entering the population and people living longer, older people are making up an increasing share of the total population. Also, migration to Slovenia is low and is not expected to be sufficient to counteract the ageing of the society. The old-age dependency ratio (the share of the population aged 65 and over relative to the population aged 15-64), is projected to rise from 25% in 2013 to 55% by 2060 (Figure 2.1, Panel A). Moreover, the share of people aged over 80 in the total population will increase from 4% in 2010 to almost 11% in 2050 (Figure 2.1, Panel B). This is faster than in many other OECD countries.

Figure 2.1. **The population in Slovenia is ageing more rapidly than in most other OECD countries**

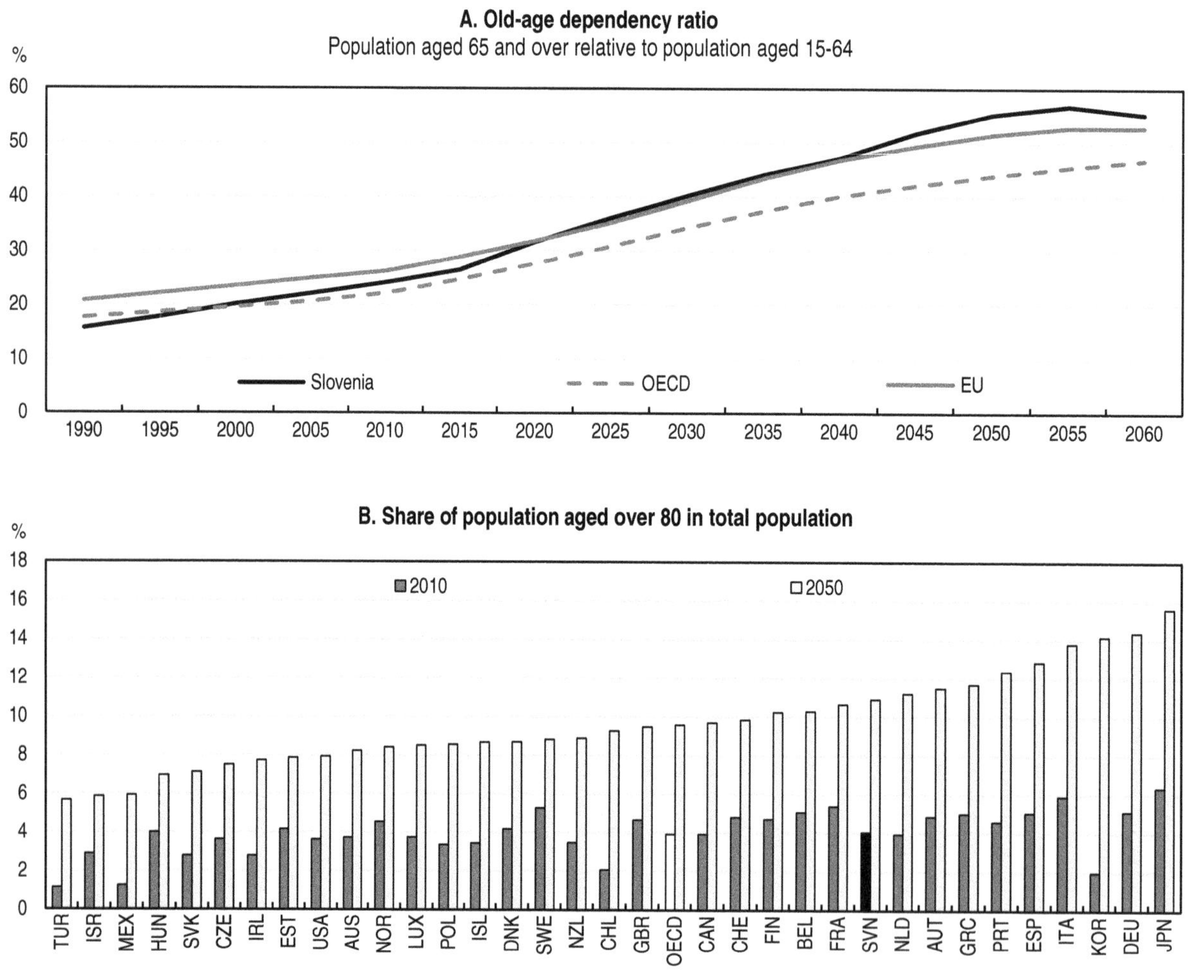

Source: UN, *World Population Prospects: The 2012 Revision.*

StatLink http://dx.doi.org/10.1787/888933205354

According to the Global AgeWatch Index, the well-being of older people in Slovenia shows a mixed picture (HelpAge International, 2014; Figure 2.2). The situation of the elderly compares favourably to many other OECD countries with respect to social connections, physical safety, civic freedom, and access to public transport, which constitute the "enabling environment" as well as "income security". In contrast, it scores below the OECD average for "health status", and is among the worst ranked with respect to "capability". The latter is the result of the low employment rate of older people, despite many older workers having completed secondary or tertiary education.

Figure 2.2. **Well-being of people aged 60 years and more**[1]

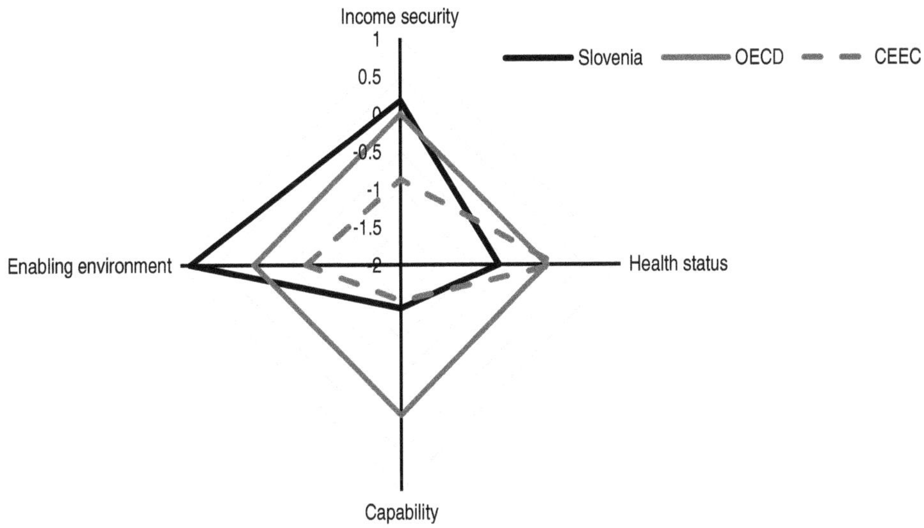

1. Each country's indicator is expressed as the difference with the OECD average and divided by the OECD standard deviation.

Source: HelpAge International (2014).

StatLink http://dx.doi.org/10.1787/888933205362

Providing older people with adequate pensions, high quality health care and gainful employment will become even more of a challenge in the coming decades. As a result of the demographic trends, Slovenia faces the prospect of a substantial increase in total age-related expenditure for pensions, as well as health and long-term care. Corresponding public expenditures are projected to rise by more than 3 percentage points by 2030 (OECD, 2014a; Figure 2.3) and more than 6 percentage points of GDP over the years 2013-60, compared with less than 2 percentage points for the European Union on average (European Commission, 2015). Hence, policy makers will need to act more strongly than in the past to rein in ageing-related outlays and to pursue efficiency-enhancing reforms of social support systems.

The remainder of this chapter falls into four parts. The next section discusses the sustainability and adequacy of pensions in Slovenia in light of the reforms that were undertaken in 2013. The following section then turns to ageing-related challenges for the health and long-term care system and how the latter might need to evolve. Subsequently, the labour force participation of different segments within the population and labour market policies are assessed, with particular attention to older workers. A brief discussion on the benefits and opportunities of an ageing population concludes the chapter.

Figure 2.3. **Age-related expenditures will exert significant pressure**

Increased spending on pensions and health, change 2015-30

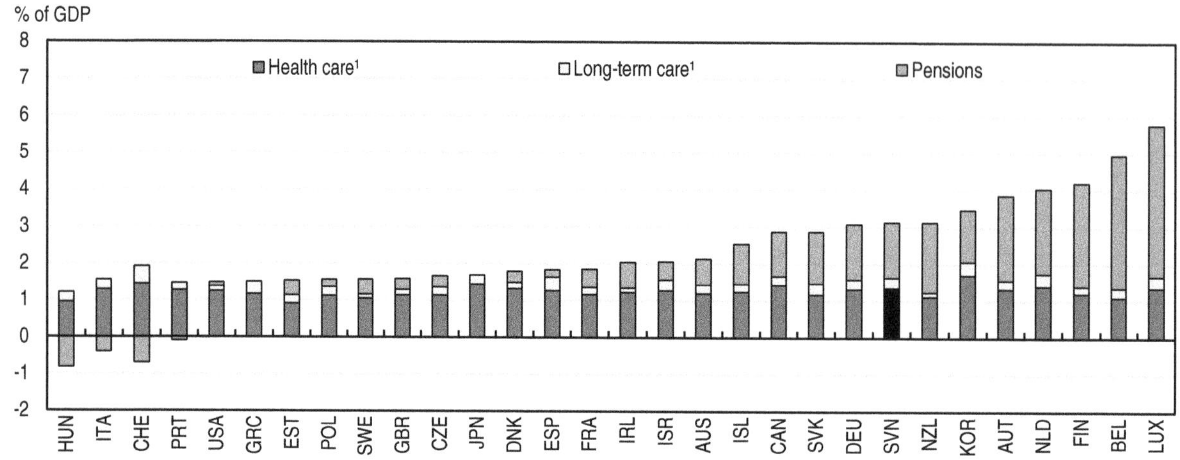

1. Based on "Cost-containment scenario", (Oliveira Martins and de la Maisonneuve, 2014). Where projections are not available over the period 2015-30, linear interpolation has been applied.

Source: Secretariat calculations based on *OECD Economic Outlook* No. 96 projections.

StatLink http://dx.doi.org/10.1787/888933205372

Making the pension system sustainable requires further policy reform

Public spending for old-age and survivor pensions is relatively high in Slovenia. In 2011, the respective expenditure amounted to 11.4% of GDP, compared with an average of 7.9% for the OECD (Figure 2.4). Several factors have contributed to the high pension expenditures, notably a relatively low average statutory and effective retirement age (Figure 2.5), short qualifying periods to receive a full pension, and longer pension drawing periods as life expectancy increased. Moreover, pension outlays in relation to GDP have risen by almost two percentage points since the global financial crisis in 2008, as year-on-year GDP growth has been negative, while the pensioner to active population ratio continued to increase.

Figure 2.4. **Public spending for old-age and survivor pensions is relatively high in Slovenia**

Public spending for old-age and survivor pensions, 2011

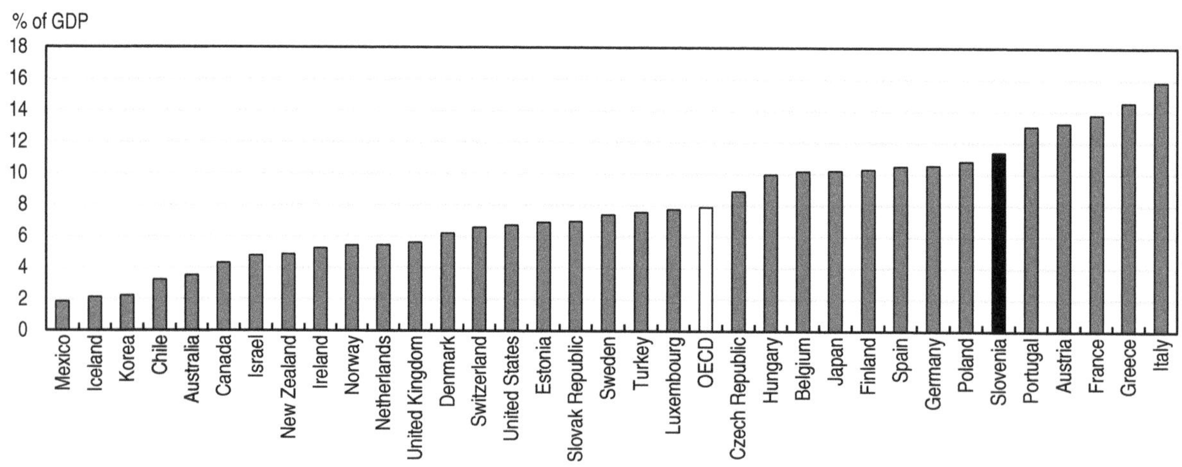

Source: *OECD Social Protection and Well-Being Database.*

StatLink http://dx.doi.org/10.1787/888933205380

Figure 2.5. **Retirement age is comparatively low**

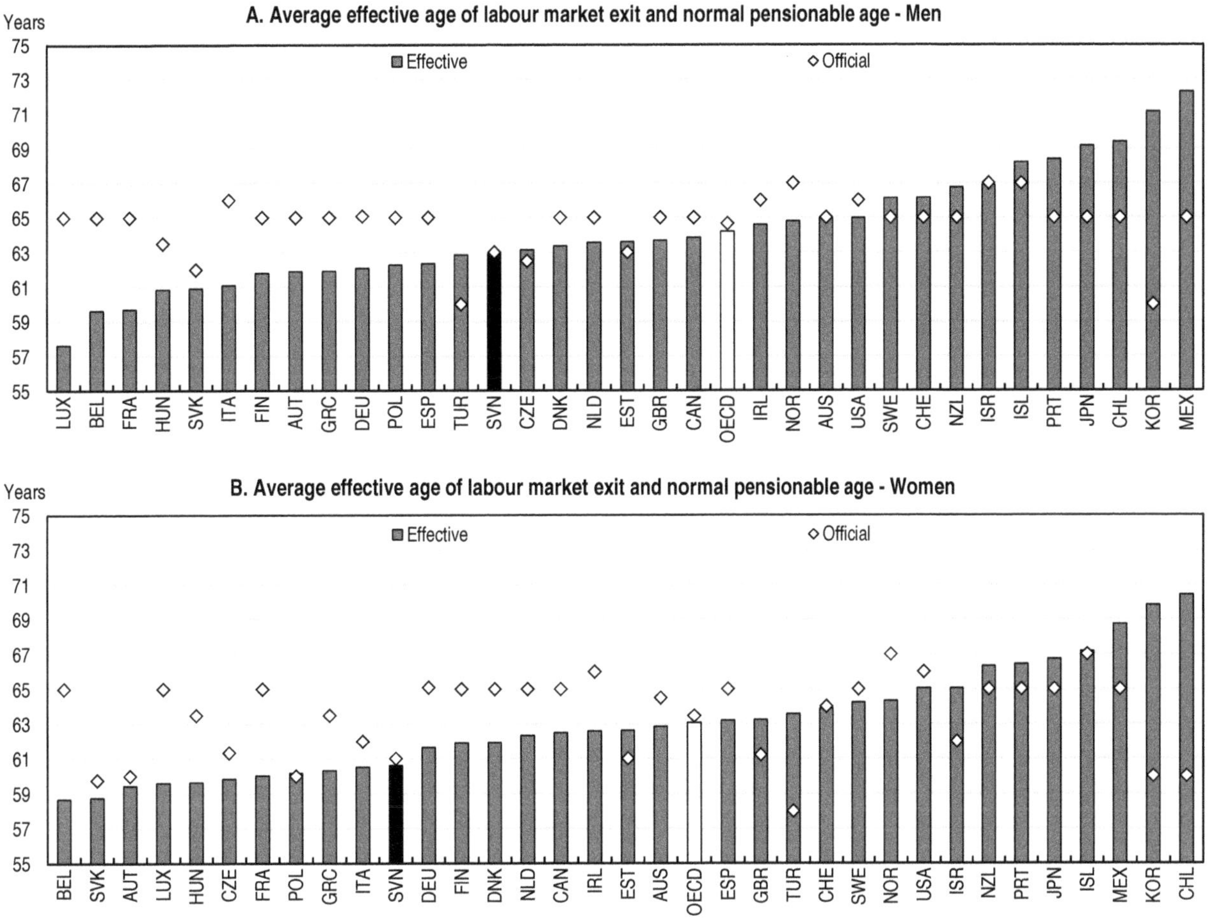

Note: Effective retirement age shown is for five year period 2007-12. Pensionable age is shown for 2012.
Source: OECD estimates based on the results of national labour force surveys and the *European Union Labour Force Survey*.
StatLink http://dx.doi.org/10.1787/888933206033

Pressures on public spending will increase

Going forward, pressure on the pension system will increase further as Slovenia's population ages rapidly. In fact, the baseline scenario of the European Commission's Economic Policy Committee projects a rise in total public pension expenditure of 3.5 percentage points of GDP for Slovenia between 2013 and 2060 (European Commission, 2015). The projection is more moderate than the OECD's pension outlook, which forecasts an increase in pension-related expenditures by 6 percentage points of GDP between 2015 and 2050 (OECD, 2014b). In any case, the increase is higher than in most other EU countries (Figure 2.6). While disability pension expenditure is expected to decrease and survivor pensions show only a moderate increase as a share of GDP, old-age pension outlays are driving the expenditure surge over time. Private pension expenditure remains of very modest importance. Slovenians have traditionally relied on the public pension system and the current policy regime does not provide strong incentives for private retirement savings.

The Government of Slovenia is aware of the pending fiscal pressures and has started to pursue reforms to increase the sustainability of the pension system. In particular, new pension legislation was implemented in January 2013 that simplified the pay-as-you-go system, strengthened the link between contributions paid and pensions received and

Figure 2.6. **Total public pension expenditure is projected to grow strongly (2013-60)**

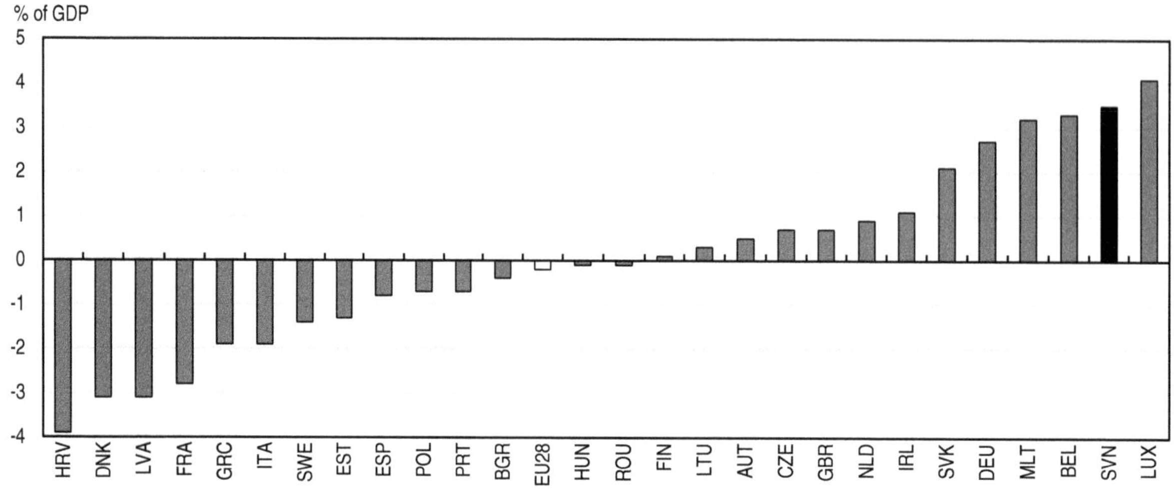

Source: European Commission, 2015 *Ageing Report.*

StatLink http://dx.doi.org/10.1787/888933205391

equalised the statutory retirement age for men and women at 65 years by 2020 (Box 2.1). These reforms are subject to transition periods from the previously existing system, but will be fully effective by 2022.

Box 2.1. **The pension reform of 2013**

The Slovenian pension system comprises two pillars. The first one is a mandatory pay-as-you-go defined benefit system, financed by contributions paid by employers (15.5% of gross wages) and employees (8.85% of gross wages) and direct transfers from the central government budget to cover any arising deficit (4.1% of GDP in 2012). The second pillar consists of private, funded schemes, which are mandatory for two groups of employees – people working in hazardous or arduous occupations and public sector employees – and voluntary for others. About two-thirds of all employees are enrolled in second pillar programmes. Overall, though, the public pay-as-you-go system is by far the dominant source of income for pensioners. Annual pay-outs from the first pillar in 2012 amounted to more than twice as much as the value of total assets of the second pillar pension funds. All pensions are in principle subject to income tax, but pensioners benefit from a 13.5% allowance, and few then have incomes that exceed the income tax entry threshold (EUR 1150 per month). As a result, only about 5% of pensioners pay income tax.

On 4 December 2012, Slovenia's National Assembly passed a new Pension and Disability Insurance Act (ZPIZ-2), which came into force on 1 January 2013. The reform makes a number of parametric and systemic changes to the previous pension legislation (ZPIZ-1), mostly with the aim of putting the system's finances on a more sustainable basis. The main reform components are listed in the following.

The retirement age is being equalised for men and women and will be gradually raised to 65 years by 2020. Under the previous system, men could retire at 63 and women at 61. The minimum insurance period to qualify for an old-age pension has been reduced from 20 to 15 years of insurance contributions.

The possibility to lower the statutory retirement age due to child care, compulsory military service or early career start was maintained, but is available only under conditions that are more restrictive than under the previous system. Also, a person may retire at the

Box 2.1. **The pension reform of 2013** *(cont.)*

age of 60 years already at a full pension, but only if he/she has 40 years of actual employment (or periods for which contributions were paid with regard to maternity, sick leave or unemployment). Under the previous system, the minimum age for receiving a full pension after 40 years of employment was 58 years.

Early retirement is now possible from the age of 60 (58 under the previous system), if a person has 40 years of pension insurance (including purchased periods, for example, for times spend for child care or in tertiary education), but is subject to a reduction in the pension by 0.3% per month of retirement before the statutory retirement age. Conversely, a bonus is provided for deferred retirement, with pensions increasing by 1% per three-month period of work beyond the statutory retirement age. The maximum pension bonus a person can obtain is limited to 12%, which corresponds to three years of additional employment.

The calculation of the pension base takes into account the 24 consecutive years of insurance that are most favourable for the individual. Under ZPIZ-1, only the best 18 years of insurance were considered. A minimum pension assessment base is defined as 76.5% of the average net wage and a maximum pension base as four times the minimum base. The scheme pays 26% of the pension assessment base for men and 29% for women, once the minimum qualifying condition (15 years of contributions) has been met. Thereafter, the accrual rate is 1.25% per year, so that the net replacement rate after 40 years of contributions is 57.25% for men and 60.25% for women.

Moreover, the pension indexation method was changed, with pensions under ZPIZ-2 now being indexed to 60% of the increase in the average gross salary paid and to 40% of the average increase in the cost of living, while in the earlier system pensions were only linked to average gross salaries.

The new pension legislation also significantly broadened the scope of employers who can enrol their workforce in a supplementary, funded pension scheme (second pillar), while benefiting from tax relief.

Furthermore, a consultative personal register of compulsory insurance was established, with the aim of providing each insured person with easily accessible information on his/her notional and actually paid contributions. This will enable the insured person to verify whether the employer has actually paid contributions for his/her pension and disability insurance.

Source: Ministry of Finance, 2013; Stanovnik and Prevolnik Rupel, 2013.

Early results from the reforms are encouraging. The Ministry of Labour, Family, Social Affairs and Equal Opportunities published a first evaluation report in April 2014 that suggests that the new measures are helping to slow the inflow of new applicants into the pension system, increase the average retirement age and raise the share of retirees that have completed the full duration of the statutory working life (MDDSZ, 2014a). The reforms of 2013 will help to reduce and stabilise public pension expenditure as a share of GDP in the short to medium term. However, the achievements have to be seen in the context of a strong inflow into the pension system and related expenditure increases just before 2013 in anticipation of the reforms. Indeed, the additional pension expenditures in the run-up to the reforms and in the context of general fiscal consolidation might have crowded out other governmental spending.

In any case, projections undertaken at Slovenia's Institute of Economic Research show that the ongoing ageing of the population will soon lead to increases in public pension

Figure 2.7. **Projected public pension expenditure under the new and old pension systems**

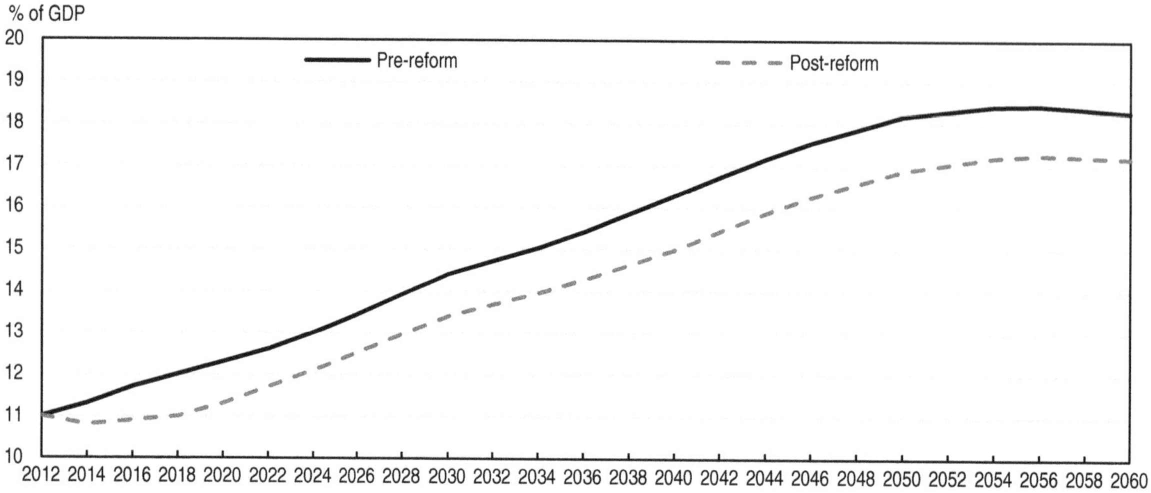

Note: Projections based on information on demographic developments as described in the European Commission's *2012 Ageing Report* (European Commission, 2012a).
Source: Majcen et al., 2012.

StatLink http://dx.doi.org/10.1787/888933205400

expenditure. While the reforms are expected to yield fiscal savings of up to 1.3% of GDP, the pre-reform expenditure to GDP ratio will be surpassed by 2020 and the ratio is projected to increase markedly thereafter (Figure 2.7). Hence further reforms will soon be needed to stabilise public pension expenditure.

Additional reforms to achieve sustainability

The funding gap could in principle be closed by measures either on the revenue or the expenditure side, or a combination thereof. However, the potential to increase revenues for the public pension system by increasing contribution rates seems limited. The average labour tax wedge in Slovenia for a single person earning average wage stands at 42.3%, substantially above the OECD average of 35.9%, and is even higher for high earners (OECD *Taxing Wages Database*). Similarly, the total public pension contribution rate of 24.4% of gross earnings puts Slovenia towards the upper end of the OECD scale (Figure 2.8). Increasing the pension contribution rates further in this context would put an additional burden on the active population and risk adverse consequences for employment, work incentives and competitiveness. Some countries have started to raise revenue to finance ageing-related expenditures by levying contributions on capital income at the personal level – as is the case in France – or use indirect energy tax revenues – as in Germany. However, given the already high top personal income tax rates in Slovenia, raising sources from capital income could come perhaps as a substitute for lowering contributions on labour incomes. The potential to increase revenues is therefore limited.

Renewed reform efforts should focus on further altering many of the parameters that were adjusted by the 2013 reform. In particular, the statutory retirement age should be gradually increased beyond 65 years to better balance contributing and pension receiving periods as life expectancy increases. Indeed, about half of OECD countries have elements in their mandatory retirement-income provision that provide an automatic link between pensions and a change in life expectancy (OECD, 2011a). The most obvious form of such links is thereby to increase the pensionable age as people live longer. This indexing of the

Figure 2.8. **Public pension contribution rates, 2012**

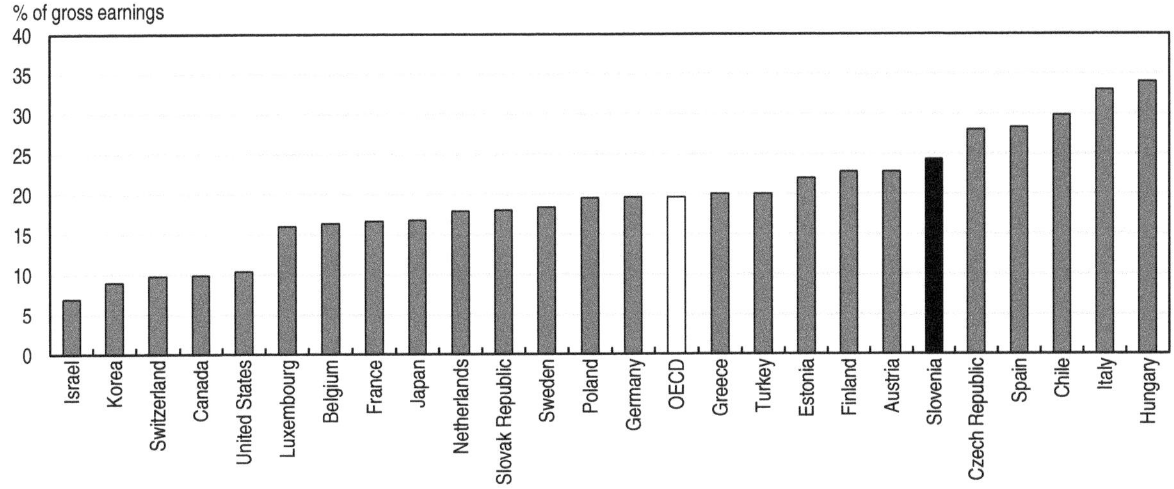

Source: OECD Pensions at a Glance 2013.

StatLink http://dx.doi.org/10.1787/888933205415

statutory retirement age to life expectancy is, for example, being introduced into the pension systems of Denmark, Greece, and Italy. Automatic adjustment means that governments no longer encounter gaps in pension financing when projections of life-expectancy change. Also, controversial political discussions on cutting future benefits could be avoided if increased life expectancy provides a direct and logical justification for the policy change.

Another avenue to stabilise pension expenditure would be to shorten the gap between statutory and early retirement ages and to better reward longer service time. Retirement choices are driven by diverse determinants related to an individual's health status, professional position, household situation, as well as socio-cultural and institutional factors (Van Erp et al., 2013), but financial aspects also play an important role. The 2013 pension reform already tightened the requirements for early retirement to some extent, but further provisions to extend the service period required to obtain a full pension and stronger incentives for older workers to remain in the labour force would help make the pension finances more sustainable. For example, limiting the entry age for early retirement to a maximum of two years prior to the statutory retirement age and imposing larger pension deductions for early retirement could make a significant contribution to the sustainability of the system (IMF, 2015).

Moreover, adjustments in the pension base have a role to play. The 2013 pension reform increased the number of years on which pensions are based from the best 18 to the best 24. Once the new pension reform is fully phased-in by 2020, a male pensioner with 40 years of contributions is expected to obtain benefits equal to 57% of the pension rating base, and a female pensioner 60%. This represents a decrease of up to 0.38 percentages points (by 2060) compared to the earlier system (Ministry of Finance, 2013). However, the 2013 reforms stopped short of adopting a system based on lifetime contributions, so that the pension base would be based on average wages rather than earnings during a period of highest wages. Moving to such an average-earnings system will tend to decrease the pension base and – unless adjustments to the accrual coefficients are made – the benefits paid out. At the same time, however, the shift to a lifetime contribution system will have distributional consequences with individuals with steep earnings growth or volatile career paths facing strong declines in their pension benefits (Disney and Whitehouse, 1999). These distributional impacts will have to be considered and potentially addressed through complementary measures.

Further, placing a greater weight on prices, rather than wages, in the indexation of pensions will lower costs over time. The 2013 pension reform introduced a mixed indexation based on 60% gross wages and 40% consumer prices. Putting additional weight on prices will make it possible to maintain the purchasing power of pensioners, while avoiding that labour productivity gains translate into higher pension expenditures. Some OECD countries, such as France, Japan, Spain, United Kingdom or United States, are only taking price inflation into account when indexing pensions. Meanwhile, Slovenia has taken *ad hoc* policy measures to contain the increase of pension outlays due to indexation as part of the government's austerity programme. Since 2010, pension indexation has been partially or completely frozen. It was reduced, respectively, to half and a quarter of nominal wage growth in 2010 and 2011, and completely frozen in 2012. In 2013, a 0.1% increase in pensions was accorded, while in 2014/15 the indexation is again fully suspended.

It is important to keep in mind, however, that containing pension costs by cutting replacement rates has implications for pension adequacy. The pension to wage ratio (net of social security contributions and personal income taxes) in Slovenia has fallen from 73% in 2001 to 62% in 2012 (Figure 2.9). The drop has been particularly pronounced since 2010, when pension indexation was partially suspended. While the replacement rates for low income workers in Slovenia continue to be in line with the OECD average (Figure 2.10), the decrease in the level of average pensions over time might raise concerns about the well-being of the lowest income groups and the effective protection of pensioners against old-age poverty.

Figure 2.9. **Pension to wage ratio (net)**

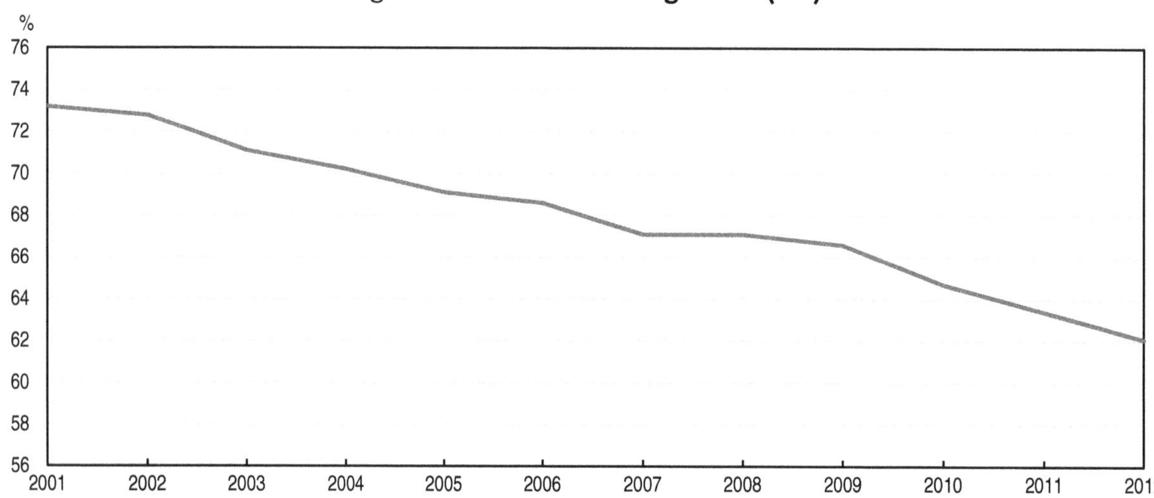

Source: Stanovnik and Prevolnik Rupel, 2013.

StatLink http://dx.doi.org/10.1787/888933205422

The relative income poverty rate of the elderly, defined as less than one-half the median income, amounts to 17% and is thus substantially higher than corresponding figures for other age groups or the OECD average at 12% (OECD, 2014c). Old-age poverty in Slovenia is not evenly distributed, but affects in particular women over 65, who are twice as likely as men to have low pension incomes (Stanovnik and Prevolnik Rupel, 2013). This gender gap is the

Figure 2.10. **Net replacement rates**

Theoretical net replacement rates at different earnings levels for full-career workers entering the labour market in 2012

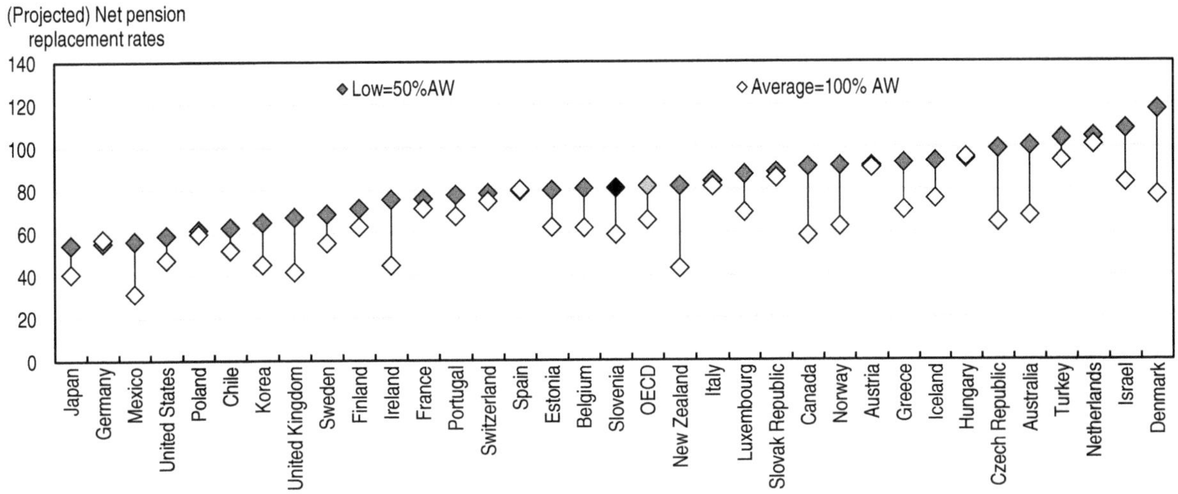

Note: "Average" and "Low" earnings levels refer to 100% average wage and 50% of the average wage, respectively.
Source: *OECD Pensions at a Glance 2013.*

StatLink http://dx.doi.org/10.1787/888933205436

result of shorter pension contribution periods by women, lower salaries earned and pension contributions made, and a higher likelihood to live in single households due to longer female life expectancy. The 2013 pension reform aligned the retirement ages and minimum contribution periods of men and women, but the effects will only be felt in the longer term, and the other two determinants of the gender gap will remain.

The level of pension benefits provided by the public pension system is generally the prime determinant of retirement-income adequacy, but there are other resources that provide incomes or benefits to retirees. In particular, many retirees in Slovenia own their homes. In fact, home ownership at 84% among individuals over 65 is among the highest in the OECD (Figure 2.11, Panel A). Unlike people of working age, older homeowners have generally paid-off their mortgages and thus fully benefit from not having to pay rent (while, however, having to assume home maintenance costs and property taxes). If this benefit is taken into account as imputed rent, the economic situation of pensioners in Slovenia improves markedly. The poverty rate falls by 60% or more compared to the assessment without imputed rent (Figure 2.11, Panel B). The findings are shown based on poverty rates with fixed and floating poverty lines. When the line is fixed, poverty is computed by comparing the incomes, augmented by net imputed rents, with the original poverty threshold calculated without imputed rent. With a floating line, poverty is computed with reference to a new income threshold that also includes the (net) imputed rent (OECD, 2013a).

A dwelling is, of course, also an asset that could be sold and the proceeds could be used to supplement the pensioners' income. Similarly, financial savings and capital income can also complement public pensions. In Slovenia, the financial assets held by pensioners are relatively modest, though, and consist to a large extent of bank deposits (OECD, 2013a). In particular, income from private funded pensions and life insurance policies – sometimes referred to as the third pension pillar – are not enhancing pensioners' income in any substantial way.

Figure 2.11. **House ownership and poverty of the elderly**

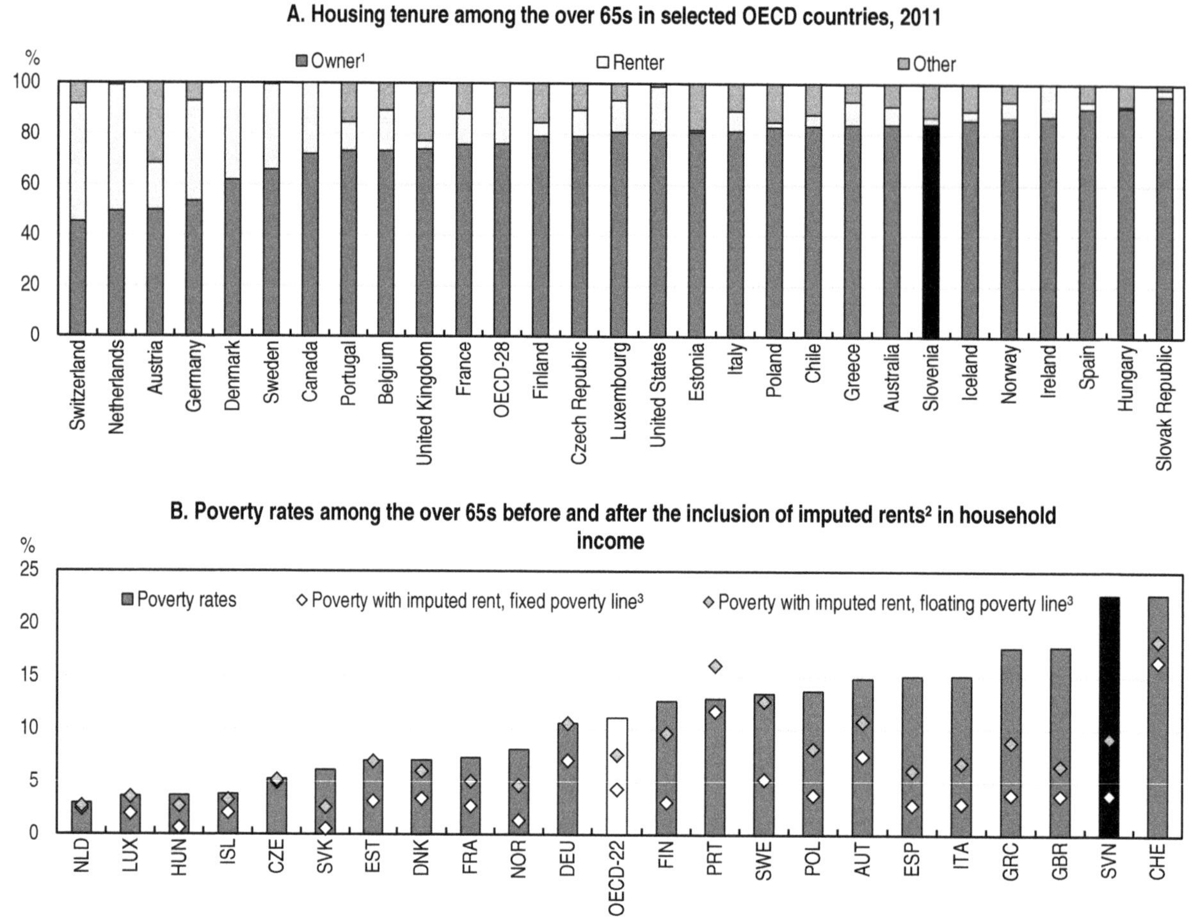

1. The category "owner" includes both outright owners and owners who are still repaying a mortgage.
2. The income stream which owners could draw from their homes and "save" by living in them is commonly termed "imputed rent".
3. When the line is fixed, poverty is computed by comparing the incomes, augmented by net imputed rents, with the original poverty threshold calculated without imputed rent. With a floating line, poverty is computed with reference to a new income threshold that also includes the net imputed rent.

Source: Pensions at a Glance 2013.

StatLink http://dx.doi.org/10.1787/888933205448

Private pensions are of minor importance

Slovenia has a second pillar in its old-age support system – supplementary pensions, which are a defined contribution plan. There are two mandatory supplementary pension schemes, which, respectively, cover employees in the public sector and workers performing arduous or hazardous tasks. These two groups are enrolled in two closed pension funds (SODPZ and ZVPSJU), which are managed by a state-owned company (Kapitalska Družba). In addition, several voluntary schemes exist that are organised by particular employers. Pension contributions from both the employer and the employee benefit from tax relief up to 5.8% of the gross wage of the employee. There is a minimum guaranteed rate of return on the paid in net premium, which should not be lower than 40% of the average annual interest on government securities with the maturity exceeding one year. The minimum return is guaranteed by the pension scheme provider over the whole period of the active participation in the supplementary pension scheme (OECD, 2011b).

Partly due to their relatively recent establishment, none of these funded pension schemes have been able to accumulate sufficient assets to provide adherents with viable supplementary pensions. Also, the public employee fund has suffered from early withdrawals, as participants took out lump sum payments after completing the minimum ten year contribution period, instead of continuing to save for old-age pensions. The poor performance of the private pension funds during the global financial crisis and the hardship many contributors experienced during that period motivated many of these withdrawal decisions (Ministry of Finance, 2013).

Moreover, the occupational pension fund had to assume unfunded entitlements when it was created, which has led to high contribution rates (10.6% of gross wages, paid by the employer) (Stanovnik and Prevolnik Rupel, 2013). Also, participation is determined by an outdated list of hazardous occupations, which does not provide employers with incentives to improve working conditions. For example, few printers are nowadays exposed to lead, so that their classification as a hazardous occupation is questionable. These shortcomings were not addressed in the 2013 pension reform. Hence, in order to improve the functioning of the occupational pension fund, the authorities should revise the list of activities that are considered arduous or hazardous, and determine the contribution rates to the occupational pension fund in accordance with actuarial principles.

Overall, the second pillar is not expected to yield substantial supplementary income for pensioners. In addition, assets in private pension funds are small and substantially below the OECD average (Figure 2.12). The European Commission forecasts the contribution from funded pensions in Slovenia to gradually grow over time, but merely reach 0.3% of GDP by 2060 (European Commission, 2012a). In this context, the authorities might want to provide incentives to strengthen the role of voluntary private pensions in order to complement the incomes of the elderly.

Slovenia no longer provides a minimum pension, but it offers means-tested minimum income support to (elderly) individuals with very low incomes. In January 2012, new social legislation took effect that modified the right to minimum pension support and transferred it from the pension insurance to a social assistance scheme, which is welcome. The maximum amount of supplementary income support for a single eligible person without any other sources of income was EUR 449.80 in 2012, and for a household with two eligible individuals it amounted to EUR 673.40 (Ministry of Labour, Family, Social Affairs, and Equal Opportunities, 2013). For comparison, the average net earnings of a single person in Slovenia amounted to EUR 976 in 2012 (Eurostat, *Labour Market Database*).

The health and long-term care systems are awaiting reform

An ageing population also has substantial implications for health care provision and related costs. Typical health expenditure profiles show average outlays as being relatively high for young children, subsequently they decrease and nudge up only gradually for most of the prime-age period, before they start to increase rapidly in older age (De la Maisonneuve and Oliveira Martins, 2013). Hence, a rising proportion of older people is placing upward pressure on overall health care spending, although other factors, such as income growth and advances in medical technology, also play a major role.

There is growing evidence that with suitable policies and programs people can stay healthy and independent well into old age and can continue to make contributions to their communities and families. Yet, the potential for an active, healthy old age is often

Figure 2.12. **Importance of pension funds relative to the size of the economy, 2013**

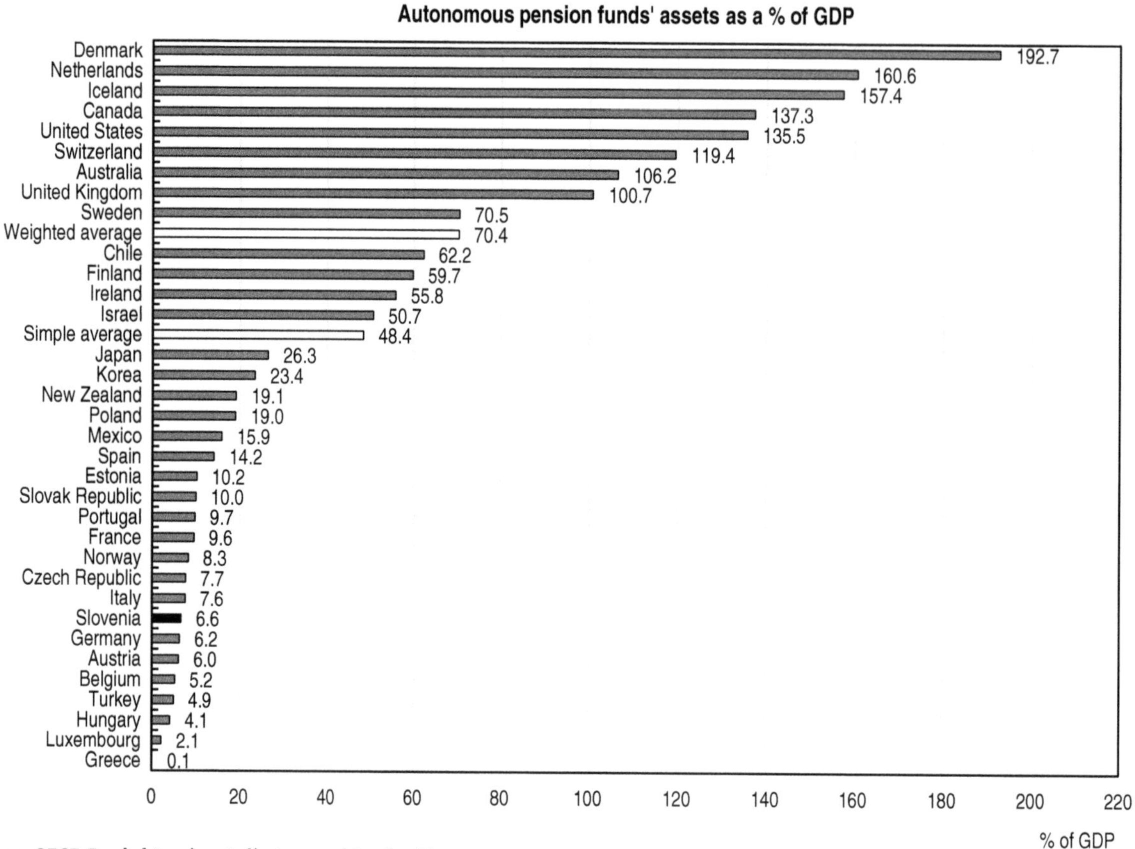

Source: *OECD Funded Pensions Indicators*; and Bank of Japan.

StatLink http://dx.doi.org/10.1787/888933205455

compromised by dementia, whose prevalence rises sharply with age. An estimated 25-30 per cent of people aged 85 or older world-wide suffer from the syndrome (WHO, 2011). Unless new strategies for prevention and management are discovered and applied, the rising number of people with dementia is expected to place growing demands on health care systems.

Moreover, many of the very old lose their ability to live independently because of physical malfunctioning that leads to limited mobility or frailty. Many require some form of permanent assistance for the most basic activities of daily living, creating a heavy economic and social burden on families and the wider community. Reducing severe disability from disease and health conditions is thus one central element for containing health care costs in an ageing society (WHO, 2011). The longer people can live independently, care for themselves and remain mobile, the lower are the costs of long-term care.

Total expenditure on health and long-term care in Slovenia amounted to 9.2% of GDP in 2012 and remains in line with the OECD average (Figure 2.13), but higher than in many countries with a similar level of GDP per capita. In 2013, the share of health expenditure in GDP dropped to 9.1% and was estimated at 9.0% in 2014. Under the European Commission's reference scenario, health care expenditure is expected to increase by 1.1 percentage points of GDP between 2013 and 2060, while outlays for long-term care would be 1.5 percentage points of GDP higher by 2060 (European Commission, 2015). The total increase in health and long-term care expenditures would, thus, amount to 2.7 percentage points of GDP by 2060

Figure 2.13. **Total current health and long-term care expenditure**

2012 or latest data available

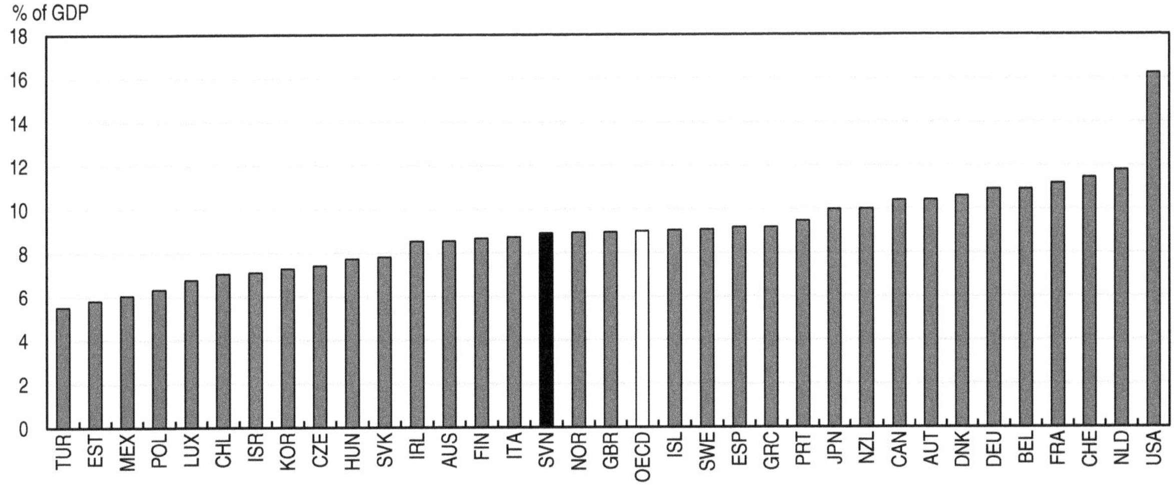

Source: *OECD Health Database.*

StatLink http://dx.doi.org/10.1787/888933205464

(Figure 2.14). Projections by the OECD predict an even stronger surge in health and long-term care expenditures (De la Maisonneuve and Oliveira Martins, 2013). Under a cost containment scenario, total health costs in Slovenia would increase by 3.6 percentage points of GDP until 2060, while in the cost pressure scenario, the expenditure hike would amount to no less than 8.2 percentage points of GDP. The "cost pressure scenario" assumes that no policy action is undertaken to curb rises in expenditure, whereas the "cost-containment scenario" assumes some policy action to rein in these expenditure pressures, such as measures to limit the growth of relative health prices.

Figure 2.14. **A big rise in health and long term care expenditures is projected in the future**

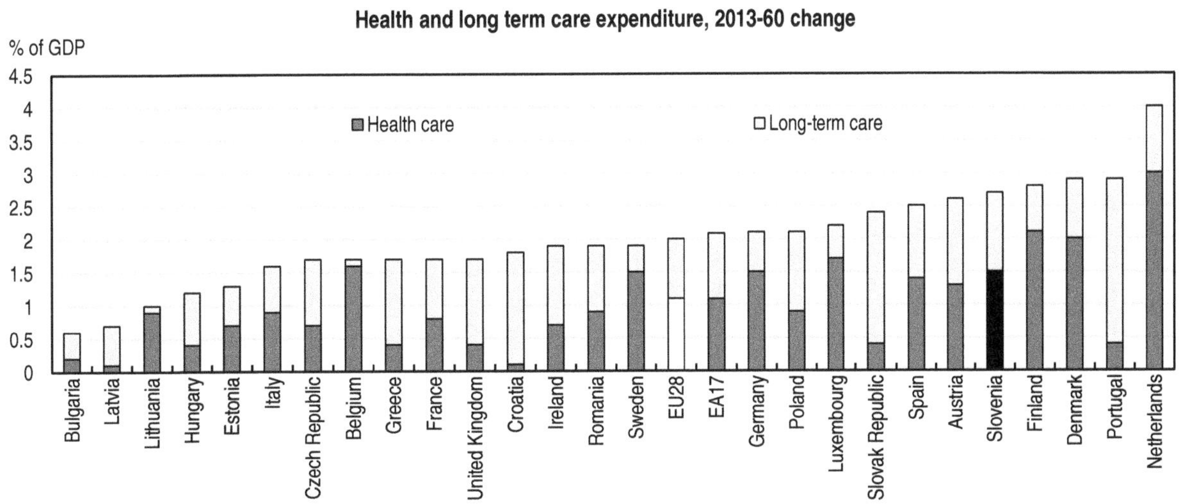

Source: European Commission, 2015 *Ageing Report.*

StatLink http://dx.doi.org/10.1787/888933204938

The current health care system in Slovenia has been in place since 1992. Health and long-term care are financed through compulsory health insurance, which is administered by the Health Insurance Institute of Slovenia (ZZZS), and through voluntary complementary insurance, which can be obtained from three private insurance companies (Vzajemna, Adriatic, and Triglav). A risk-equalisation scheme among the three insurance companies was introduced in 2005 based on open enrolment and equal risk premiums in order to avoid discrimination according to age, gender and health status. The compulsory insurance gives the insured access to free coverage of basic treatments within the public provider network against a fixed share of their gross wages (7.09% paid by employers plus 6.36% paid by employees), pensions (5.65%) or incomes. The voluntary complementary insurance, which individuals can purchase against a flat fee (at around EUR 27 per month in 2012), covers most or all expenses that are not fully reimbursed by the compulsory insurance. In addition, individuals can buy private supplementary insurance that provides access to additional medical services (or decide to pay for such services out-of-pocket). The coverage of compulsory health insurance is virtually universal, while 95% of the population buy voluntary complementary insurance.

Rising costs and the economic downturn following the global financial crisis of 2008 have resulted in the emergence of severe financial constraints for the Health Insurance Institute of Slovenia. These have been tackled through short-term austerity measures, such as rate cuts for health care service provision, lowering of reimbursement rates from the compulsory insurance system, and augmentations in contribution rates for the voluntary complementary insurance. As a consequence, the accessibility to health care services has decreased, both in terms of lower affordability and increased waiting times. In particular, the share of private health care funding gradually increased from 26% of total expenses in 2008 to 28% in 2013 (Stanovnik and Prevolnik Rupel, 2013), and the number of patients on waiting lists increased from 39 000 in 2011 (across 52 services monitored) to 76 000 in 2014 (47 services monitored) (Ministry of Health, 2015).

Some of the cost drivers seem endemic to the system. Despite recent growth in the number of general practitioners, their share among all doctors is still low (Figure 2.15) and the allocation of resources is skewed to more costly specialist care. A third of overall healthcare spending is on inpatient care, and more could be done to further develop ambulatory care (OECD, 2013b). The Commission for the Prevention of Corruption reports

Figure 2.15. **The share of general practitioners among all doctors is low**

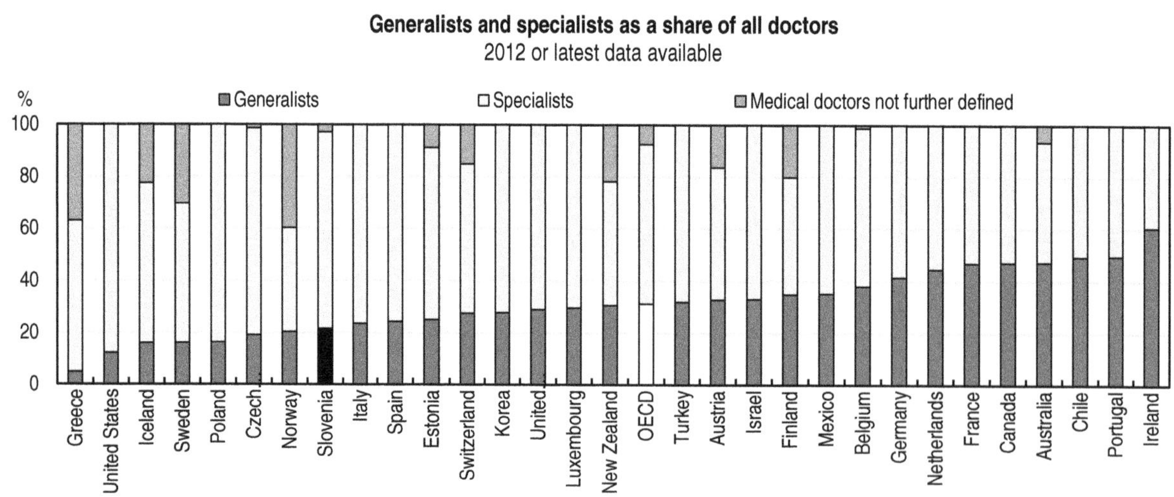

Source: OECD Health Care Resources Database.

StatLink http://dx.doi.org/10.1787/888933205471

that the public health system is inefficient in its public procurement and susceptible to conflicts of interest. The decentralised Slovenian health providers pay significantly higher prices for the equipment and materials in comparison to their counterparts in many EU countries (CPC, 2014). Also, research findings using the OECD's Data Envelope Analysis methodology suggest that, overall, the Slovenian health care system achieved only a 52% efficiency score relative to frontier countries, such as Chile, Israel, Italy and Japan (IMF, 2015).

In this context, the Insurance Institute of Slovenia has undertaken several cost-cutting initiatives, notably the classification of drugs by categories, negotiations with suppliers to reduce the prices of medicines, expansions of the lists of mutually interchangeable drugs, the determination of the highest recognised prices/costs of medicines, and the introduction of new therapeutic groups. Moreover, to increase efficiency and transparency, the Ministry of Health has started to centralise the procedures for purchasing of drugs and pharmaceutical products, and this practice is planned to be extended to medical equipment.

The government is undertaking a comprehensive review of expenditure at state and local government levels, direct and indirect budget users and municipality-owned providers of facilities and services, scheduled for the first half of 2015. The aim of the assessment is to evaluate the potential for improving the cost-effectiveness and quality of service delivery and to identify institutional reforms and marked-based mechanisms that could generate synergies and cost savings. The findings of the review will serve as inputs into a comprehensive health sector reform that the government intends to launch towards the end of 2015.

The health insurance system in Slovenia has a number of redistribution elements. There is no upper contribution threshold for the compulsory health insurance, so that high income employees pay much more into the insurance pool than would be actuarially needed to cover their health risks. Pensioners face a lower contribution rate than employees and despite higher contributions from the self-employed since the beginning of 2014, they contribute less than comparable wage earners. Moreover, the voluntary complementary insurance consists of a flat fee, which represents a heavy burden on low income individuals. Hence, contribution rates of different groups within society might need to be reviewed in order to reduce or avoid distortions in the system.

The Slovenian government already addressed one distortive exemption from social contributions when it reformed the treatment of student work in early 2015. In Slovenia, many young high school or university graduates used to have problems in entering the labour force. For entry-level positions, companies preferred to hire student workers on temporary contracts, as they provided flexibility and did not require contributions to the social security system. This practice led to increased unemployment among young graduates and extended study periods (OECD, 2013b). From February 2015, students will have to make a 15.15% contribution to the pension system, while employers have to pay 8.85% in pension contributions and 6.36% in healthcare insurance contributions. Also, the minimum wage for student workers was fixed at EUR 4.50 per hour, which is 10% below the regular minimum wage.

Another element in need of reform is the voluntary complementary health insurance. It currently covers the full remaining part of the costs of most treatments that are not fully reimbursed by the compulsory health insurance. Hence, neither medical practitioners nor patients have an incentive to ensure that the treatments and drugs prescribed are effective and necessary. In this context, the authorities should reform the system to limit insurance cover to a basket of proven and effective drugs and services and let patients pay for any additional treatments they desire out-of-pocket or through private insurance.

Long-term care deserves the attention of policy makers

The health care system reform will also provide an occasion to put the financing and delivery of long-term care (LTC) services on a more solid basis. Several reform proposals have been under discussion since 2004, and in 2012 a working group with representatives from different ministries and stakeholders has been established to undertake detailed preparatory work regarding a comprehensive LTC reform (Nagode et al., 2014).

The current LTC system is rather complex, fragmented, and non-transparent. Long-term care is provided from within the general health and social care systems and paid for out of resources from the compulsory health insurance, the pension insurance, central and local government tax revenues, and private out-of-pocket contributions (about 25% of total LTC costs). Similarly, the regulations governing the sector are spread across several social security laws, and the oversight of LTC activities is split between the Ministry of Labour and the Ministry of Health. Patients often need to interact with different government services to claim benefits and might be subject to several differing needs assessments. A unifying framework is missing, social care and health care interventions are not always well co-ordinated, and there is an uneven regional distribution of LTC providers, with a notable undersupply in rural areas (Stanovnik and Prevolnik Rupel, 2013).

With expenditure on LTC as a share of GDP projected to more than double over the next 50 years (European Commission, 2015), developing an integrated care system and an adequate financing arrangement seems important to improve transparency and to better monitor the service quality and economic efficiency in the sector. Several types of funding arrangements have been under discussion (Dominkuš and Gracar, 2011). Proposals include schemes that break out a part of the compulsory health insurance and devote it to LTC, set up a private but compulsory LTC insurance, or introduce an LTC tax. Within the OECD, there has been a trend towards adopting a collectively financed system that provides universal eligibility for a basic package of care (Colombo et al., 2011), while leaving room for private top-up insurance (or out-of-pocket payments). A broader base for the LTC levy that does not only comprise the working-age population but also pensioners would thereby offer the advantage of mitigating the levy-induced increase in labour costs, ensuring greater funding stability, and enhancing the spirit of solidarity across generations.

LTC in Slovenia is currently oriented towards institutional care (Figure 2.16). As the latter is very expensive, a move towards home care is likely to generate substantial savings, while improving the quality of life of old people (OECD, 2013b). The government has already taken measures to further develop community-based services, such as day care centres and smaller residential units, and to unify health and social home care services. However, institutional care continues to benefit from higher public cost coverage and better services, while home care patients have to assume their living costs and have access to a more limited scope of care services. Also, home care patients often have access to only one service provider within their municipalities (Prevolnik Rupel et al., 2010), so that there is limited choice and competition. In some Northern European countries, patients have been receiving vouchers that they can use to contract those providers that offer a service package that bests suits their needs. The Slovenian authorities might want to explore this option as a cost-reducing and patient-friendly measure.

Another weakness of the existing LTC-system in Slovenia that should be addressed in the context of the upcoming reform is lack of support for healthy and active ageing programmes. While life expectancy at 77 years for men and 83 years for women is above the EU average, the number of healthy life years is below the EU benchmark (Figure 2.17).

Figure 2.16. **Slovenia is oriented toward institutional long term care**

% of population aged 65+

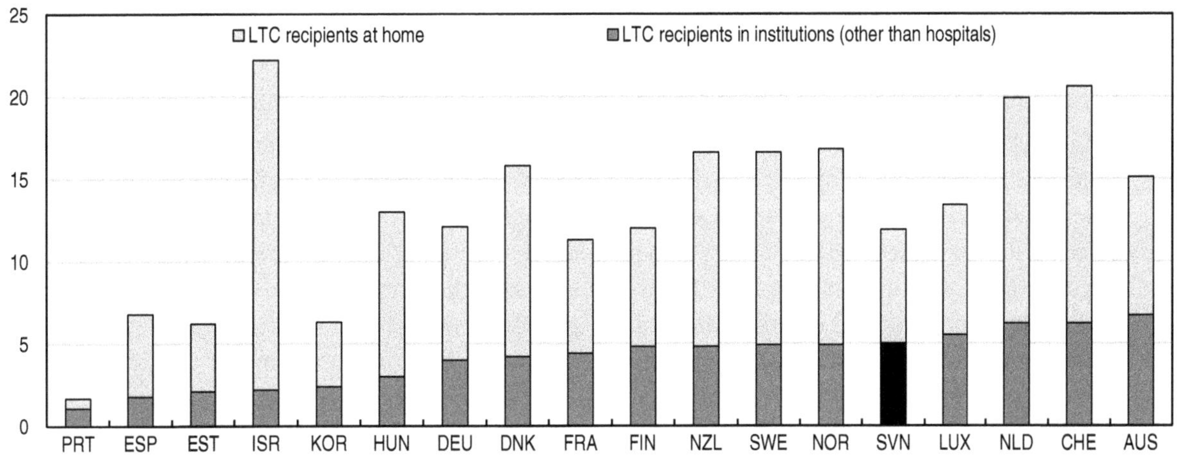

Source: *OECD Long-Term Care Resources and Utilisation Database.*

StatLink http://dx.doi.org/10.1787/888933205485

Figure 2.17. **Life expectancy (LE) and healthy life years (HLY) at birth, by gender, 2012**

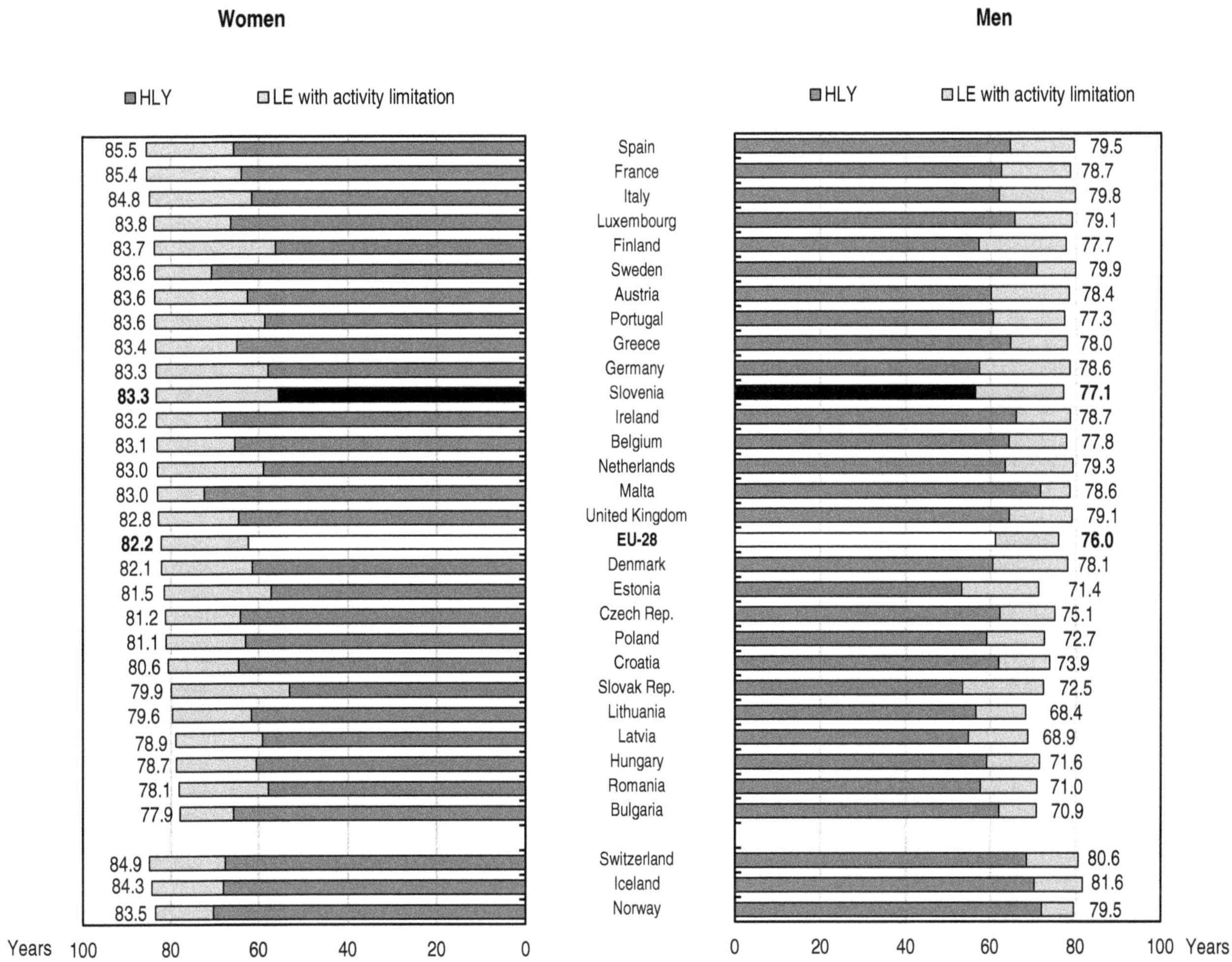

Source: *OECD Health at a Glance: Europe 2014.*

StatLink http://dx.doi.org/10.1787/888933205491

Preventive and rehabilitative care is underdeveloped and so is the use of advanced information and communication technologies in LTC. Also, Slovenia does not have a single specialised palliative care facility. Investments in these areas would certainly improve the welfare of the elderly and might also help to contain LTC-costs.

Demographic trends will have profound implications for the labour market

The ageing of the population in Slovenia will also have marked effects on the labour market. As the cohort of the elderly expands, the active population shrinks in relative terms. The share of the working-age population (aged 15 to 64) in the total population in Slovenia is projected to fall by almost 15 percentage points by 2060, compared with a drop of less than 11 percentage points for the European Union as a whole. One remedy to counter this trend would naturally be for people to extend their working lives, as encouraged also with the 2013 pension reform. Yet, this represents a major challenge, since the labour force participation rate of older workers (aged 55-64) is currently very low in Slovenia. Indeed, it is the lowest in the European Union and the second lowest in the OECD (Figure 2.18). Getting older workers to remain professionally active will require strengthening financial incentives to continue working, tackling employment barriers on the side of employers, and improving the employability of older workers (OECD, 2006).

Figure 2.18. **Labour force participation rate of older workers, 2013**

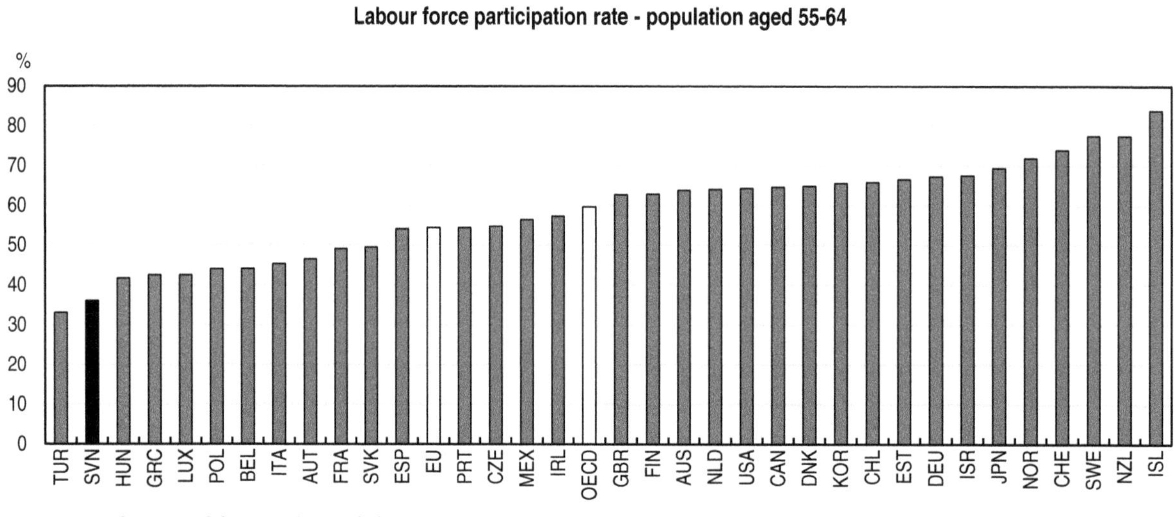

Source: *OECD Short-Term labour Market Statistics Database.*

StatLink http://dx.doi.org/10.1787/888933205500

Reducing explicit or implicit taxes on continued work will incentivise older people to remain in the active workforce. Slovenia used to have a very high implicit marginal tax on continued work (Kierzenkowski, 2013), which contributed to the very low labour force participation of older workers. Both the pension reform of 2013 and the labour market reform of 2013 contain measures to address this issue and encourage continued employment of older workers. In particular, the pension reform increases the statutory and minimum retirement ages and provides benefits in the form of higher pension pay-outs for continued work beyond the normal retirement age and penalties for early retirement. The labour market reform introduces the possibility of temporary work for pensioners. Moreover, during the financial crisis several targeted measures, including the partial exemption from payment of social security contributions, were introduced to encourage the hiring of older workers on a permanent basis.

The 2013 pension reform also tightened the requirements for early retirement. While the possibility to lower the statutory retirement age due to child care, compulsory military service or early career start was maintained, this pathway into early retirement is available only under conditions that are more restrictive than under the previous system. Yet, conditions to retire early could also be tightened for special pension regimes, such as those available to policemen, firemen, pilots, and miners (OECD, 2013b).

Analysis using the OECD pension model suggests that the 2013 pension reform has strengthened to some extent the incentives for older workers to remain in the labour force. In particular, the net pension wealth of an individual from staying in a job is higher now than it used to be under the previous policy (Figure 2.19). The change in net pension wealth measures the level of the pension promise from remaining in employment for an

Figure 2.19. **Changes in net pension wealth**

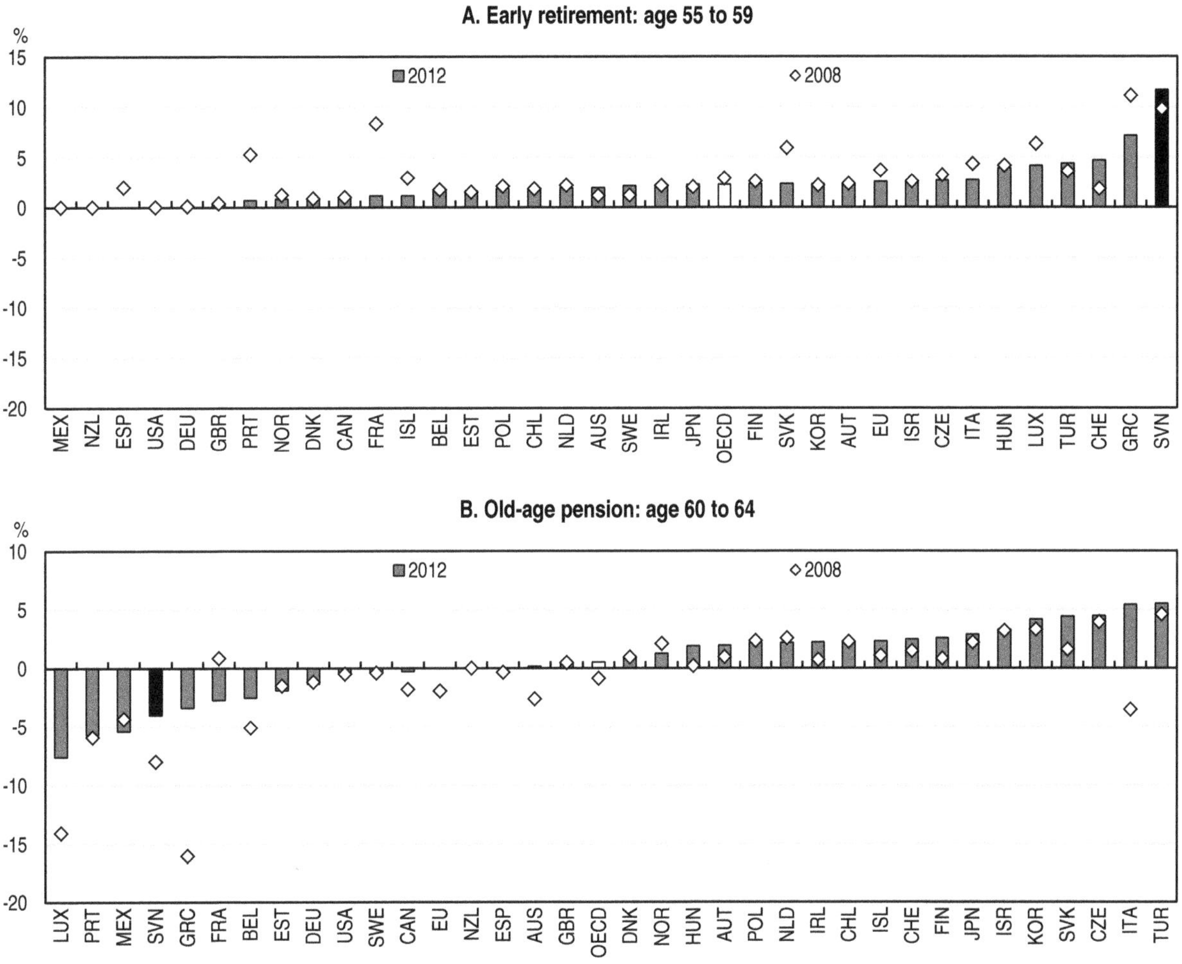

Note: The analysis labelled as 2012 is based on parameters and taxes for 2012, but long term legislated rules that were known at the time of publication are taken into account. In particular, the pension reform of 2013 for Slovenia is reflected in the calculations.
The change in pension wealth is a measure of the incentive to remain in the workforce for an additional period. It measures the level of the pension promise from remaining in employment for an additional year. The calculation is the annual average increase in males' pension wealth when working from age 55 to 59 (early retirement) and from age 60 to 64 (old-age pension). Net pension wealth is the present value of the flow of pension benefits, taking account of the taxes and social security contributions that retirees have to pay on their pensions. It is measured and expressed as a multiple of gross annual individual earnings in the respective country. See OECD (2013), *Pensions at a Glance 2013: OECD and G20 Indicators* for additional details.
Source: OECD, *Pension Models.*

StatLink http://dx.doi.org/10.1787/888933205517

additional year. The calculation is the annual average increase in males' pension wealth when working an additional year at age 55 to 59 (early retirement) or at age 60 to 64 (old-age pension). It represents the present value of the flow of pension benefits, taking account of the taxes and social security contributions that retirees have to pay on their pensions. It is affected by life expectancy and by the age at which people take their pensions, as well as indexation rules. The indicator is measured as a multiple of annual gross earnings.

Indeed, in the age group of the 55 to 59 year olds, Slovenia provides the strongest incentives to remain in the labour force across all OECD countries. Conversely, beyond the age of 60, there is relatively little benefit to stay in a job and an additional year of employment actually leads to a decline in net pension wealth. These findings are driven by the extension of the statutory contribution period to 40 years and the system of, respectively, penalties and bonuses that apply to early or deferred retirement. With a 40 year contribution period, an individual who is assumed to start work at age 20 can retire at a full pension at age 60. Every additional year of work then has relatively little impact on the pension level. There is a maximum 12% increase in the pension for three years of deferral, but this incentive is low by OECD standards and no additional benefit exists for working beyond three years. The actuarially neutral level of pension increases per year of additional work has been estimated at around 6-8% for OECD countries (Queisser and Whitehouse, 2006). Hence, further incentives would be needed to entice older workers to stay active in the labour market.

Strict employment protection legislation can have both beneficial and detrimental effects on the employment rate of older workers. On the one hand, high dismissal costs may help to keep older workers in their job; while on the other hand, it raises the cost of hiring and thus may reduce the number of recruitments. The net impact is unclear, but some surveys have found that strict employment protection legislation tends to depress the hiring and retention rates of older workers (Daniel and Siebert, 2004; OECD, 2006). The 2013 labour market reforms were a decisive step in loosening dismissal legislation and Slovenia's legislation on employment protection is now just slightly more rigid than the average OECD country (Figure 2.20). This lowering of dismissal costs might also help to support the employment of older workers. Also, the reform introduced new measures, such as the gradual increase in the age from which workers benefit from special termination protection, that will also help increase the employability of older workers.

Yet, increasing the employment rate of older workers will also require overcoming the sometimes negative attitudes towards older workers and some misconceptions about their ability. Employers are often reluctant to hire older workers or retain them in their jobs because older employees are considered as having low technological skills, being slow in processing information, and lacking openness to new ideas (European Commission, 2012b). In Slovenia, age discrimination at work seems to be particularly pronounced (Figure 2.21). In this context, life-long learning and targeted training programs to older workers could help them adapt to new tasks and technologies and, thus, enhance their employability. Training can furthermore facilitate shifts of workers from arduous jobs to less exacting work after a certain age. In the same vein, programs that encourage employers to improve working conditions, so that the workplaces and working hours are more accommodating for older workers could encourage the latter to stay in the labour force for longer.

In Slovenia, the Ministry of Labour, Family, Social Affairs and Equal Opportunities has been pursuing the "Employ.me" initiative since 2009 to promote the employment of

Figure 2.20. **Protection of permanent workers against individual and collective dismissals, 2013**

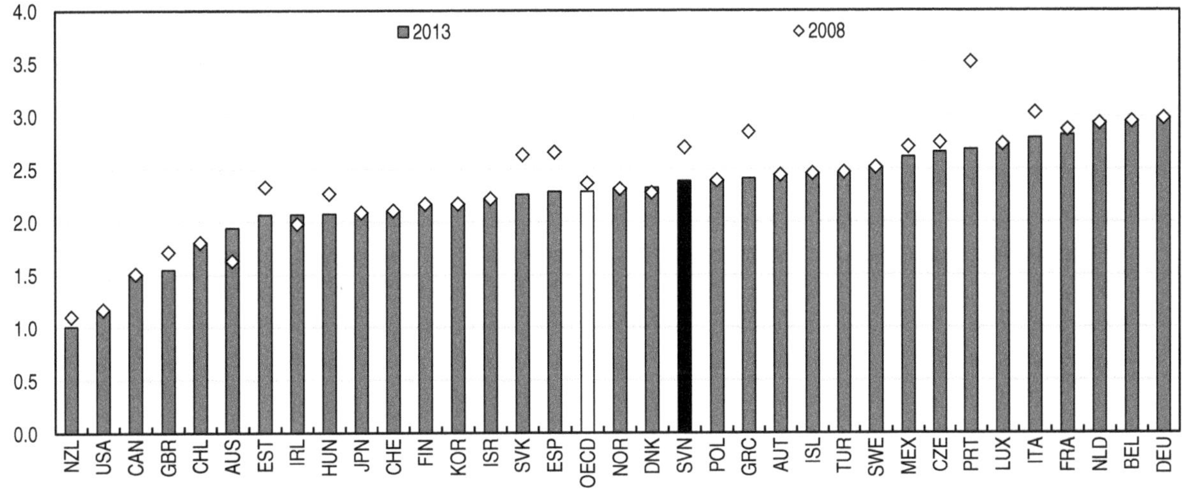

1. The OECD indicator of employment protection legislation (EPL) for regular employment measures the procedures and costs involved in dismissing individual regular employees. The indicator runs from 0 to 6, representing the least to most restrictive EPL.

Source: OECD Employment Protection Database, 2013 update.

StatLink http://dx.doi.org/10.1787/888933205527

Figure 2.21. **Percentage of workers over 55 who report having been subject to age discrimination at work**

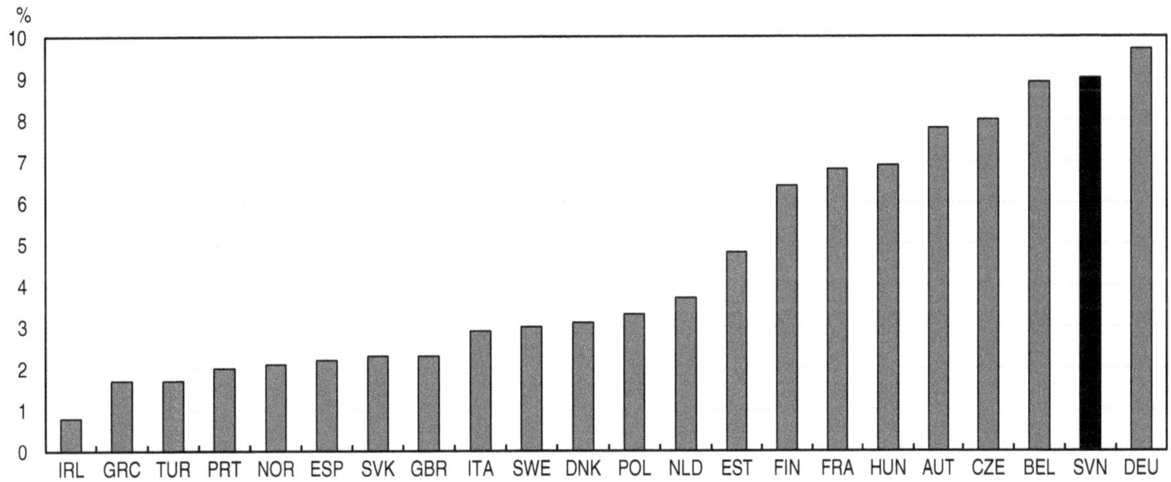

1. Percentage of workers over 55 years old who report having been subject to age discrimination at work.

Source: European Working Conditions Survey, 2010.

StatLink http://dx.doi.org/10.1787/888933205535

disadvantaged unemployed individuals, including older persons. This active labour market policy provides employers with a EUR 5 000 subsidy if they hire an individual from the target group for at least 12 months under full time working arrangements. The matching of disadvantaged unemployed individuals with the employers' job descriptions is done by the Employment Service of Slovenia, while the final selection of candidates is left to the employers. Over the period 2009-2013, about 15 000 disadvantaged unemployed people found employment with the subsidy, including about 1 500 individuals that were older than 55 years. For comparison, 102 000 individuals were unemployed in 2013 (Eurostat – *Labour Market Database*). Half of those included in the Employ.me scheme were still employed with the same or another employer 12 months after the subsidy expired (MDDSZ, 2014b). Since 2009, approximately EUR 60 million have been paid to employers, of which 85% were co-financed by the European Social Fund.

An ageing society also provides opportunities

The ageing of the population in Slovenia will transform the society markedly and presents challenges across several dimensions, including income sustainability, social services, labour market adjustments, and infrastructure provision in rural areas. At the same time, the changing demographics also offer benefits and opportunities. For example, the elderly tend to be more law abiding, so that crime rates might fall. Older people are often positively inclined towards environmental protection, energy saving, and recycling initiatives, so that the resource footprint of the population might decrease. They also have spare time and are willing to volunteer and provide free or low-cost services to their communities.

Moreover, an ageing society provides market opportunities for firms that develop products and services for the elderly. The expanding health and long-term care sector will provide additional employment prospects and create business for supplementary services and products, from stair lifts to wheelchairs. Catering to a growing population of the elderly can help local enterprises to discover products and services that can subsequently be exported to other markets. Slovenia has a number of dynamic enterprises that produce goods and services for the elderly and seem well placed to benefit from the growing global market of senior customers. For example, a number of young companies in the Technology Park Ljubljana are focused on producing goods and services for the elderly, often using advanced information technology. For example, Socinet offers the communication platform LINKEDAGE, which provides networking access to social infrastructure and makes it possible for elderly individuals to remain independent for longer; Mobili provides tracking devices that can emit distress calls in the case of emergencies; MKS specialises in tele-care solutions for frail and disabled people living at home who need additional support for their independent living; MESI offers screening tools for peripheral arterial disease; and DRUGI specialises in developing mobile device interfaces for older or disabled individuals.

Many affluent pensioners have time to travel and enjoy holidays, including during off-peak periods. Slovenia's tourism sector seems well placed to cater to this group of customers. Tourism already accounts for about 5% of GDP, employs more than 33 000 workers, and contributes almost 40% to Slovenia's services exports (OECD, 2014d). Most inbound tourists come from Italy, Austria, Germany, Croatia, and Serbia – all nearby countries that will experience population ageing and will, hence, see the number of elderly increase over the coming decades. The World Travel and Tourism Council expects foreign tourist arrivals in Slovenia to increase by 3% annually over the next ten years (WTTC, 2014). In order to exploit the elderly tourism market, Slovenian service providers in collaboration with the authorities will have to cater to the specific demands or older customers. For example, the latter often place a premium on good security and appreciate the existence of tourism-oriented policing units. Tourism locales will also want to review their physical structures for easy accessibility and ensure that the size of print that they use in information brochures is easy to read for ageing eyes. Finally, health-oriented offerings, such as wellness spas, are generally very much appreciated by older travellers.

Recommendations on pensions, health care, long-term care, and labour market reforms

Key recommendations

- Increase the statutory and minimum pension ages and link them explicitly to life expectancy. Calculate pension rights over lifetime contributions.
- Thoroughly reform the health sector to improve efficiency, including of organisational and governance structures and public procurement.

Further recommendations

- Increase the weight of inflation in the pension indexation rule.
- Revise the list of occupations for the supplementary occupational pension fund and set the contributions in line with actuarial principles.
- Strengthen the role of voluntary private pensions in order to complement the income of the elderly.
- Equalize the contribution rates of different population groups to the compulsory health insurance and move coverage for health-critical services from the voluntary complementary insurance to the compulsory insurance system.
- Ensure transparent and sufficient funding for long-term care, based on contributions from the working-age population and pensioners.
- Develop home care by creating a level playing field with institutional care in the accessibility to health services, and by giving patients more freedom to organise their own care.
- Help older workers adapt to new tasks and technologies through life-long learning and targeted training programmes, and facilitate shifts of workers from strenuous jobs to less extorting work after a certain age.

Bibliography

Colombo, F., A. Llena-Nozal, J. Mercier and F. Tjadens (2011), *Help Wanted? Providing and Paying for Long-Term Care*, OECD Publishing.

CPC (2014), *Annual Report 2013*, Commission for the Prevention of Corruption (in Slovenian).

Daniel, K. and W.S. Siebert (2004), "Does Employment Protection Reduce the Demand for Unskilled Labor?", *IZA Discussion Papers*, No. 1290.

De la Maisonneuve, C. and J. Oliveira Martins (2013), "A Projection Method for Public Health and Long-Term Care Expenditures", *OECD Economics Department Working Papers*, No. 1048, OECD Publishing.

Disney, R.F. and E.R. Whitehouse (1999), "Pension Plans and Retirement Incentives", Pension Reform Primer series, *Social Protection Discussion Paper*, No. 9924, World Bank, Washington, DC.

Dominkuš, D. and I. Gracar (2011), "Closing the Gap – In Search for Ways to Deal with Expanding Care Needs and Limited Resources", *Comment Paper*, Peer Review in Social Protection and Social Inclusion and Assessment in Social Inclusion, October.

European Commission (2015), *The 2015 Ageing Report. Economic and Budgetary Projections for the EU28 Member States* (2013-2060).

European Commission (2014), "The 2015 Ageing Report. Underlying Assumptions and Projection Methodologies", European Economy, No. 8.

European Commission (2012a), "The 2012 Ageing Report. Economic and Budgetary Projections for the 27 EU Member States" (2010-2060), European Economy, No. 2.

European Commission (2012b), "Active Ageing", Special *Eurobarometer* 378.

HelpAge International (2014), *The Global AgeWatch Index: Insight Report.*

IMF (2015), "Republic of Slovenia: Selected Issues", *IMF Country Report*, No. 15/42. Washington, DC.

Kierzenkowski, R. (2013), "Restructuring Welfare Spending in Slovenia", *OECD Economics Department Working Papers*, No. 1061, OECD Publishing.

Majcen, B, M. Čok, J. Sambt, T. Turk, N. Stropnik, G. Dekkers, V. Prevolnik Rupel, V. Lavrac, N. Kump and M. Ogorevc (2012), "Izgradnja kombiniranega mikrosimulacijskega modela in modela generacijskih računov", Inštitut za ekonomska raziskovanja, Ljubljana.

Ministry of Finance (2013), "Country Fiche on Pension Projections", *Update for the Peer Review*, Ljubljana.

Ministry of Health (2015), "Additional Information and Clarifications Regarding Waiting Periods and eHealth", Follow-up after the meeting between the Ministry of Health and the European Commission, Ljubljana.

Ministry of Labour, Family, Social Affairs and Equal Opportunities (MDDSZ) (2014a), "Učinki Pokojninske Reforme in Nadaljnji Koraki", Ljubljana.

Ministry of Labour, Family, Social Affairs and Equal Opportunities (MDDSZ) (2014b), "Zaposli.me/ Spodbujanje zaposlovanja težje zaposljivih brezposelnih oseb", *http://ec.europa.eu/social/ main.jsp?catId=1080&langId=en&practiceId=30.*

Ministry of Labour, Family, Social Affairs, and Equal Opportunities (2013), "Additional Clarification on Article 23 – The Right of Elderly Persons to Social Protection – in Respect of the Question Posed by the European Committee of Social Rights", *Document* RAP/RCha/SLO/12(2013)Add, European Social Charter.

Nagode, M., E. Zver, S. Marn, A. Jacović and D. Dominkuš (2014), "Long-Term Care – Use of the International Definition in Slovenija", *IMAD Working Paper*, 2/2014, Vol. XXIII.

OECD (2014a), "Growth Prospects and Fiscal Requirements Over the Long Term", in OECD, OECD Economic Outlook, Vol. 2014, Iss. 1, OECD Publishing, Paris, DOI: *http://dx.doi.org/10.1787/eco_outlook-v2014-1-44-en.*

OECD (2014b), OECD Pensions Outlook 2014, OECD Publishing, Paris, DOI: *http://dx.doi.org/10.1787/ 9789264222687-en.*

OECD (2014c), "Slovenia: Reforms for a Strong and Sustainable Recovery", *Better Policies*, OECD Publishing, Paris, DOI: *http://dx.doi.org/10.1787/9789264215894-en.*

OECD (2014d), "Slovenia", in OECD, OECD Tourism Trends and Policies 2014, OECD Publishing, Paris, DOI: *http://dx.doi.org/10.1787/tour-2014-35-en.*

OECD (2013a), Pensions at a Glance 2013: OECD and G20 Indicators, OECD Publishing, Paris, DOI: *http:/ /dx.doi.org/10.1787/pension_glance-2013-en.*

OECD (2013b), OECD Economic Surveys: Slovenia 2013, OECD Publishing, Paris, DOI: *http://dx.doi.org/ 10.1787/eco_surveys-svn-2013-en.*

OECD (2011a), Pensions at a Glance 2011: Retirement-income Systems in OECD and G20 Countries, OECD Publishing, Paris, DOI: *http://dx.doi.org/10.1787/pension_glance-2011-en.*

OECD (2011b), *Slovenia: Review of the Private Pension System*, OECD Publishing.

OECD (2006), Live Longer, Work Longer, OECD Publishing, Paris, DOI: *http://dx.doi.org/10.1787/ 9789264035881-en.*

Oliveira Martins, J. and C. de la Maisonneuve (2014), "The Future of Health and Long-Term Care Spending", *OECD Journal: Economic Studies*, OECD Publishing.

Prevolnik Rupel, V., M. Ogorevc and B. Majcen (2010), "The Long-Term Care System for the Elderly in Slovenia", *ENEPRI Research Report*, No. 87, European Network of Economic Policy Research Institutes.

Queisser, M. and E.R. Whitehouse (2006), "Neutral or Fair? Actuarial Concepts and Pension-System Design", *OECD Social, Employment and Migration Working Papers*, No. 40, OECD Publishing, DOI: *http:/ /dx.doi.org/10.1787/351382456457.*

Stanovnik, T., and V. Prevolnik Rupel (2013), "Pensions, Health and Long-Term Care: Slovenia", *ASISP Country Document*, Brussels.

Van Erp, F., N. Vermeer and D. van Vuuren (2013), "Non-Financial Determinants of Retirement", *CPB Discussion Paper*, No. 243.

World Health Organisation (2011), *Global Health and Ageing*, Geneva.

World Travel and Tourism Council (2014), *Travel and Tourism Impact 2014: Slovenia*, London.

Chapter 3

Restoring the financial sector and corporate deleveraging

Excessive credit growth, poor risk assessment and lax lending standards in the run up to the 2008 global crisis led to unsustainable debt build-up in banks and related corporates. A weak framework for the governance of largely state-owned banks is likely to have contributed to the misallocation of credit. Furthermore, there were weaknesses in the banks' risk management systems and banks often didn't properly adhere to regulations and guidance given by the supervisor. Following the results of the stress tests and the Asset Quality Review, in December 2013, the major state-owned banks were recapitalised at a cost of around 11% of GDP, and part of their non-performing loans (NPLs) transferred to the Bank Asset Management Company (BAMC). Banks nevertheless remain weak, with still high NPLs, and corporations are highly leveraged. For successful restructuring and liquidation of assets, BAMC needs to act independently, transparently, with corporate governance of highest standards. Privatisation can improve corporate governance and closer supervision can ensure better compliance by banks. Insolvency legislation was thoroughly reformed in 2013 and should be implemented effectively to help return the healthy parts of the economy to invest and grow again.

The banking sector was hit hard by the boom-bust credit cycle. A combination of low interest rates, overly optimistic growth expectations and a massive inflow of foreign wholesale funding raised the loan-to-deposit ratio close to 180% in 2008 (Figure 3.1, Panel A). The credit-to-GDP ratio more than doubled between 2003 and 2011 to 58% of GDP, although it remained below the levels seen in Ireland, for example. The loans were mainly directed to the corporate sector as household indebtedness remained low. The unwinding of the lending boom and the large drop in economic activity increased non-performing loans (NPLs) to 18% of total loans at the end of 2013 (Figure 3.1, Panel B), mostly in the large

Figure 3.1. **The banking sector was hit hard by the boom-bust credit cycle, but restructuring efforts have resulted in improvements**

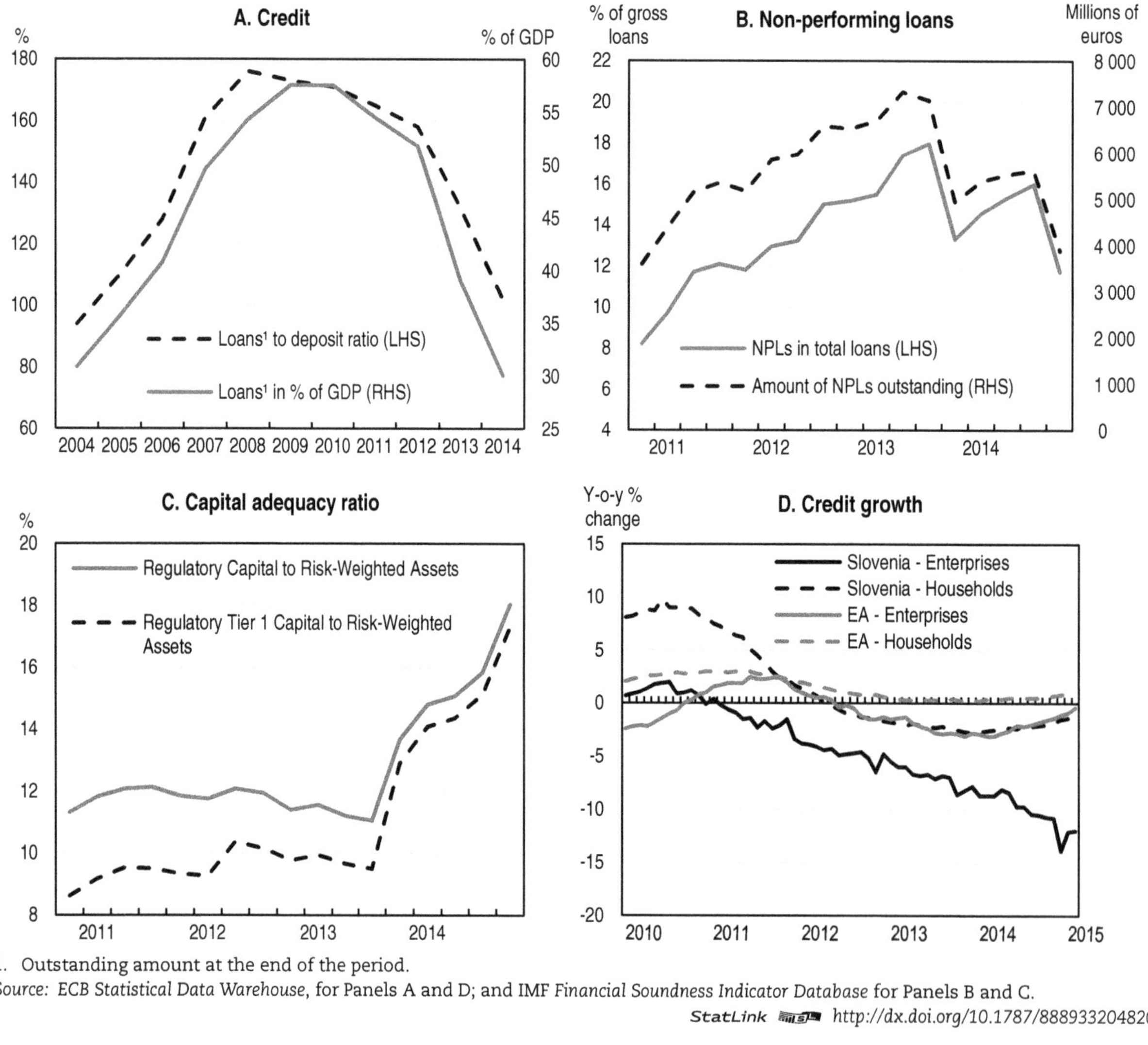

1. Outstanding amount at the end of the period.

Source: *ECB Statistical Data Warehouse*, for Panels A and D; and IMF *Financial Soundness Indicator Database* for Panels B and C.

StatLink http://dx.doi.org/10.1787/888933204820

state-controlled banks. The deterioration in asset quality left Slovenian banks poorly capitalised and ill-equipped to extend further credit to the private sector, holding back investment and consumption (Figure 3.1, Panels C and D).

In late 2012, the authorities became more resolute about restructuring the increasingly troubled state-owned banking sector as the related uncertainty led to a sharp rise in sovereign spreads and funding difficulties. Previous attempts, over 2011 and 2012, to boost capital of the large state banks by EUR 0.7 billion had failed to make them viable. In December 2012, the parliament adopted amendments to the Banking Act entrusting Bank of Slovenia with additional resolution powers, and passed the Act Defining the Measures of the Republic of Slovenia to Strengthen Bank Stability that, among others, established conditions for setting up a Bank Asset Management Company (BAMC). In addition, in September 2013, Bank of Slovenia announced a supervised winding down of two small private banks, together accounting for 4.5% of total assets (IMF, 2014), that had been facing recurrent losses and failed to raise adequate capital.

BAMC was established to have a key role in managing, liquidating and restructuring bad assets. In March 2013, BAMC was incorporated as a state owned company with the principal goal of recovering the highest possible value for the transferred assets, thereby minimising the cost to the budget of banking sector restructuring (BAMC, 2014). By law, BAMC can issue up to EUR 4 billion of government-guaranteed bonds (about 11% of GDP) to acquire the impaired assets of banks. BAMC has the legal instruments and the power to seek quick resolution of impaired assets, for example, by restructuring the company when it holds more than 50% of claims. Bankruptcy procedures where BAMC is involved are to be concluded within six months. BAMC can acquire additional assets from other banks to facilitate corporate restructuring, but has to purchase them at market prices. The law stipulates the life-span of the BAMC at five years – until the end of 2017 – after which the remaining assets are to be transferred to the Slovenia Sovereign Holding (SSH) (BAMC, 2014; IMF, 2014).

The asset transfers and bank restructuring were complicated and delayed due to pricing concerns. Any transfer of assets from banks to asset management companies comes under the scrutiny of European Commission Directorate General for Competition (DG Comp). The transfers need to abide by the EC rules for state aid to avoid using public funds to compensate private losses. Fair pricing based on credibly estimated market value is important on one hand for banks to appropriately recognise the past losses, and on the other hand to offer a restructuring vehicle (BAMC in this case) an opportunity to make profit. Given rising uncertainties and the seeming unwillingness of the authorities and banks to fully recognise the size of the losses, the European Commission and the ECB insisted that Slovenia perform a comprehensive Stress tests and Asset Quality Review (AQR) of 8 Slovenian banks, undertaken by independent experts.

The announcement of the results of the stress tests, in December 2013, gave an important push to bank resolution. Under the adverse scenario, total capital needs of the banks stood at EUR 4.8 billion (about 13% of GDP) (Bank of Slovenia, 2013). The European Commission approved new recapitalisations for the two largest state-owned banks (NLB, NKBM) (European Commission, 2013). The European Commission also temporarily approved the rescue aid for Abanka (the third-largest state-owned bank) and authorities recapitalised the two small private banks undergoing resolution. The Bank of Slovenia also identified a group of banks that were given some time to boost their capital on the market. If unsuccessful the authorities promised to chip in. The authorities furthermore committed to fully privatise NKBM and Abanka, and to reduce the state ownership in NLB to 25% plus one share in the medium term. The capital of the BAMC was increased to ensure its smooth operations. The exercise, despite costly for the budget, significantly reduced uncertainty and calmed the financial markets. The sovereign bond yields that had been edging up to 7% over the summer and autumn of 2013, dropped below 5% soon after the announcement of the results, and subsided further ever since.

In 2014, measures to stabilise the banking sector continued. After the European Commission confirmed the restructuring plan for Abanka it was capitalised for another EUR 243 million in October, as initially planned. In October 2014, the authorities received two binding offers for NKBM, and the bank was expected to be sold in the first quarter of 2015, but there are delays. The winding-down of the two smaller domestic banks could be finalised ahead of time, with the full repayment of deposits and the return of the banking licences still in 2015. A smaller bank, Banka Celje, was recapitalised in December 2014 at a cost of EUR 190 million, and is eventually to be merged with Abanka. Since December 2013, the state has provided close to EUR 4 billion of capital to banks in total (11% of GDP).

The physical transfers of the loan files to the BAMC from NLB and NKBM have been completed while the Abanka transfer was finalised in the first half of 2015. In total, the three large state-owned banks and another small bank are transferring EUR 4.86 billion in assets to the BAMC, at the transfer value of EUR 1.56 billion, or with a 68% average haircut. BAMC has acquired additional corporate exposures at market prices from two smaller domestic banks in wind-down and further transfers from Banka Celje (European Commission, 2014a). Only about half of corporate NPLs have been transferred to the BAMC (IMF, 2015a), so there is room for further transfers. Foreign NPLs – consisting of lending to companies and subsidiaries of domestic banks in the Balkans – have not been transferred to the BAMC and constitute close to one quarter of total remaining NPLs (European Commission, 2015).

Restructuring has stabilised the banking sector, but there are still weaknesses. Despite the transfers of impaired assets to the BAMC, the level of non-performing loans on banks' balance sheets remains elevated (Figure 3.2, Panel A). The level of provisioning however is higher than before and NPLs pose a lower risk to the solvency of banks (European Commission, 2015). The recapitalisations boosted capital, but capital ratios are not high compared to banks in other euro area countries (Figure 3.2, Panel B). The results of the ECB's Comprehensive Assessment of European banks' balance sheets, announced in October 2014, showed a small capital shortfall under the adverse scenario for NLB and NKBM, amounting to less than 0.2% of GDP. But the report (ECB, 2014) states that the banks will not require additional recapitalisation, as after the restructuring efforts so far, both banks returned to profit, and they will be able to cover the capital shortfalls from retained earnings. Yet, profitability remains low and credit activity to the corporate sector is still declining (Figure 3.2, Panels C and D). To return the banking sector to health in a sustainable manner, a stronger and better co-ordinated policy action is needed.

Enhancing the role of BAMC in dealing with bad assets

BAMC was established to recover bad assets, while the remaining cleaned-up banks could focus on normal banking operations. As reported in the *2013 Economic Survey*, banks were initially unable or unwilling to deal with their bad loans. The average monthly ratio of written-off loans to overdue loans was only 0.2% in the first nine months of 2012, so banks would require 40 years to clean up their loan portfolios (OECD, 2013a). Similarly, the

Figure 3.2. **The banking sector remains weak and credit activity is subdued**

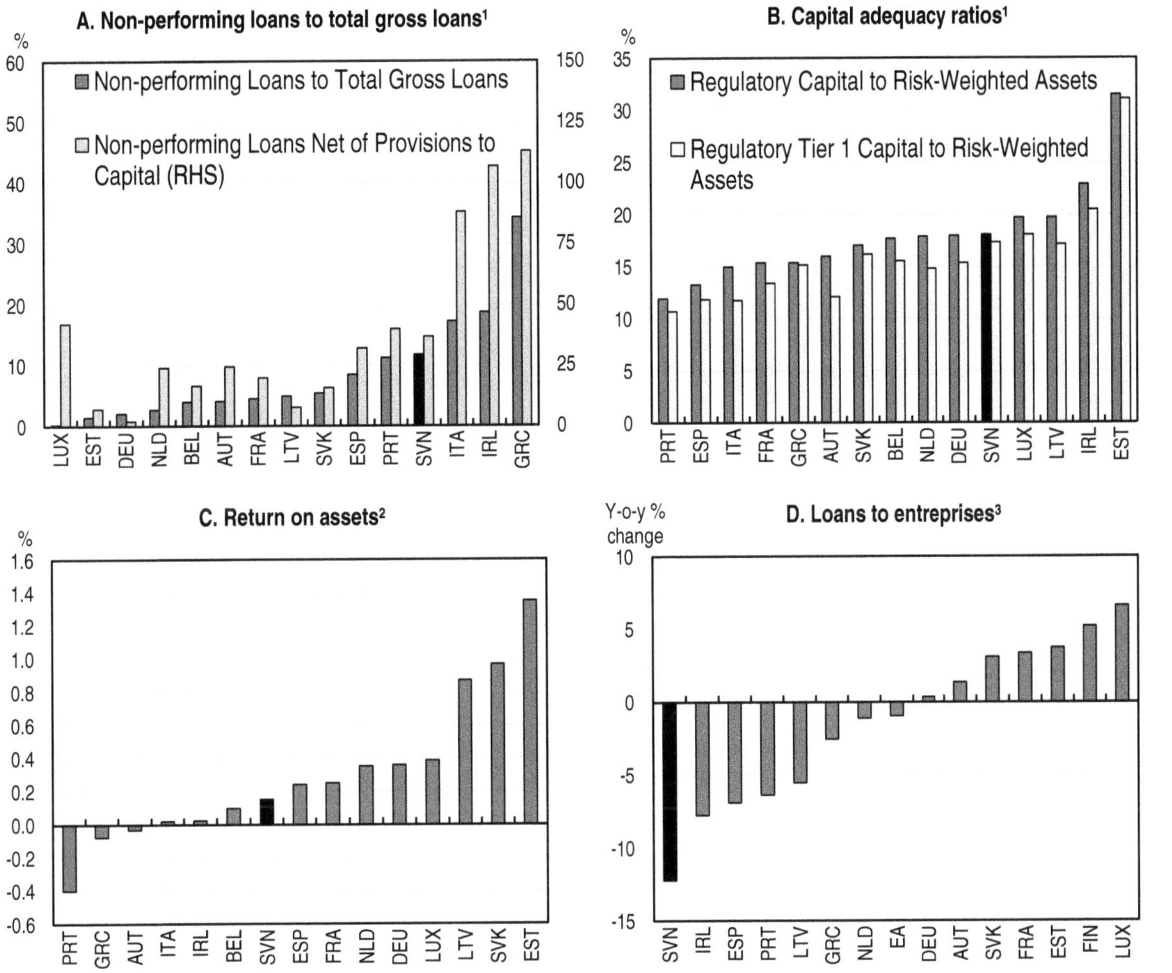

1. 2014 Q4 or latest data available.
2. Average return on assets in the four quarters of 2014, except for France and Germany whose data refers to 2013.
3. Average of annual growth rates between November 2014 and February 2015. Loans adjusted for sales and securitisation of all types of maturity.

Source: IMF *Financial Soundness Indicator Database*, for Panels A, B and C; and ECB *Statistical Data Warehouse*, for Panel D.

StatLink http://dx.doi.org/10.1787/888933204831

BAMC in its *2013 Annual Report* notes that the transfer prices for NPLs calculated and suggested by the banks themselves in spring 2013 were substantially overvalued.

A separate asset management company (AMC) to tackle bad assets allows banks to focus on core business while the AMC concentrates on asset recovery. A separate agency can exploit economies of scale in consolidating scarce skills and resources, and has enhanced bargaining power versus debtors. The disadvantage of taking assets away from banks is some loss of institutional knowledge about borrowers. Another disadvantage is that banks can provide additional financing, which can be important for restructuring (Klingebiel, 2000; Woo, 2000). For AMCs to successfully and effectively do their task, it is important that a country has an effective legal system and adequate insolvency regulation, and sound financial regulatory and supervisory framework. Professional management, political independence, a skilled resource base, appropriate funding, good information and management, and transparency in operations and processes are also key (Klingebiel, 2000; Woo, 2000). Finally, a stable macroeconomic environment can restore the viability of some nonperforming assets.

Klingebiel (2000) reviews experience of seven countries (Ghana, Finland, Mexico, Spain, Sweden, the Philippines and the USA) that established AMCs to address the overhang of bad debt in the economy, and concludes that they have a mixed record. Laeven and Valencia (2008) find that AMCs have been set up in 60% of crises, but similarly report that they appear largely ineffective in resolving distressed assets. In practice, selling off assets of unviable bankrupt institutions had a higher rate of success than corporate restructuring. Moreover, when the assets acquired were mostly real estate related, the process was more successful. When AMCs only had a small fraction of the banking system on their balance sheets, it was easier to maintain its independence from political pressures (Klingebiel, 2000).

In the case of Slovenia, about two thirds of the BAMC's exposures are in default. BAMC is to acquire the collateral – mostly real estate but also equity and company assets – and sell it to the private sector. The other exposure is corporate assets that have a viable core activity but need to be financially and operationally restructured (European Commission, 2014a). From experience of other countries, the task of corporate restructuring can be more challenging, and especially so in Slovenia where there are numerous complex, inter-connected group loans with several bilateral contracts and conflicting interests (Bank of Slovenia, 2014a). To speed up the process, policy makers should create an environment where the BAMC can successfully take a lead with its strong expertise.

To do this, more assets should be transferred from banks to the BAMC. All assets in a company group should be transferred, so that the BAMC will have a majority position *vis-à-vis* other creditors. This will expedite the restructuring process and increase recovery prospects. Care should be taken, however, not to make the BAMC too big and thus susceptible to political influence. According to Klingebiel (2000), the successful cases of AMCs in Spain, Sweden and the USA each held assets below 10% of total financial assets in the economy. This translates to the maximum size of BAMC of approximately EUR 6 billion, which is beyond the current limit of EUR 4 billion stipulated by law. BAMC in co-ordination with the authorities should decide strategically which are the most urgent and important cases in the economy to be restructured, and ensure that additional exposures are transferred. This will also alleviate the problem of NPLs on banks' balance sheets. But action needs to be taken swiftly. Past experience shows that ambiguity on what additional assets may or may not be eventually transferred to the AMCs limits banks' incentives to engage in corporate restructuring of assets remaining on their balance sheets (Klingebiel, 2000).

Independence and professionalism are also very important for success (Klingebiel, 2000). Restructuring companies requires specialised expertise which is highly valued on the market. BAMC therefore needs to have freedom to set its own remuneration policy to attract adequate talent. By Slovenian law, the BAMC is established as a company with a board of directors, a one-tier versus a two-tier (a supervisory board and a management board) governance structure. One-tier structure allows for greater influence of the single shareholder – the government – on operations. It is important to preserve adequate independence of the BAMC over its life span and the authorities should consider establishing a two-tier governance structure within the BAMC.

Extending the life-span of the BAMC would reduce pressure for fire sales and enhance its independence. The BAMC was created with a 5-year life. Due to past delays and to avoid any fire sales, this should be extended, but past experience shows that some time limit is good. AMCs are created to expedite restructuring and not delay it. There can be a tendency to prolong the process under unrealistic expectations of a turnaround in asset values. The authorities are planning to change legislation in order to extend the life of BAMC to 2022, which is a step in the right direction.

The governance of BAMC could be strengthened. The Slovenian Corruption Prevention Commission (CPC) and the Court of Audit in their reports voiced concerns about conflict of interest, significant corruption risks and irregularities in the BAMC with respect to hiring of external consultancies, remuneration policies, internal processes and corporate governance. The reports also urged the Ministry of Finance to ensure better supervision of the BAMC. Successful AMCs in the past have relied on a detailed set of directives and guidelines to its staff and contractors that covered a wide range of operations, including asset management and disposition, contract policies, bidding procedures and marketing. This minimised the possibility of fraud and made policy and cost evaluation more transparent and expedited the resolution process (Klingebiel, 2000). Steps should be taken to strengthen corporate governance of the BAMC, and to ensure that it adheres to highest standards. BAMC has taken measures to strengthen its own governance in 2014 by adopting strategic guidelines and a business strategy for asset management.

Successful restructuring and disposal of assets importantly rely on sound financial institutions and available markets to sell the assets. Deep and liquid capital markets help in this regard. However, in Slovenia fresh equity is scarce, BAMC cannot lend money to companies, while banks are weak and in the process of deleveraging. In fact, the authorities are planning to change the law to enable BAMC to lend to companies, which will facilitate restructuring. In addition, more openness to privatisation and foreign investors could bring more fresh capital. Swift restructuring of the banking sector and resumption of credit activity is equally important. BAMC can use tools at its disposal to encourage banks to lend afresh to viable restructured companies, for example by putting up its collateral for fresh loans or assigning super-seniority status. Foreign funds specialising in turning around companies could enter the market to buy viable companies and/or inject fresh money into companies. There are special funds under the umbrella of the EBRD that specialise in this and could be used more.

Improving bank supervision and business practices of banks

The 2013 *Economic Survey* argued that the weak framework for the governance of state-owned banks is likely to have contributed to poor credit standards, excessive risk taking and misallocation of credit. The Slovenian Corruption Prevention Commission reported (CPC, 2013) that corrupt practices in allocation of credit had been wide spread in the state dominated banking system. Several chief executive officers cited political interference as one of the reasons for their decision to resign. The planned privatisations are welcome in this regard as they are expected to improve corporate governance. However, the decision to retain a blocking minority shareholding should be dropped. Especially if remaining shares are widely held, a controlling stake opens the door to political interference.

The risk management in banks should be of higher standard and bank supervisor should more closely monitor banks' adherence to regulations and guidance. The AQR from December 2013 identified several weaknesses in the banks' risk management systems (European Commission, 2014b). The data integrity validation highlighted deficiencies in IT systems and paper records, with significant gaps in several loan files. Most of the banks did not assign rating classes in line with the regulations issued by the Bank of Slovenia and in many instances the collateral valuations were out of date. The BAMC (2014) likewise notes that credit files received from the banks were in many cases incomplete and of poor quality.

The risk management in banks should be of higher standard and bank supervisors should more closely follow that regulations and guidance are properly followed by the banks.

The ECB Single Supervisory Mechanism, in place from November 2014, will bring unified supervisory methodologies and standards at the Eurosystem level. New legislation was adopted in March 2015 in line with EU directives, to introduce capital shock absorbers, enhanced risk management and bank governance requirements, and improved transparency of bank operations through additional disclosure and assessment of systemic risks. Furthermore, a bank resolution fund has been established, to be financed by banks and managed by the central bank. To foster higher standards of the risk management and non-performing exposures management in banks, the Bank of Slovenia has introduced number of measures, such as additional reporting of banks and requirements for individual plans for non-performing exposure management. The absence of credit information sharing between banks is also likely to have contributed to poor risk outcomes (OECD, 2013a). According to the Bank of Slovenia, the Central Credit Registry is being upgraded to better support supervisory tasks (Bank of Slovenia, 2014a), which is welcome.

Recent macroprudential measures to address systemic risks are welcome. In 2014, the institutional framework for macroprudential oversight of the financial system was established by the Bank of Slovenia. The Financial Stability Committee sets recommendations to safeguard the stability of the financial system by early identification of systemic risks and takes preventive measures. The Bank of Slovenia has adopted two macroprudential instruments. The first places a cap on deposit interest rates and imposes a capital add-on requirement for exceeding this cap. This instrument mitigated income risk, by contributing to a reduction in passive interest rates, in the context of banks' competition for stable sources of funding. The second instrument limits the annual change in gross loan-to-deposit ratio (of the non-banking sector), in order to slow down the pressure on deleveraging in the banking sector. The aim is to encourage banks to moderate the contraction of lending to the non-banking sector (Bank of Slovenia, 2014b).

Improved insolvency framework to speed up corporate restructuring

Corporate indebtedness is high (Figure 3.3, Panel A), despite debt reduction since 2009 (Figure 3.4, Panel A). Profitability is low due to high interest burden and the bank funding cost of Slovenian corporates remains elevated (Figure 3.4, Panel B). The debt is concentrated in a few companies (Bank of Slovenia, 2014b; European Commission, 2014b; Damijan, 2014; IMAD, 2014a). Companies with financial debt exceeding EBITDA (earnings before interest, taxes, depreciation and amortisation) by a factor of five account for about 80% of financial debt, but represent only one third of companies (Figure 3.3, Panel B). State-owned and state-controlled enterprises are also highly leveraged and continue to be at risk of default (European Commission, 2015). Many companies, however have been able to tap alternative sources of funding at lower cost. Slovenia therefore does have a healthy core of companies, often export-oriented, which did not over-borrow and even improved their business since the crisis (IMAD, 2014a). However, despite the concentration of excessive debt, the deleveraging has been shown to affect negatively the overall economy via lower activity and investment (IMAD, 2014b). Moreover, unlike in other vulnerable countries where the economic distress was concentrated in the real estate and construction sectors, in Slovenia the pattern is rather cross-sectorial, with many service sectors also affected (European Commission, 2014b).

Figure 3.3. **The debt overhang is concentrated in a few companies**

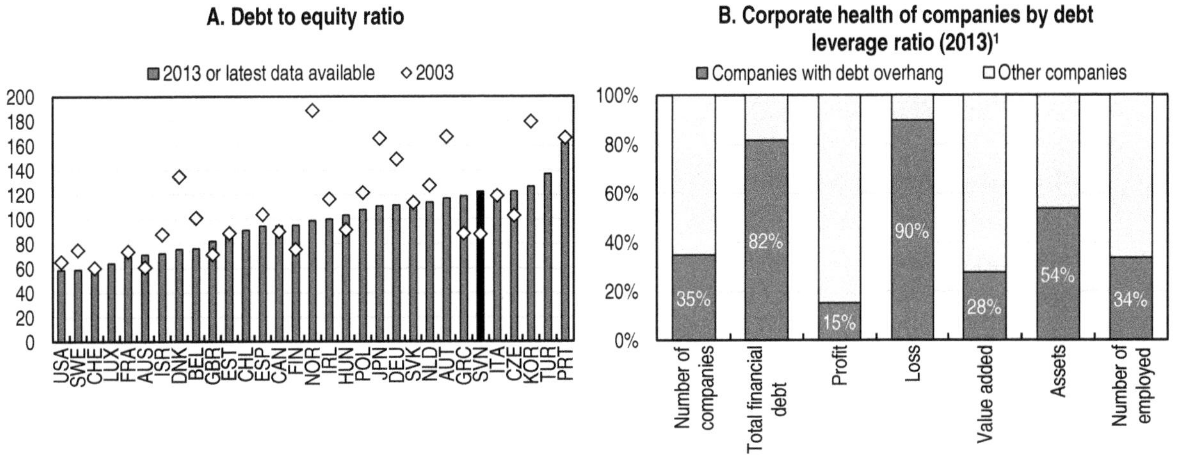

1. Companies with debt overhang are those with negative EBIDTA (earnings before interest, tax, depreciation and amortisation) and those with debt leverage ratio (financial debt over EBITDA) larger than 5.

Source: *OECD Financial Indicators Database*, for Panel A; and Calculations by IMAD, based on raw micro level data (firm-by-firm) from AJPES, for Panel B.

StatLink http://dx.doi.org/10.1787/888933204848

Figure 3.4. **Deleveraging has been under way, while corporates still face elevated funding costs**

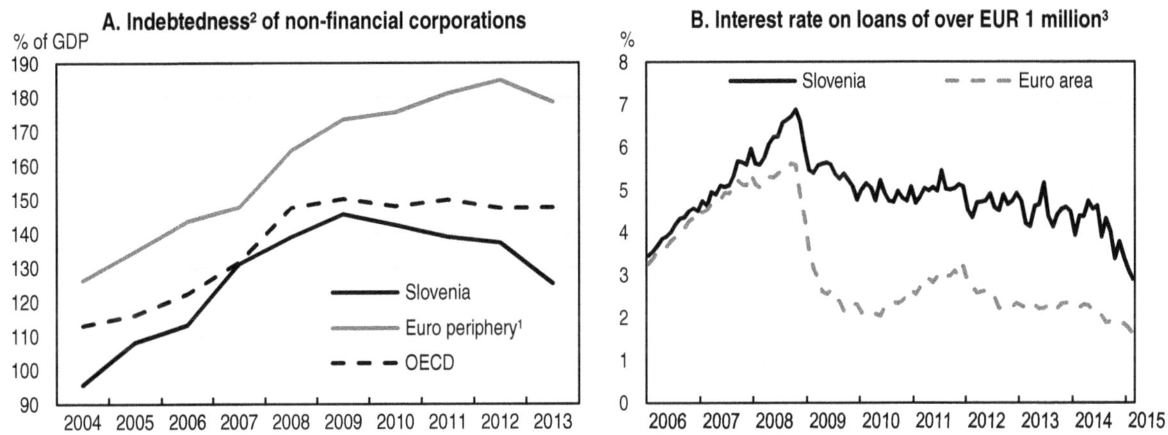

1. The euro periphery is composed of Greece, Portugal, Spain and Ireland.
2. Debt is defined as all liabilities that require payment or payments of interest or principal by the debtor to the creditor at a date or dates in the future. It comprises of all debt instruments except for shares, equity and financial derivatives.
3. Interest rate on loans to non-financial corporations of amount over EUR 1 million.

Source: *OECD Financial Indicators Database*, for Panel A; and *ECB Statistical Data Warehouse*, for Panel B.

StatLink http://dx.doi.org/10.1787/888933204852

European Commission (2014b) found that between 2007 and 2012, Slovenia's expenditures on state aid to the real economy more than tripled, to 1.3% of GDP. Yet, many of the companies that received aid still ended up in financial difficulties. Given the fiscal pressures, Slovenia needs to shift from subsidising troubled companies to providing a framework for swift liquidation of unviable companies and effective restructuring of viable ones. In addition, dynamic credit and equity markets that are able to support growth of healthy parts of the economy are needed. Attracting equity through privatisation and entry of foreign investors could enhance corporate deleveraging, while strengthening corporate governance. The authorities are already replacing subsidies by low cost loans to companies. Slovenia has taken measures to improve its framework for liquidation and restructuring of companies. Furthermore, in January 2015, the government appointed a task force for corporate restructuring and deleveraging, comprising government and central bank officials, tasked with monitoring and co-ordinating restructuring and deleveraging of companies, and proposing measures to make the processes more effective. However, further improvements could be made.

Protracted insolvency procedures

Resolving insolvency in Slovenia is very time consuming and recovery rates are low. At a time when Slovenia faces a large burden of non-performing loans and an overleveraged corporate sector, this is especially harmful. According to the Doing Business Survey (World Bank, 2015), it takes on average 2 years to complete a standard bankruptcy procedure (involving a main secured creditor and several unsecured ones). As mentioned in the *2013 Economic Survey*, the duration is much longer – three or more years – for large complex businesses with numerous creditors. The duration of insolvency procedures is crucial because recovery rate decreases with time. While in Slovenia investors can recover only about 50% of assets, best practices show that it is possible to achieve recovery rates above 90% (Finland, Japan and Norway). Such high rates are achieved by rapid bankruptcy procedures that last 5 to 11 months. Hence, decreasing the duration of the insolvency procedures should be the priority of the bankruptcy framework.

In Slovenia, insolvency procedures are often initiated too late, usually when it is already impossible to save the enterprise. According to Slovenian law, a company that is balance sheet insolvent (value of assets is smaller than the sum of liabilities) can challenge its creditor in court if it demonstrates that it can still meet its obligations. Therefore, insolvent companies that succeed in refinancing their loans can stay insolvent for prolonged periods of time before applying for bankruptcy. Although the law obliges insolvent firms to apply for bankruptcy and sets sanctions for violations, in practice there were no sanctions against such fraudulent behaviour (OECD, 2013a).

Improved insolvency procedures can facilitate credit activity and entrepreneurship

Public policies and programmes related to insolvency procedures can create a business environment that helps entrepreneurs save viable businesses and create more companies and employment. It is important that entrepreneurs are not discouraged from starting a company due to fear of bankruptcy and failure, even if their last attempt failed. Research shows that businesses set up by re-starters grow faster than businesses set up by first timers in terms of turnover and jobs created (European Commission, 2011).

In Slovenia, there is stigma of failure. In surveys, when presented with the statement "Entrepreneurs who failed should have a second chance", 32% of respondents disagree with the statement, the highest percentage among the 33 countries and twice the average (OECD, 2013b). Perhaps this is because the public perceives that bankruptcies are associated with fraud. The government should therefore actively pursue policies to reduce stigma of failure and create an environment that does not discourage fresh start of failed non-fraudulent entrepreneurs. The systematic recognition of honest vs. dishonest entrepreneurs is essential. In the UK for example, dishonest entrepreneurs are identified by the behaviour prior to or during the bankruptcy process (reckless expenditure of credit, paying family members, "evaporation" of assets, etc.) and are then liable for prosecution (European Commission, 2011).

Effective systems for secured and unsecured creditors to protect their rights are important also to facilitate credit activity. Slovenia scores low on the "getting credit" component of the *Doing Business Survey* (World Bank, 2015). It is at the bottom of the high-income OECD country group on the strength of legal rights, which measures the degree to which collateral and bankruptcy laws facilitate lending. According to the Global Competitiveness indicators (World Economic Forum, 2014), access to financing is identified as the most problematic factor for doing business in the country. On the ease of access to loans Slovenia is one of the worst performing countries, ranking 140 out of 144. Certainly, such a low score is a consequence of plethora of reasons: the high corporate leverage, the unhealthy balance sheets of banks and the prolonged crisis. Nevertheless, further improvements in insolvency procedures would be one important step in resolving the credit crunch environment.

In 2013, the parliament passed important reforms to facilitate early restructuring of viable companies. The new framework provides for preventive restructuring of viable large and medium-sized companies that could become insolvent within a year. The new framework gives more powers to creditors. Creditors holding at least 20% of financial claims may demand court-mandated debt restructuring and creditors' restructuring plan has precedence over a potential rival plan by the debtor. Furthermore, smaller creditors now enjoy better protection. An absolute priority rule has been introduced to ensure that if equity is zero, debtor equity will be eliminated, preventing existing owners from blocking the restructuring process. The amendment also improved corporate restructuring features, such as debt-for-equity swaps and corporate spin-offs, to facilitate viable firms continuing as a going concern (IMF, 2014). The overall procedure of court-mandated debt restructuring has been simplified by broadening the scope of companies eligible for a "simplified procedure", which besides micro companies now applies also to small companies. To speed up liquidation of companies after a bankruptcy, auction-style asset sale has been improved.

The amendment significantly improves the corporate insolvency regime and, if properly implemented, can facilitate the rehabilitation of viable firms. During 2013-14, about 30 compulsory settlements were completed per year, simplified compulsory settlements increased from 10 in 2013 to 90 in 2014. Furthermore, in 2014, 8 pre-insolvency restructuring proceedings were concluded for the first time. Nevertheless, corporate bankruptcy procedures remain widespread, amounting to close to 1 000 per year in 2013-14, twice as many as in 2012 (IMF, 2015a). The effectiveness of the reform should be closely monitored and evaluated based on appropriate indicators at aggregate level, such as recovery rates in all types of insolvency procedures (European Commission, 2014c; IMF, 2014). Indeed, Slovenia has already started evaluating the reform (European Commission, 2015). Institutional capacity could also be improved further to promote successful implementation. The number of judges specialised in commercial law is low. The number of insolvency administrators is insufficient and many lack relevant knowledge in the areas of accounting and finance. Furthermore, there is lack of meaningful co-operation between judges and insolvency administrators (IMF, 2015a and 2015b).

Slovenia could achieve speedy and cost effective debt settlement also via better use of voluntary out-of-court restructuring. In view of overburdened courts and their limited capacity, promoting voluntary out-of-court restructuring is a good alternative. *2013 Economic Survey of Slovenia* reports that although allowed under the Slovenian insolvency law, out-of-court restructuring is not explicitly regulated and average time of such restructuring is high in international comparison. Because the process of out-of-court financial restructuring is not legally defined, the Slovenian Banking Association in co-operation with the Bank of Slovenia and the Ministry of Finance drafted the "Slovenian principles of the financial restructuring of corporate debt". As has been recently done in Spain and Portugal for SMEs, additional incentives could be introduced to promote the use of out-of-court restructuring. Debt hair-cuts should be permitted for such procedures and tax and social security should be equalised with other liabilities. A public mediator agency with electronic platform can facilitate mediation by reducing paperwork bureaucracy.

Improving the judiciary

The judiciary has been slow to deal with cases despite recent improvements in procedures. Slovenia has made progress in accountability of judges and efficiency of the judicial system. In 2008, the Supreme Court established a computerised case management system (Judicial Data Warehouse), which has improved the management of human resources between courts, speeding up litigation and reducing the backlog (OECD, 2013a). European Commission (2014a) assesses, however, that despite the improvements in the functioning of the court system the length of trials remains long. The backlog of enforcement cases is also still high in comparative terms. In 2012, there were 8.3 pending enforcement cases per 100 inhabitants in Slovenia compared to the EU median of 0.3. Given the difficult economic situation, insolvency cases have risen in numbers. Consequently, in bankruptcy cases against legal entities the clearance rate fell from 83% in 2012 to 67% in 2013, leading to a 32% increase in the number of pending cases. Nevertheless, the proportion of insolvency proceedings involving legal entities resolved within nine months of filing improved from 57% in 2009 to 63% in 2013 (European Commission, 2014a).

Independence of the judiciary could be improved. According to the Global Competitiveness Indicators (World Economic Forum, 2014), the Slovenian judiciary ranks low on perceived judicial independence from government, citizens, or firms. Among OECD countries, only Mexico, Spain, Turkey and Slovak Republic rank lower. The 2014 EU Justice Scoreboard reports that among the EU countries Slovenia has the highest number of judges per capita and one of the highest general government expenditures on law courts as percentage of GDP. While low perception of the judicial system may partly be a consequence of open attacks on some decisions by judges in the recent past, the perception had been low even before. It is the responsibility of all branches of government to ensure respect of the judiciary. Obviously, the foremost responsibility rests with the judicial branch itself that needs to improve quality, independence and efficiency of the justice system.

Recommendations on restoring the financial sector and corporate deleveraging

Key recommendations

- Enhance the leading role of the Bank Asset Management Company to ensure swift restructuring of companies and effective liquidation of assets.
- For the most important firms to be restructured, ensure that all assets in a company group are transferred to the Bank Asset Management Company.
- Bank Asset Management Company should maintain its independence and ability to attract highly professional staff, while adhering to the highest standards of corporate governance and transparency.

Recommendations on restoring the financial sector and corporate deleveraging *(cont.)*

- Monitor the implementation of the new insolvency regulation and improve institutional capacity by training judges and insolvency administrators. Make out-of-court restructuring faster and more attractive.

Other recommendations

- Privatise state-owned banks without retaining blocking minority shareholdings.
- In the context of the single supervisory mechanism framework, the bank supervisor should more closely monitor banks' adherence to regulations and guidance, and encourage banks to improve their risk management.
- Enhance corporate deleveraging by raising equity through privatisation and attracting foreign investors, thus strengthening also corporate governance.
- Set up a system for systematic recognition of honest vs. dishonest entrepreneurs during bankruptcy. Actively pursue policies to reduce stigma of failure and create an environment that encourages fresh start.
- Improve quality, independence and efficiency of the justice system. All branches of government should ensure respect of the judiciary.

Bibliography

BAMC (2014), *Annual Report 2013*, Bank Assets Management Company.

Bank of Slovenia (2014a), *Policy Strategy Paper for Slovenia*, Ljubljana, 17 July.

Bank of Slovenia (2014b), *Financial Stability Review*, May.

Bank of Slovenia (2013), "Report on Comprehensive Review of the Banking System and Associated Measures", *Press Release*, 12 December.

CPC (2013), *State of Corruption in Slovenia, 2013*, Commission for the Prevention of Corruption (in Slovenian), *https://www.kpk-rs.si/upload/t_datoteke/Ocena_stanja_korupcije_v_RS.pdf*.

Damijan, J.P. (2014), "Corporate Financial Soundness and its Impact on Firm Performance: Implications for Corporate Debt Restructuring in Slovenia", *European Bank for Reconstruction and Development Working Paper*, No. 168.

ECB (2014), *Aggregate Report on the Comprehensive Assessment*, October.

European Commission (2015), "Country Report Slovenia 2015", *Commission Staff Working Document*, Brussels, 26.5.2015.

European Commission (2014a), *Slovenia: Review of Progress on Policy Measures Relevant for the Correction of Macroeconomic Imbalances*, November.

European Commission (2014b), "Macroeconomic Imbalances, Slovenia 2014", *Occasional Papers*, 187, March.

European Commission (2014c), "Assessment of the 2014 National Reform Programme and Stability Programme for Slovenia", *Commission Staff Working Document*.

European Commission (2013), "State Aid: Commission Approves Rescue or Restructuring Aid for Five Slovenian Banks", *Press Release*, Brussels, 18 December.

European Commission (2011), "A Second Chance for Entrepreneurs: Prevention of Bankruptcy, Simplification of Bankruptcy Procedures and Support for a Fresh Start", *Final Report of the Expert Group*, Enterprise and Industry Directorate-General, European Commission.

IMAD (2014a), *Autumn Forecast of Economic Trends 2014*.

IMAD (2014b), "Indebtedness and Deleveraging of Slovenian Firms", *Economic Issues*.

IMF (2015a), "Republic of Slovenia: 2014 Article IV Consultation", *IMF Country Report*, No. 15/41, February.

IMF (2015b), "Legal and Institutional Challenges in Corporate Insolvency. Republic of Slovenia: Selected Issues", *IMF Country Report*, No. 15/42, February 2015.

IMF (2014), "Republic of Slovenia: 2013 Article IV Consultation", *IMF Country Report*, No. 14/11.

Klingebiel, D. (2000), "The Use of Asset Management Companies in the Resolution of Banking Crises", *World Bank Policy Research Working Papers*, No. 2284, World Bank.

Laeven, L. and F. Valencia (2008), "Systemic Banking Crises: A New Database", *IMF Working Papers*, No. 08/224.

OECD (2013a), OECD Economic Surveys: Slovenia 2013, OECD Publishing, Paris, DOI: *http://dx.doi.org/10.1787/eco_surveys-svn-2013-en*.

OECD (2013b), Entrepreneurship at a Glance 2013, OECD Publishing, Paris, DOI: *http://dx.doi.org/10.1787/entrepreneur_aag-2013-en*.

Woo, D. (2000), "Two Approaches to Resolving Nonperforming Assets During Financial Crises", *IMF Working Papers*, No. 00/33.

World Bank (2015), *Doing Business Survey 2015*.

World Economic forum (2014), *Global Competitiveness Report 2014-2015*.

ORGANISATION FOR ECONOMIC CO-OPERATION AND DEVELOPMENT

The OECD is a unique forum where governments work together to address the economic, social and environmental challenges of globalisation. The OECD is also at the forefront of efforts to understand and to help governments respond to new developments and concerns, such as corporate governance, the information economy and the challenges of an ageing population. The Organisation provides a setting where governments can compare policy experiences, seek answers to common problems, identify good practice and work to co-ordinate domestic and international policies.

The OECD member countries are: Australia, Austria, Belgium, Canada, Chile, the Czech Republic, Denmark, Estonia, Finland, France, Germany, Greece, Hungary, Iceland, Ireland, Israel, Italy, Japan, Korea, Luxembourg, Mexico, the Netherlands, New Zealand, Norway, Poland, Portugal, the Slovak Republic, Slovenia, Spain, Sweden, Switzerland, Turkey, the United Kingdom and the United States. The European Commission takes part in the work of the OECD.

OECD Publishing disseminates widely the results of the Organisation's statistics gathering and research on economic, social and environmental issues, as well as the conventions, guidelines and standards agreed by its members.

OECD PUBLISHING, 2, rue André-Pascal, 75775 PARIS CEDEX 16
(10 2015 12 1 P) ISBN 978-92-64-23222-8 – 2015-02

www.ingramcontent.com/pod-product-compliance
Ingram Content Group UK Ltd.
Pitfield, Milton Keynes, MK11 3LW, UK
UKHW051504290926
15471UKWH00008B/1402

9 789264 232228